T0208632

国家汉办/孔子学院总部
Hanban/Confucius Institute Headquarters

Zhuangzi

Collection of Critical Biographies of Chinese Thinkers

(Concise Edition, Chinese-English)

Editors-in-chief: Zhou Xian, Cheng Aimin

Author: Bao Zhaohui
Translator: Thomas Mitchell
Reviser: Wang Zhengwen
Expert: Shi Yunlong

Nanjing University Press

《中国思想家评传》简明读本 — 中英文版 —

主 编 周 宪 程爱民

国家汉办/孔子学院总部
Hanban/Confucius Institute Headquarters

庄 子

著 者 / 包兆会
译 者 / Thomas Mitchell
审 校 / 王正文
审 读 / 石云龙

南京大学出版社

Editor: Rui Yimin
Cover designed by Zhao Qin

First published 2010
by Nanjing University Press
No. 22, Hankou Road, Nanjing City, 210093
www.NjupCo.com

©2010 Nanjing University Press

Chinese Library Cataloguing in Publication Data
The CIP data for this title is on file with the Chinese Library.

ISBN10: 7-305-07177-5(pbk)
ISBN13: 978-7-305-07177-5(pbk)

《中国思想家评传》简明读本（中英文版）

编 委 会

主　任　许　琳　张异宾
副主任　马箭飞　周　宪
编　委　（按姓氏笔画为序）
　　　　马箭飞　王明生　左　健　许　琳　吕浩雪　张异宾
　　　　周　宪　周　群　金鑫荣　胡　豪　夏维中　徐兴无
　　　　蒋广学　程爱民
主　编　周　宪　程爱民

Editorial Committee

of

Collection of Critical Biographies of Chinese Thinkers

(Concise Edition, Chinese-English)

Executive Director: Xu Lin, Zhang Yibin

Associate Director: Ma Jianfei, Zhou Xian

Members of Committee: Cheng Aimin, Hu Hao, Jiang Guangxue

　　　　　　　　　　　Jin Xinrong, Lü Haoxue, Ma Jianfei, Wang Mingsheng

　　　　　　　　　　　Xia Weizhong, Xu Lin, Xu Xingwu, Zhang Yibin

　　　　　　　　　　　Zhou Qun, Zhou Xian, Zuo Jian

Editors-in-chief: Zhou Xian, Cheng Aimin

Books available in the collection

Confucius
《孔子》
978-7-305-06611-5

Laozi
《老子》
978-7-305-06607-8

Emperor Qin Shihuang
《秦始皇》
978-7-305-06608-5

Li Bai
《李白》
978-7-305-06609-2

Cao Xueqin
《曹雪芹》
978-7-305-06610-8

Du Fu
《杜甫》
978-7-305-06826-3

Zhuangzi
《庄子》
978-7-305-07177-5

Sima Qian
《司马迁》
978-7-305-07294-9

Mencius
《孟子》
978-7-305-07583-4

Mozi
《墨子》
978-7-305-07970-2

总序

General Preface

China is one of the cradles of world civilization, enjoying over five thousand years of history. It has produced many outstanding figures in the history of ancient thought, and left a rich philosophical heritage for both the Chinese people and the entire humanity. The fruit of these thinkers was to establish unique schools that over the long course of history have been continuously interpreted and developed. Today much of these thoughts are as relevant as ever and of extreme vitality for both China and the rest of the world. For instance, the ideal of "humaneness" and the concept of "harmony" taught by Confucius, the founder of Confucianism, have been venerated without ceasing by contemporary China as well as other Asian nations.

Ancient Chinese dynasties came and went, with each new dynasty producing its own scintillating system of thought. These rare and beautiful flowers of philosophy are grounded in the hundred schools vying for attention in pre-Qin times and the broad yet deep classical scholarship of Han and Tang times and in the simple yet profound occult learning of the Wei and Jin dynasties together with the entirely rational learning of Song and Ming Neo-Confucianism. The fertile soil of religious belief was Buddhism' s escape from the emptiness of the sensual world and Daoism' s spiritual cultivation in the search for identification with the immortals. The founders of these systems of thought included teachers, scholars, poets, politicians, scientists and monks— they made great contributions to such disparate cultural fields in ancient China as philosophy, politics, military science, economics, law, handicrafts, science and technology, literature, art, and religion. The ancient Chinese venerated them for their wisdom and for following moral paths, and called them sages, worthies, saints, wise men, and great masters, etc. Their words and writings, and sometimes their life experiences, constitute the rich matter of ancient Chinese thought distilled by later generations. The accomplishments of Chinese thought are rich and varied, and permeate such spiritual traditions as the harmony between humans and nature, the unification of thought and action, and the need for calmness during vigorous action, synthesizing the old and innovating something new.

Nanjing University Press has persisted over the last twenty years in publishing the 200-book series, *Collection of Critical Biographies of Chinese Thinkers*, under the general editorship of Professor Kuang Yaming, late honorary president of Nanjing University. This collection is the largest-scale project of research on Chinese thinking and culture undertaken since the beginning of the twentieth century. It selected more than 270 outstanding figures from Chinese history, composed their biographies and criticized their

中国是世界文明的发源地之一，有五千多年的文明史。在中国古代思想史上，涌现出了许许多多杰出的思想家，为中华民族乃至整个人类留下了丰富的思想遗产。这些思想成果独树一帜，在漫长的历史中又不断地被阐释、被发展，很多思想对于今天的中国乃至世界而言，仍然历久弥新，极具生命力。比如，儒家学派创始人孔子"仁"的理念、"和"的思想，不仅在当代中国，在其他亚洲国家也一直备受推崇。

古代中国朝代更迭，每一个朝代都有灿烂夺目的思想文化。百家争鸣的先秦诸子、博大宏深的汉唐经学、简易幽远的魏晋玄学、尽心知性的宋明理学是思想学术的奇葩；佛教的色空禅悦、道教的神仙修养是宗教信仰的沃土；其他如经世济民的政治、经济理想，巧夺天工的科技、工艺之道，风雅传神、丹青不老的文学艺术……都蕴涵着丰富的思想。这些思想的创造者中有教师、学者、诗人、政治家、科学家、僧人……他们在中国古代的哲学、政治、军事、经济、法律、工艺、科技、文学、艺术、宗教等各个文明领域内贡献巨大。古代中国人尊敬那些充满智慧、追求道德的人，称呼他们为圣人、贤人、哲人、智者、大师等，他们的言论、著作或被后人总结出来的经验构成了中国古代思想的重要内容，在丰富多彩中贯穿着天人合一、知行合一、刚健中和等精神传统，表现出综合创新的特色。

南京大学出版社坚持20余年，出版了由南京大学已故名誉校长匡亚明教授主编的《中国思想家评传丛书》，这套丛书共200部，是中国20世纪以来最为宏大的中国传统思想文化研究工程，选出了中国历史上270余位杰出人物，为他们写传记，

intellectual accomplishments; all in all, it is a rigorous and refined academic work. On this foundation, we introduce this series of concise readers, which provides much material in a simple format. It includes the cream of the crop of great figures relatively familiar to foreign readers. We have done our best to use plain but vivid language to narrate their human stories of interest; this will convey the wisdom of their thought and display the cultural magnificence of the Chinese people. In the course of spiritually communing with these representative thinkers from ancient China, readers will certainly be able to apprehend the undying essence of thoughts of the Chinese people.

Finally, we are deeply grateful for the support from Hanban/ Confucius Institute Headquarters, and the experts from home and abroad for their joint efforts in writing and translating this series.

Editors

November 2009

评论他们的思想成就，是严肃精深的学术著作。在此基础上推出的这套简明读本，则厚积薄发，精选出国外读者相对较为熟悉的伟大人物，力求用简洁生动的语言，通过讲述有趣的人物故事，传达他们的思想智慧，展示中华民族绚烂多姿的文化。读者在和这些中国古代有代表性的思想家的心灵对话中，一定能领略中华民族思想文化生生不息的精髓。

　　最后，我们衷心感谢国家汉办/孔子学院总部对本项目提供了巨大的支持，感谢所有参与此套丛书撰写和翻译工作的中外专家学者为此套丛书所做的辛勤而卓有成效的工作。

编者

2009年11月

目录
Contents

引言

Introduction

During the Spring Autumn and Warring States Periods there lived a great many pre-Qin scholars, including Laozi, Confucius, Mencius, Zhuangzi, Xunzi❶ , Han Fei, and more.This was a time characterized by a multitude of great thinkers, among whom Zhuangzi was distinguished as being particularly brilliant. Without him, Chinese cultural history would be much shorter, Chinese artistic history would seem boring and dull, and Chinese philosophical history would lack freshness and uniqueness.

Zhuangzi lived from about 368 B.C. to 286 B.C.. Hailing from the town of Meng in the state of Song (located in today' s northeast Shangqiu in Henan Province), Zhuang was his surname and Zhuang Zhou his full name. He was a contemporary of Mencius of Zou in Shandong (who lived from about 372 B.C. to 289 B.C.) as well as Aristotle of ancient Greece (who lived from about 384 B.C. to 322 B.C.).

Compared with other great pre-Qin thinkers, Zhuangzi' s life was simple and impoverished. He fished in Pu River, sang while he walked along the banks of small ponds, lived in ramshackle alleys, married, had children, and lived by weaving straw sandals. He preferred to, " play in filth rather than be bridled by statesmen," he did not insist on possessing anything, and did not exert himself to be successful in anything. He was indifferent and contemptuous towards such worldly things as wealth, distinction, fame, and great accomplishments. His life is primarily recorded in Sima Qian' s *Record of the Grand Historian: Biography of Laozi and Han Fei* as well as some sections of his own work, *Zhuangzi*.

Like Zhuangzi, Mozi (who lived from about 480 B.C. to 420 B.C.) was a philosopher of humble birth. As such, he was similar to Zhuangzi in both philosophical views and social position. Mozi was adept at handicrafts, an art which would later become his career. He referred to himself as *bi ren*, meaning " humble man," and was referred to by others as the " patched clothes scholar" and " lowly man." Mozi had a deep understanding of the misery of the laboring class, which caused him to be ardently opposed to the principle of, " the rich insulting the poor and the noble despising the lowly," and instead advocated " mutual love and mutual benefit" (*see Mozi: Universal Love*). He believed that this " universal love" would, " give food to the hungry, clothes to the naked, rest to the weary, and order to the chaotic." However, there were some differences between him and Zhuangzi. For instance, in order to promote his philosophy, Mozi accepted disciples from far and wide, and his trusted followers numbered in the hundreds. In his day, Mohism was a powerful and dynamic school of thought, even rivaling Confucianism, the major school of

　　在春秋战国时期，诞生了一大批先秦诸子，如老子、孔子、孟子、墨子、庄子、荀子、韩非子❶等。这是群星灿烂的时代。庄子在其中显得特别耀眼，也卓尔不群。中国文化史缺少了他，文化史就少写了许多；中国艺术史缺少了他，显得无趣和寡味；中国思想史缺少了他，减少了新颖和独特。

　　庄子（约前368—前286），名周，宋国蒙（今河南商丘东北）人。与他同时代的有山东邹人孟子（约前372—前289），古希腊的亚里士多德（Aristotle，前384—前322）。

　　在先秦诸子中，庄子一生平淡，也贫穷。他垂钓在濮水，行吟在泽畔，住陋巷、娶妻、有子女，以编草鞋为生。他追求的是"宁游戏污渎之中自快，无为有国者所羁"的生活，不强求一切，也不苦心经营。尤其对世俗汲汲所求的富贵显达、功名事业，他无动于衷，反而有些远之、鄙之。他的生平主要记载在司马迁《史记·老子韩非列传》及《庄子》的一些篇什中。

　　作为同是战国时期的平民思想家，与庄子思想倾向和社会出身相近的要数墨子（约前480—前420)。墨子，平民出身，精通手工技艺，是小手工业者。他自称"鄙人"，被人称为"布衣之士"和"贱人"。墨子对劳动人民的悲惨生活有深切的体会，因此，他激烈反对"富侮贫，贵傲贱"，主张"兼相爱，交相利"（《墨子·兼爱》)，认为这样可使"饥者得食，寒者得衣，劳者得息，乱者得治"。但他与庄子还有些不同，他为宣传自己的主张，广收门徒，一般的亲信弟子达数百人

---

❶ 译者注：古时指有学问的男人，也指老师，如孔子、孟子和墨子。

❶ Translator's note: " zi " means " master." It is the ancient title of respect for a learned or virtuous man such as Kongzi (Confucius), Mengzi (Mencius) and Mozi.

thoughts. He once successfully prevented the state of Chu from invading the state of Song by defeating Gongshu Ban❶ in debate. While a senior official of Song, he traveled for many years in the kingdoms of Qi, Zheng, Wei, Chu, Yue and others, advocating his political ideas.

In his whole life, Zhuangzi was never as active and influential as Mozi. Though he worked for a time as a minor official in charge of a lacquer tree orchard, most of his life was spent in distant lands developing his philosophy. He had very few followers: though in the chapter of *Zhuangzi* entitled " The Mountain Tree" there are records of his disciples traveling with him through the mountains and in the chapter " Lie Yu Kou" it is written that his disciples planned on giving him an elaborate funeral, yet in all these records we only find the name of one follower: Lin Qie.

In the Spring Autumn and Warring States Periods, Zhuangzi distinguished himself from many other renowned thinkers of various schools of thought such as the Confucians headed by Confucius and Mencius, the Mohists headed by Mozi, and the Legalists such as Han Fei. He did so by not passionately advocating political and social policies and by not traveling around and promoting his own philosophies. For instance, in order to promote the concept of " benevolent government," Zhuangzi' s contemporary Mozi maintained regular contact with King Hui of Liang (ruled from 369 B.C. to 319 B.C.), King Xuan of Qi (ruled from 319 B.C. to 301 B.C.) and the head of the state in which Zhuangzi lived, Lord Yan of Song (lived from 338 B.C. to 298 B.C., ruled from 288 B.C. to 286 B.C.), and even carried out political reform in the state of Song. Zhuangzi did not concern himself with sweeping historical narratives, barely mentioning earthshaking events such as political coups, battles, and the diplomatic intrigues of the Warring States Period in his writings. Instead, he focused on the destiny of individuals in a world full of absurdity, turbulence, war, death, uncertainty and misery. His goal was to discover the way by which people can find happiness and freedom during their short lives. Zhuangzi suggested that this was best accomplished by " free and easy wandering."

This was Zhuangzi: his life is worthy of our study.

之多，在当时形成了声势浩大的墨家学派，可以与当时同样为显学的儒家学派相抗衡。他还曾和公输般❶论战，成功制止了楚国对宋国的侵略战争。他曾做过宋国大夫，长期奔走于齐、郑、卫、楚、越等诸侯国之间，宣传他的政治主张。

庄子没有墨子生前轰轰烈烈，一段时期曾做过管理漆园的小吏，更多时候一个人在僻处自说。他的弟子也很少，虽然《庄子·山木》中记载庄子在山中行走时有他的弟子相随，《庄子·列御寇》中记载庄子临终的时候，弟子们想要厚葬他，但明确记载庄子弟子有名有姓的只有一个——蔺且。

在春秋战国时期，庄子也不像儒家的孔子和孟子、墨家的墨子、法家的韩非子那样热衷于提出安邦定国的政治策略，开出安定社会秩序、拯救天下苍生的社会药方，也没像他们那样到处游说，推广自己的政治理想。比如，与他同时期的孟子，为了推广其"仁政"，与梁惠王（前369—前319在位）、齐宣王（前319—前301在位），以及庄子所在国元首宋君偃（前338—前298，前288—前286在位）等都有过直接的交往，还曾到宋国搞过政治改革。庄子也不关注历史的宏大叙事，甚至在他的书中也很少正面记载发生在战国时期的那些惊天动地、改天换地的大事件，比如宫廷政变、征战杀伐、政治外交，而是关注在这个荒谬、动荡，到处战争杀戮，充满人生无常和苦难的世上，个人如何安身立命，个人如何在有限的生存空间中活得快乐和自由。庄子的回答是"逍遥游"。

这就是庄子。他的一生值得我们寻味。

---

❶ 译者注：公输般，中国古代的能工巧匠，即"公输子"。因为他是鲁国（今山东）人，所以通常也被叫做鲁班。

❶ Translator's note: Gongshu Ban, known as the father of builders in ancient China, he was also referred to as the Master Gongshu (Gongshuzi). Because he was from the State of Lu (today's Shangdong), records most commonly refer to him as Lu Ban.

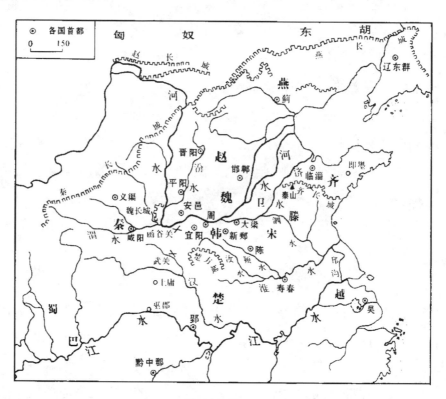

战国形势图

Map of the Warring States Period

一　庄子时代

Chapter Ⅰ　The Time of Zhuangzi

The time of Zhuangzi was a time of war and slaughter.

During the Warring States Period, incessant wars were fought for wealth, land, and domination of China. In their struggle to conquer their rivals economically and militarily, the Chinese states all underwent various degrees of reform.

In the state of Wei, Lord Wen (in office from 445 B.C. to 396 B.C.) assigned Li Kui to take charge of political reform. He also incented farming and fighting, the construction of irrigation systems, and promoted economic development, all of which caused the state of Wei to become the first powerful state of its time. In 356 B.C., King Xiao of Qin employed Shang Yang to carry out political reform, causing the state to grow rapidly in power. That same year, the state of Qi also underwent political reform and became stronger. King Dao of the state of Chu (ruled from 401 B.C. to 381 B.C.) charged Wu Qi with reforming state affairs, and though this did not produce great results, it did preserve the state's original position as a great power. During the constant wars, the state of Yan also increased in power. The competition between these seven states came to define the condition of the Warring States Period.

In order to obtain more land, population, and tax revenue, the wars between states began to intensify, and the scale of the conflicts began to escalate. For example, in 341 B.C. at the battle of Maling, fought between the states of Wei and Qi, Wei mobilized 100,000 soldiers. In 293 B.C., the great general of Qin, Bai Qi, delivered a crushing defeat to the army of Wei at Huayang, beheading 150,000 soldiers. Because the various states employed mandatory conscription during the Warring States Period, all farmers within the age limit could be forced to join the army during times of war. Because of this, a large battle would involve tens or even hundreds of thousands of men and horses, and the scale of battles became larger than ever before.

In the chapter "In the World of Men," Zhuangzi describes the carnage of war. Through the character Yan Hui, he explained that in his time, there were many kingdoms like the state of Wey. The monarchs of these states acted arbitrarily and dogmatically. They were reckless in the administration of their kingdoms, viewing the commoners' lives to be as worthless as weeds. On a whim, they would send commoners to their deaths; consequently the corpses of commoners were piled high on the fields of battle. To mock the cruelty of these bloody wars, Zhuangzi created the character Crippled Shu to explain how commoners would escape being drafted into the army. Crippled Shu was extremely ugly: his chin was pulled back under his navel, his shoulders were higher than his head, his guts were piled on top, and his legs pressed on his

庄子的时代是战争和杀戮的时代。

战国时期，为了财富、土地和雄霸天下，各国之间的战争非常频繁。为了能在战争中靠经济、军事实力战胜对手，各国进行了不同程度的改革。

魏国由于魏文侯（前445—前396在位）任用李悝变法，改革政治、奖励耕战、兴修水利、发展经济，最早成为强国。公元前356年，秦孝公任用卫鞅变法，秦国强盛起来。同年，齐国也进行政治改革，国势也强盛起来。楚国在楚悼王（前401—前381在位）时任用吴起变法，虽然没有取得很大成果，但它保持了原来就是强国的地位。燕国也在战争中渐露头角。于是，形成了七强并立的形势。

为了夺取更多的土地、人口和税收，国与国之间的兼并战争更激烈，战争规模更大了。公元前341年，魏与齐之间的马陵之战，魏国动用了"十万之军"。公元前293年，秦国大将白起大败魏军于华阳，斩首15万。战国时期，由于各国已普遍实行郡县征兵制度，作战时所有及龄农民都有可能被强迫编入军队。因而，一场大战往往动用几万、几十万人马，战争规模达到了前所未有的地步。

庄子在《人间世》篇中对战争的杀戮有所描述。他借着颜回的口告诉我们这样一个历史事实：在庄子时代，像卫国这样的诸侯国很多。这些国的国君行事独断，治理自己的国家十分轻率，视百姓的性命如芥草，轻易就让百姓去送死，在战争中死去的百姓尸横遍野。同时也通过塑造"支离疏"这一人物形象来说明当时百姓对征兵的逃避。支离疏，人长得丑陋不堪，

ribs. Because he was so handicapped, he could wander around the field used for drafting soldiers, waving good-bye to all the soldiers leaving for war. ❶

War and death were not only in the background of Zhuangzi's life, but they were also integral pieces of the inconstant, cruel, and violent world which he saw. It was this cruel reality that contributed to Zhuangzi's decision to withdraw from "law of the jungle" world which he inhabited.

In the time of Zhuangzi, scholars became the most active social class.

During the Warring States Period it was common practice for scholars to travel extensively. In intrastate affairs, these traveling scholars helped to prosper and rule the state; in interstate affairs, they were also adept at negotiating the interests of the various states. Consequently, it became common for all levels of the governing class, from local wealthy families to the dukes and kings of great countries, to recruit these traveling scholars. The nobility realized that in obtaining one truly great scholar, it would be possible for them to obtain all of China. With able men in their employ, they could realize their dreams of greatness, accumulate the wealth of all under heaven, and enlarge the land of their states. For instance, the state of Yan was once one of the weakest of the seven great kingdoms. When King Zhao of Yan came to power, he planned to grow his strength, declaring that he would be courteous to the wise and spend any price to recruit worthy scholars. Because of this policy, many talented men came to the state of Yan: Su Qin arrived from Zhou, Zou Yan came from Qi, Yue Yi came from Zhao, and Qu Jing from Chu. The state of Yan became stronger with each passing day.

For traveling scholars, this was a time of rare opportunity to develop their ambitious plans. As long as they proved their usefulness to their respective lords, it was enough for them to have just one small talent to be kept on at court. Even men who resorted to petty, under-handed schemes could be received by lords such as Lord Mengchang of Qi. Traveling scholars gave council and formulated plans, traveled around to advance their lords' interests, and managed political or economic affairs. If able to win the appreciation of their lord, even those of humble birth were able to experience a meteoric rise in their careers, possibly becoming permanent chancellors in court. Wei Yang, for example, began as a retainer of Gongshu Cuo, the prime minister of Wei. After coming to Qin, he attracted the attention of King Xiao of Qin, eventually rising to the highest position in the government, *da liang zao* ❷ .

头缩在肚脐下面，双肩高过头顶，五脏挤在背上，两腿紧靠肋旁。因残疾，官府征兵时他可以大摇大摆地在征兵场所闲逛。❶

战争、杀戮不仅构成了庄子生存的一个背景，也是庄子看待这个无常、残酷、暴力的世界的一个组成部分，并一定程度上促使庄子作出退出这个弱肉强食、遵从丛林法则的世界的决定。

庄子的时代，士成为最为活跃的社会阶层。

战国时代，游士之风盛行。由于游士对内可以兴邦治国，对外可以通过游说平衡各国利益关系，所以小到地方豪门贵族，大到诸侯王公，都盛行纳士。王公贵族也确实意识到，得一人才可以得天下，有用之才可以帮助他们圆强国之梦，聚天下之财，并万里之地。比如，燕国原是七雄中较弱的国家。燕昭王即位后，奋发图强，"卑身厚币以招贤者"，很多人才都跑到燕国去：苏秦"从周归燕"、邹衍"从齐归燕"、乐毅"从赵归燕"、屈景"从楚归燕"。燕国日趋强盛起来。

对游士来说，这也是一个千载难逢，可以让自己大展宏图的时代。只要对效忠的主人有用，有一技之长都可以，所以连鸡鸣狗盗之徒都被孟尝君收在门下。这些游士或为主人出谋划策；或奔走游说；或经办某项事务，若得主人赏识，原来出身卑微的，也许一夜之间就能飞黄腾达，被提拔为朝廷的执政大臣。如卫鞅，本是魏相公叔痤的家臣，入秦之后说动了秦孝公，做到了秦国一人之下万人之上的最高官职——大良造❷。

---

❶ 参见庄子《庄子全集》，Watson Burton译，纽约：哥伦比亚大学出版社1968年版。网址：Terebess Asia Online. http://www.terebess.hu/english/chuangtzu.html.
❷ 译者注：官名。战国初期为秦的最高官职，掌握军政大权。

---

❶ Zhuangzi. *The Complete Works of Chuang-Tzu*. Trans. Watson Burton. New York: Columbia University Press, 1968. Terebess Asia Online. http://www.terebess.hu/english/chuangtzu.html.
❷ Translator's note:The supreme officer of Qin in the early Warring States Period, who possessed the military power.

Because the various states of the Warring States Period were constantly searching for talented men to recruit, traveling scholars had ample opportunity to put their talents on display. If one was unable to be fully appreciated in one land, he could travel to a distant state where he could compete for a position in the government. Consequently, there were many men who worked for one state one day and another state the next. There were even some who helped one state attack another, only to later switch sides and help the second state counterattack the first. For instance, in 333 B.C., Gongsun Yan of Wei left his home state to become the *da liang zao* of King Hui of Qin. In 330 B.C., Gongsun Yan defeated the armies of Wei at Diaoyin (located in modern southern Ganquan County in Shanxi Province), capturing the Wei general Long Jia and forcing the state of Wei to cede its land west of the Yellow River to Qin. The next year, Zhang Yi of Wei was employed by the state of Qin, and Gongsun Yan fled back to Wei where he became a general.

At the time of the Warring States, Lord Mengchang of Qi, Lord Pingyuan of Zhao, Lord Xinling of Wei, Lord Chunshen of Chu, and Lü Buwei, Marquis of Wenxin in Qin, each had over 3,000 scholars in their employ. The Ji Xia Academy located in the state of Qi accepted many worthy scholars, at times as many as a thousand men. It was also the school where Mencius and Xunzi studied. Of course, there were also imitation scholars. One example of an imitation scholar can be found in the story of "The Terrible Flutist Who Made the Right Number," a story which originated from the Warring States period, specifically during the reign of King Xuan of Qi. King Xuan sought to gather talented musicians from all over China, and demanded that 300 musicians play at each performance. Among his musicians there was a scholar who lived to the south of the capital city (a land referred to as "nan guo" in ancient Chinese). The man boasted of his musical prowess to King Xuan. After hearing the scholar's boastful remarks and without any audition, King Xuan happily allowed the scholar to join his musicians, even offering him delicious food every day. In reality, the scholar couldn't play the flute at all; he was just there to bring the number of musicians to 300. After the death of King Xuan, the next king, King Min, preferred listening to each musician one at a time. Afraid of what could happen, the deceitful scholar decided to flee the court.

In terms of domestic politics, traveling scholars assisted the monarch in ruling and managing the state, promoted political reform, and rectified the administration of the officials. In the areas of administration and management of commoners, the local nobility most often employed Legalist policies. The most representative of these included Li Kui of Wei, Wei Yang of Qin, Wu Qi

正因为战国时期各诸侯都在广罗人才，游士施展才华就有了很多机会。若这边不能慧眼识明珠，不被赏识，就可以远走他乡，在异地博得一官半职。所以，那个时期，今天在这个国家做官，明天就跑到另一国家高就的人，比比皆是。有的人甚至今天帮助这一国攻打另一国，明天反过来，帮助另一国攻打这一国。如，公元前333年秦惠王任用魏人公孙衍为大良造。前330年，公孙衍打败魏军于雕阴（今陕西省甘泉县南），俘虏了魏将龙贾，迫使魏国把河西献给秦国。第二年，魏人张仪入秦，公孙衍又跑回到魏国做了将领。

当时，齐国的孟尝君、赵国的平原君、魏国的信陵君、楚国的春申君、秦国的文信侯吕不韦，所养的士多达三千人。齐国的稷下学官广纳贤士，最多时达一千多人。孟子、荀子都去过那里。当然，其中也有"冒牌"的。"滥竽充数"这则故事讲述的就是齐宣王时代，齐宣王招聚天下音乐人才，每次吹奏必三百人在列，其中有个南郭处士向齐宣王推荐自己很有音乐才华，齐宣王仅听一面之辞，也没经过考核，就高高兴兴地把他纳入乐团，并为之提供丰盛的食品。那个处士实则不会吹竽，却混在吹竽的队伍里充数。宣王死，湣王立，好一一听之，处士选择了逃跑。

游士对内，主要协助统治者治理国家，进行政治改革，整顿吏治。尤其在整顿吏治和管理百姓方面，地方诸侯往往采纳

of Chu, Shen Buhai of Han, and Zou Ji of Qi (all of whom were in power between 400 B.C. and 350 B.C.). These powerful officials promoted Legalist philosophies, advocating the strict enforcement of the law in bringing order to the state. They viewed the law as an effective tool for centralizing state power and for strengthening their rule over the peasants. Shen Buhai said, "He who sees on his own is called intelligent, he who hears on his own is called wise. He who is able to act on his own will rule all under heaven (*Han Fei: Collection of Other Stories Part III*)." By this, he meant that when dealing with ministers and government officials, the ruler should pretend to not hear, not see, and not know what is going on. He should not reveal his own desires, wisdom, or discernment. In so doing, he could prevent his ministers from guessing his intentions, flattering him to obtain favors, or concealing their own intentions. He advocated using secretive plots to control government officials and rule the people, as well as using the rule of law to strengthen the qualification, assessment, and supervision of ministers.

In terms of education, the various states employed Confucian policies. At the time of Zhuangzi, Confucianism and Mohism were very influential. In particular, the Confucian concepts of "righteousness and benevolence" and "benign government" were very attractive to the states of the time. Thus, they employed Confucian philosophies to deceive and curry favor with the common people. For instance, Lord Wen of Wei employed Li Kui and other Legalists as generals and ministers of his state, all the while calling the Confucian scholars Bu Zixia and Tian Zifang his teachers and promulgating Confucian teachings. Because Mohists advocated equality and love in human relationships and sought to ensure that the commoners would have food to eat, clothes to wear, and time to rest from work, many ordinary citizens supported Mozi's teachings. Followers of Mohist teachings were known for their strict organization and discipline. They had to obey their higher-ranking superiors, and they were willing to brave all sorts of hardships to complete their missions. Mohists who made great contributions to Mohism were called *juzi*, or "hard iron implements." One such juzi, named Meng Sheng, helped Lord Yangcheng of Chu protect his holdings. Later, Lord Yangcheng participated in a rebellion in opposition to the Wu Qi Reform and was forced to flee, his land being taken over by the king of Chu. Meng Sheng took 183 disciples who fought and died in his defense. However, after peace was re-established, these kinds of armed groups became an unstable element in society, resulting in the government banning Mohist organizations after the Western Han Dynasty. As Mohism gradually exited the historical stage, Confucianism, because of its

的是法家的政策。最典型的是公元前400—公元前350年左右，
魏国的李悝、秦国的卫鞅、楚国的吴起、韩国的申不害、齐国
的邹忌等先后推广法家思想，主张通过厉行法治来达到治国的
目的，把法看成实行中央集权的有效工具，通过法治加强对广
大农民的统治和整顿吏治。申不害说："独视者谓明，独听者
为聪。能独断者，故可以为天下主。"（《韩非子·外储说右上》）
意思是说，大王与臣民打交道过程中装作没听见、没看见、不
知道，不暴露自己的欲望、智慧和观察力，使臣下无从猜测国
君的意图，无从讨好取巧，无从隐藏自己，也就是要用阴谋权
术来驾驭臣下和统治人民，用法治加强对臣下的考核和监督。

　　诸侯国在教导方面则采用儒家的政策。在庄子时代，儒家
和墨家思想很有影响力，尤其儒家思想所讲究的"仁义"和
"王道"对各诸侯国都有吸引力，各诸侯国利用儒家这一套思
想对百姓进行欺骗和笼络。如魏文侯一方面起用李悝等法家为
将相，另一方面，尊儒家卜子夏为"师"，并敬重本国儒者田
子方等人，宣扬儒家思想。墨家提倡人与人之间平等相爱，要
使普通老百姓有饭吃、有衣穿，劳动时有休息时间，所以底层
百姓跟随者众。信奉墨家学说的人以严密的组织性、纪律性著
称，所有的墨者都必须服从上级领导，为任务可以赴汤蹈火。
墨家学派对墨家有成就的人称"钜子"。钜子孟胜替楚国的阳
城君守卫封国，阳城君后因参加反对吴起变法叛乱出逃，他的
封国被楚王收回，孟胜竟带了一百八十三个弟子为他殉身。但
是，一旦社会安定下来，这种带有武装性质的集团就成了社会
不稳定的因素。所以西汉以后，政府对墨家的思想和墨家组织
进行禁止。墨家渐渐在历史上淡出舞台，而儒家思想因着对

softening and numbing effects on the commoners, began to be actively promoted by the government.

In terms of foreign politics, traveling scholars primarily negotiated on behalf of the kingdoms in which they served. Because of the incessant warfare between states and the resulting conflicts of interest, interstate relations were often tense requiring frequent negotiations.

During the Warring States period, the two dominant foreign policy strategies were "vertical coalitions" and "horizontal alliances." "Vertical coalitions" ❶ referred to several weak countries banding together to attack one strong country in order to prevent being annexed by the stronger country. "Horizontal alliances" ❷ referred to a strong country winning over a few weak countries and attacking other weak countries in order to annex their territory. Those traveling scholars who became accustomed to political battles became adept at forming "vertical coalitions or horizontal alliances." In this time of "vertical coalitions" and "horizontal alliances," diplomacy was extremely important. In particular, Zhang Yi of Qin became very successful at forming "horizontal alliances," thus achieving his goal of annexing foreign territory. The structure of "vertical coalitions and horizontal alliances" was very complex and many ministers of great states participated in forming these coalitions or alliances.

In the process of making a name for themselves, traveling scholars were naturally caught up in all kinds of political battles and conflicts of interest, forcing them to frequently risk their lives. Because of this lifestyle, worry and anxiety were written on their faces instead of cheerfulness and happiness. In the chapter of *Zhuangzi* "In the World of Men," Zhuangzi records the story of the revered Ye Zigao who was ordered to serve as an envoy to the state of Qi and the impossible choice he faced.

Ye Zigao was very depressed, because if he was unable to complete the tasks given to him by the king of Chu, he would suffer a terrible punishment. But if he were to finish the tasks, he would have to work himself almost to death. In the end, no matter what he did, there would be horrible consequences.

百姓具有怀柔和麻痹的性质，遂成为历代政府着力推广的一种思想。

游士对外，主要代表宗主国进行各种外交斡旋。由于国与国之间的战争杀戮、利益冲突，导致相互之间关系紧张，所以需要有各种外交斡旋。

战国时代的诸侯国对外政策是"合纵"与"连横"。所谓"合纵"❶，即"合众弱以攻一强"，就是许多弱国联合起来抵抗一个强国，以防止被强国兼并；所谓"连横"❷，即"事一强以攻众弱"，就是由强国拉拢一些弱国来进攻另外一些弱国，以达到兼并土地的目的。游士中担任纵横家的就是适应这种政治斗争的需要而产生的。这是"合纵"与"连横"的时代，政治外交特别重要。张仪在秦国推行连横策略获得成功，达到了对外兼并土地的目的。合纵连横的形势很复杂，不少大国的大臣和纵横家参与合纵、连横活动。

游士为了谋取功名与利禄，自然要卷入各种政治斗争和利害冲突中，就要冒着各种生命危险。于是，写在他们脸上的是焦虑和忧愁，不是生命的快乐和悠然。庄子《人间世》篇记载了叶公子高出使齐国所面临的两难选择的故事，道出了其中一二。

叶公子高非常忧愁，因为楚王交托给他的任务若不完成，就有惩处的祸患；若要把交托的事情办成，自己肯定要鞠躬尽瘁、呕心沥血，忧劳成疾，结果，不论事情成或不成，都有后

---

❶ 译者注：战国时期，七国中相对弱小的五国联合起来。五国土地南北相连，故称合纵。

❷ 译者注：战国时期，七国中相对强大的齐国和秦国联合起来。两国土地东西相连，故称连横。

---

❶ Translator's note:These alliances were called "vertical coalitions" because the weaker 5 of the 7 warring states were positioned geographically north-south, thus making an alliance between them appear vertical on a map.

❷ Translator's note:These alliances were called "horizontal alliances" because the stronger 2 of the 7 warring states (Qi and Qin) were positioned geographically east-west, thus making their wars appear horizontal on a map.

From the time Ye Zigao was commanded to serve as an envoy, the heat caused by his anxiety forced him to drink ice water at night in order to cool his body down. Even before beginning to carry out his orders, his body's equilibrium was already thrown out of balance, and his health suffered. Added to this was his fear that he would be unable to complete the tasks given to him and would have to face the terrible punishment of the King of Chu.

This illustrates the two difficult choices faced by traveling scholars. They could choose to make their livelihood outside the political arena, and be, in a sense, like wild ducks in a pond which are not kept in a cage but are rather free to move about as they wish. However, this life entailed poverty, requiring them to move constantly in search of their next meal. Their other choice was an official career, but there they would be locked in a figurative cage and forced to listen to the orders of their master, to like what their master liked and base their standards on their master's standards. If they failed, they faced harsh punishments. On the other hand, there were also benefits; at least they did not have to worry about food or clothing. Unfortunately, during the Warring States Period, the vast majority of traveling scholars chose the second life. As the political strategist Su Qin said, "Scholars live for wealth and glory, taking the pleasure of their masters, fine things, and official positions" as their highest goals (from *The Book of the Warring States: First Book of Qin*). This is the weakness of human nature.

Honest, upright scholars, on the other hand, refrained from aiding tyrants. However, if one were to point out the mistakes of a tyrant or disobey his wishes, he would face grave punishment, possibly even death. There are many historical instances of this, such as when Emperor Jie of Xia executed Guan Longfeng and when Emperor Zhou of Shang executed Bi Gan, forced the viscount of Wei to leave court, and enslaved the viscount of Ji. Because of this, followers of Daoism often chose to live outside the political system in order to protect their lives. They chose a simple, rustic lifestyle, relying on their own labor, escaping from politics, and enjoying the simple pleasures of life. Many Daoist hermits such as the Old Man carrying weeding device, Chang Ju, and Jie Ni all urged Confucius not to promote his philosophy of benevolent government to the monarchs of China, because by so doing he risked being killed. We read of one instance of this near the end of the chapter "In the World of Men," when Zhuangzi writes of the hermit Jie Yu of Chu who exhorted Confucius saying, "Oh Confucius! When the world has the Way, you can still be a part of mainstream society and teach your philosophy. But now the world does not have the Way, and all you can do is protect your life by avoiding

患。叶公子高自从接到出使齐国的命令后，晚上就要靠喝冰水解热，真是忧心如焚啊！他还未接触到真正的事务，就开始出现阴阳失调，身体有了问题。再加上他很怕交代的事情将来不能完成，要面临楚王的惩罚，所以实在是忧愁交织啊！

这对游士来说，面临着人生两种选择，一是选择在仕途外谋生，如水泽里的野鸡，不被关在笼子里，可以自由自在地在水泽里走来走去，但意味着贫穷，也许走十步才啄到一口食，走百步才能喝到一口水；另一种选择在仕途中发展，但要关在笼子里被驯养，听从主人的各种命令，以主人的喜好为自己的喜好，以主人的标准为自己的标准，否则会面临主人的惩罚，当然也有回报，就是不愁穿，不愁吃。悲哀的是，战国时代大多数游士选择了后一种人生。用纵横家苏秦的话说，士人活着就是竭力追逐富贵尊荣，以所谓"说（悦）人主"、"出其金玉锦绣，取卿相之尊"（《战国策·秦策一》）为最高目标。这也许是人性的弱点。

对那些心地正直的人来说，总不能帮助暴君为虎作伥。但，若指出暴君的过错，违背他们的意愿，就有可能面临杀身之祸，历史上就有夏桀杀了关龙逢，商纣杀了比干，微子去之，箕子为之奴的历史事实。所以，为保护自身安全计，遵循道家思想生活的人，往往选择的是不在政治体制里与暴君共舞，而是选择一种简朴的生活，靠自身的劳作，享受平凡中的幸福。很多道家的隐居者，比如靠农耕养活自己的荷蓧丈人、长沮、桀溺都劝孔子，不要到处在国君面前推广自己的仁义，这很容易招致杀身之祸的。《人间世》篇的末尾，也记载了楚国隐居者接舆对孔子的劝告："孔子啊，孔子，天下有道，你还可以融入体制，你可以成就教化，但现在是天下无道，你唯一可做的就是在不损害自己品性的前提下怎样保全自己的性命，免遭刑罚。

punishments without harming your moral character. It is dangerous to go about flaunting your moral uprightness all over the place like that and attracting attention to yourself, you must be more discreet, more discreet."

The world at the time of Zhuangzi was not only full of death and chaos, but also moral debauchery. The kings of many states were fatuous and many prime ministers were treacherous.

Among traveling scholars, there were those who were untrustworthy and hypocritical, such as Zhang Yi. In 328 B.C., Zhang Yi masterminded a "horizontal alliance" for the state of Qin which brought the states of Han and Wei under its banner, and forced the heir princes of these two states to present themselves in the Qin court. At the same time, he sent Prince Sang to take the Wei city of Puyang, only to implore King Hui of Qin to return Puyang to the state of Wei. He then sent Prince Yao as a "hostage" to Wei. Afterwards, Zhang Yi traveled to Wei, where he advised the king of Wei to not be rude to Qin. The state of Wei had no choice but to cede 15 counties to Qin in order to mend relations with Qin. Another example is Li Si. Like Han Fei, Li Si was also a disciple of Xunzi, but because Li Si was jealous of Han Fei's talent, he sought for ways to bring about Han Fei's destruction. When Han Fei was sent to Qin as an envoy, Li Si slandered him, forcing Han Fei to poison himself in prison. How lamentable is the conflict between friends!

Among traveling scholars, there were those whose only concern was for their own future, caring only about national power and personal gain without a thought for moral correctness. Lord Meng Chang was an example of such a man. About 310 B.C., the son of Tian Ying of Qi, Tian Wen (also called Lord Meng Chang) became prime minister. After 10 years of gradually building up his personal power, in 301 B.C., Tian Wen became the true ruler of Qi, to the point that "when one hears of Qi, one only hears of Tian Wen and not of the king." In 301 B.C., Lord Meng Chang successfully negotiated a "vertical coalition" uniting Qi, Han, and Wei against Chu, defeating the Chu armies. Chu surrendered to Qi, and even Qin began to be afraid of Qi, hastily mending its relations with Qi. In 299 B.C., the state of Qin invited Lord Meng Chang to become the prime minister of Qin. Because such a deal would be damaging to the state of Zhao, it prevented Qin from employing Lord Meng Chang, sending a Zhao minister, Lou Huan, to be prime minister of Qin instead. This brought Qin, Zhao, and Song into an alliance against Qi, Han, and Wei. Fearing the potential alliance, King Zhao of Qin attempted to assassinate Lord Meng Chang. Lord Meng Chang, however, fled from Qin, returning to Qi. A few years after having returned to Qi, he incited one nobleman named Tian Jia to

你那样到处展示自己的德行，到处惹别人的注意，是很危险的，要收敛一些，要收敛一些。"

庄子时代不仅是战争杀戮之乱世，昏上奸相之浊世，也是道德败坏之衰世。

游士中不守信用、表里不一的，如张仪。公元前328年，张仪在秦国采取联合韩、魏的连横策略，迫使韩、魏太子来朝。同时派公子桑攻取魏国的蒲阳，却又请求秦惠王将蒲阳还给魏国；又将公子繇作为"人质"送到魏国。然后，张仪前往魏国，劝说魏惠王不可以对秦国无礼，魏国只好把上郡十五个县在内的地方一起献给秦国，与秦和好。再如李斯。李斯与韩非子同为荀子门下弟子，但因李斯嫉妒韩非子才华，结果韩非子出使秦国时，遭李斯谗害，被迫在狱中服毒自杀。真是同门相煎何急！

游士中只为自己前程考虑，藉国家权势济个人私欲没有道德立场的，如孟尝君。公元前310年左右，齐国田婴的儿子田文即孟尝君当上了相国，经过十年培植自己的势力，至公元前301年，田文在齐国专权，以至于"闻齐之有田文，不闻有其王"。公元前301年，孟尝君合纵成功，齐、韩、魏三国联合起来攻楚，大败楚军。楚向齐屈服，秦国也恐惧起来，和齐国修好。公元前299年，秦请孟尝君入秦为相。赵国因为秦、齐两大国联合不利于己，便促使秦国免除孟尝君相位，由赵国派遣楼缓入秦为相，于是秦、赵、宋三国和齐、韩、魏形成了两个对立的集团。于是，秦昭王要杀死孟尝君。孟尝君逃离秦国，

start a rebellion. The rebellion failed, and Lord Meng Chang was forced to flee again, this time to Wei where he became prime minister to the king of Wei. Once he was in the state of Wei, Lord Meng Chang formulated another "vertical coalition" with Zhao and Qin to attack Qi.

Rulers were equally inconstant. King Min of Qi wanted to attack the state of Song and take the great commercial city of Ding Dao. He made a temporary alliance with Zhao to attack Qin, then turned around and allied with Qin to attack Zhao, all to prevent Qin and Zhao from interfering with his ambitions of territorial growth.

What these men wanted was profit and balance of power, not honesty and regulations.

Because of this, there were unending cat and mouse games of war between the various states. In 354 B.C., the State of Wei attacked Zhao. Zhao was unable to repel the assault and had no choice but to implore Qi for aid. At the Battle of Guiling (in modern Changyuan in Henan Province), Qi routed the Wei armies. 10 years after, Wei and Zhao allied against Han. Han was unable to beat back the invaders, and asked for help from Qi. At the Battle of Maling (in modern southwest Fan County, Henan Province), Qi once again routed the Wei armies. After this, Wei had no choice but to admit defeat, bow down in submission to Qi, and swear fealty to Qi. However, this angered neighboring Chu, who felt that Wei, like the state of Qi, was the rightful land of the supreme king of Zhou. By taking Wei as a vassal, Qi was showing disdain for Chu. This caused Chu to preemptively attack Qi in order to save face. Wei said the war was justified and it would be best if Chu won to erase the shame of defeat at Maling. However, though Wei supported Qi on the surface, it provided aid to Chu under the table.

It is easy to see that profit was the motivating factor for all sides of the conflict as well as the deciding factor in the decision to attack or retreat. Traveling scholars came to value profit over trust and personal desires over ameliorating the condition of the commoners. Upright men refrained from this kind of behavior, avoiding contact with those who engaged in such depravity. Zhuangzi's contemporary Qu Yuan wrote in his epic poem *The Lament(Li Sao)*: "Truly to craft alone their praise they paid; The square in measuring they disobeyed; The use of common rules they held debased; With confidence their crooked lines they traced! In exile rather would I meet my end, Than to the baseness of their ways descend." ❶ By this he meant that as secular men have always excelled at being opportunistic, they had no qualms in abandonning the law. Outright rejection of moral standards, insatiable lust for evil, and frequent

回到齐国。回到齐国几年后，孟尝君指使贵族田甲发动叛乱。叛乱失败后，孟又被迫流亡魏，在魏昭王那里担任相国。到魏后，孟尝君又与赵、秦等商议，合纵攻打齐国。

国君也是这样。齐湣王想要攻打宋国，夺取大商业城市定陶。他忽而与赵联合发动合纵攻秦，忽而与秦联合攻赵，目的是防止秦、赵等国对它的领土扩张进行干涉。

他们要的是利益与平衡，而不是诚信与规则。

由于此，国与国之间经常玩猫捉老鼠的战争游戏。公元前354年，魏国攻打赵国，赵国扛不住，只好向齐求救，齐在桂陵之地(今河南长垣)大败魏。过了十来年，魏与赵联合起来攻打韩，韩吃不消，向齐求救。齐在马陵（今河南范县西南）又大败魏。这下魏只好服输，向齐卑躬屈节，称臣。不过，邻国楚国生气了，感觉齐竟然把万乘之国魏以臣相待，说明不把自己放在眼里，于是主动出击齐国。楚为"面子"问题向齐开战。魏说，打得好，最好楚胜，以报马陵战败之耻辱。不过，魏表面上要支持齐，暗地里则投靠楚。

可见，是利益牵动着各方的神经，并作出进与退的选择。在这种重利益，轻诚信，重个人私欲，轻天下百姓安危的时代背景下，游士逐利、变节之风盛行。正直的人对此不屑为，也不屑与之为伍。与庄子同时代的屈原在《离骚》中这样宣告："固时俗之工巧兮，偭规矩而改错；背绳墨以追曲兮，竞周容以为度。……宁溘死以流亡兮，余不忍为此态也！"❶意思是

---

❶ 诗歌英译引自杨宪益、戴乃迭的译文。

❶ Poem translated by Yang Hsien-yi and Gladys Yang.

association with other evil people became commonplace. To reiterate the words of the poem, "I would rather die anonymously in lonely exile than speak hypocritical flatteries in the ears of King Huai!"

The Warring States Period was a time of upheaval throughout China where profit ruled supreme. It was in this cruel world that Zhuangzi, the greatest philosopher and poet of his time, began his life in searching for dream and ideal with a sensitive, honest heart and inquisitive spirit. His quest was to find a place where he belonged-a spiritual homeland that he could call his own.

说，世俗之人本来就善于投机取巧，他们可随意背弃法度不走正道；放弃正道去追求邪曲啊，争着同流合污且习以为常。……我宁愿在孤独的流亡中溘然死去，也决不在怀王面前阿谀奉承!

战国成了"天下熙熙，皆为利来；天下攘攘，皆为利往"的时代。庄子，一代圣哲和诗人，就在这样的时代背景下，带着正直和敏感的心，好学求问的精神，开始踏上寻梦的人生，去寻找真正属于自己的精神家园，去开辟属于自己的心灵故乡了。

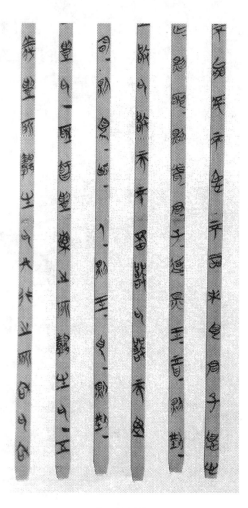

战国竹简
Bamboo Writing Tablets of the
Warring States Period

二 青少年时期（约前368—前350）

Chapter Ⅱ　　Adolescence(About 368 B.C.−350 B.C.)

Zhuangzi was born during the Warring States Period, in the town of Meng in the State of Song. Today, Meng is located northeast of modern Shangqiu in Henan Province, about 30 or 40 *li* from the city of Shangqiu itself. There was a well-known river, called the Bian River, which flows west to east and passes about 15 *li* to the north of Meng. In this region, the land was very fertile, the landscape was beautiful and clear, and rivers and streams made a colorful patchwork across the land.

Because of its favorable position and natural beauty, in the Han Dynasty, Emperor Wen of Han made this land the fief of his favorite son Liu Wu, known as King Xiao of Liang. King Xiao of Liang was the second son of Emperor Wen of Han, he was made king of Suiyang in 176 B.C.. During the Han Dynasty, the capital of the state of Liang was at Suiyang (south of Shangqiu in Henan Province). At the time, the State of Liang had an extensive frontier region, with fertile land, fruitful trees, and rare animals. As one of the most powerful vassal states of the Western Han Dynasty, Suiyang became a major north-south transportation hub. In 154 B.C., the Rebellion of the Seven States erupted in opposition to the rule of the Western Han Dynasty. Liu Bi, King of Wu and Liu Wu, King of Chu, among others, personally led great armies against Suiyang, attempting to clear a road to attack the imperial capital Chang'an. King Xiao of Liang commanded 100,000 men in defending Suiyang for three months, giving the Western Han Emperor enough time to gather his troops. After putting down the Rebellion of the Seven States, Emperor Jing of Han was so deeply grateful to his brother King Xiao of Liang for his courageous defense of Suiyang that he granted him the right to use the same banners and flags as the emperor and allowed him the honor of riding in the same carriage as the emperor[1] . The State of Liang became one of the strongest feudal states under the Han Dynasty.

At the time of King Xiao of Liang, the State of Liang was also a center of culture. Among the hangers-on of King Xiao of Liang, were many talented writers, such as the renowned author Mei Cheng, the essayist Zou Yang, the poet Wu Yanji, and more. Liang's celebrated reputation even attracted the great poet Sima Xiangru, who preferred to stay with King Xiao of Liang rather than follow Emperor Jing of Han.

This was the land of Zhuangzi's birth. It is easy to see that this outstanding philosopher, who was also an unmatched literary genius, did not develop out of nothing, but rather grew up under the influence of local culture.

庄子是战国时期宋国蒙人。蒙在今河南商丘东北，离河南商丘不远，大概三四十里的路程。有一条著名的汳水河，自西向东从蒙城北边十五六里处经过。这一带，土壤肥沃，山清水秀，风景秀丽，水网星罗棋布。

所以在汉代，汉文帝特别把这个地方作为他的爱子梁孝王刘武的封地。梁孝王为汉文帝的第二个儿子，公元前176年被封为睢阳王。汉时梁国的首都在睢阳（河南商丘之南）。当时，梁国疆域辽阔，土地肥沃，充满奇果佳树，珍禽异兽，是西汉中期势力最大的几个藩国之一。睢阳也是当时南北的交通枢纽。公元前154年，西汉发生吴楚七国之乱，吴王刘濞、楚王刘戊等亲率大军攻打睢阳，企图打通西进京都长安之路。梁孝王拥兵十万，死守睢阳城三个月，给西汉王朝得以重整旗鼓的机会。吴楚七国之乱被平定后，梁孝王因守睢阳有功，深得汉景帝厚爱，赐弟弟天子旌旗并与他同辇❶，梁孝王所在的梁国也成为汉王朝中最强大的诸侯国之一。

梁国在当时也是文化艺术中心。梁孝王门客中很多人皆善属辞赋，有著名的作家枚乘、散文家邹阳、写赋高手吴严忌等。连司马相如也慕名而去，宁愿待在梁孝王身边，而不愿跟随当朝皇帝汉景帝。

庄子就出生在这样一个地方。我们可以想象，这么个旷代哲人同时又是绝世文豪，他不是横空出世而是有着地方文化的

---

❶ 译者注：中国古代的皇帝拥有至高无上的权力。不经皇帝恩准，没有人可以像他那样穿龙袍、举天子旌旗、驾黄辇。

❶ Translator's note:In ancient China the emperor had supreme power; no one was allowed to wear dragon robes like his, fly his banner or ride in his carriage.

How great is the influence of environment in the development of talent!

In addition to the nourishment of local culture provided to the young Zhuangzi, his social status as a descendent of nobility might also have set him apart from the other children and given him the opportunity for a better education and exposure to many literary works.

At the time of Zhuangzi, private school education gradually became more and more popular. Nevertheless, still very few people were able to receive an education. As such, few people chose professions involving reading and writing. Books were not widely disseminated, primarily because it was extremely difficult to copy books onto bamboo writing tablets. It was also very difficult for private individuals to accumulate books, because books were heavy and expensive. For instance, *The Book of Changes*, written during the Warring States Period, was written on bamboo which was cut into smaller pieces called bamboo writing tablets. After drying the tablets over a fire, one could write on them. Bamboo writing tablets were of certain length and width. Only one line of characters (between eight and a couple of dozen characters) could be written on one piece of bamboo. Books were made of many writing tablets connected by a strong cord. An old proverb, "the leather cord breaks three times," tells of Confucius studying *The Book of Changes* so diligently that the leather cord holding the book together snapped several times.

How many bamboo writing tablets did it take to make a book? On average, each tablet was about 23 centimeters long, equal to one *chi*❶ in ancient China. Each was about 1 centimeter wide and 0.2 or 0.3 centimeters thick, holding about 20 characters. Using this calculation, *The Book of Changes*, which was about 24,000 characters long, would require 1,200 bamboo writing tablets, and *Zhuangzi*, with over 100,000 characters, would require at least 5,000 tablets. When we have understood this, it is not surprising for us to learn that in the chapter of *Zhuangzi* entitled "The World," we read of Zhuangzi's learned friend Hui Shi, who produced over five carts of works written on bamboo writing tablets.

Beginning with Confucius, more and more private schools were founded, which increased the number of people who had access to education. By the time of the Warring States, these private schools had become commonplace. Zhuangzi had the good fortune of studying at a private school while he was young, making friends with his elder classmate Hui Shi. The characters of the two boys were revealed when the teacher asked what they wanted to do when they grew up: Hui Shi said he wanted to make great contributions to his country by becoming an important political figure. Later, Hui Shi did as he

养育。真是一方水土养育一方人才啊！

　　不仅地方文化滋养着青少年时期的庄子，而且有可能作为贵族后裔的他，与其他普通小孩不同的地方，在于他从小有接受良好教育和博览群书的机会。

　　在庄子时代，私学之风渐盛，但即便如此，能够接受教育的人还是很有限，毕竟识字读书仅是少数人的志业。书籍在当时也不普及流行，原因是写在竹简上的书籍抄写、流传非常不便。私人藏书也十分困难。书很重，价格也昂贵。以《易经》为例，春秋战国时的书，主要是以竹子为材料制造的，即把竹子破成一根根竹签，称为"竹简"，用火烘干后在上面写字。竹简有一定的长度和宽度。一根竹简只能写一行字，多则几十个字，少则八九个字。一部书要用许多竹简，这些竹简必须用牢固的绳子之类的东西编联起来才能阅读。有一成语叫"韦编三绝"，说的是孔子勤读《易经》，竟然把编联简书的牛皮绳磨断了多次。

　　一部书要用多少根竹简呢？若以普通材质的竹简为例，一般一根竹简长23厘米左右，相当于当时的一尺❶，宽1厘米，厚0.2或0.3厘米不等，平均每根可以书写20字左右。若以此文字密度计算的话，用每根一汉尺长的竹简，一部24 000字左右的《易经》，它的书写共需要1 200支竹简，《庄子》一书十余万字，至少需要5 000支竹简。《庄子·天下》篇提到庄子的朋友惠施博学好问，用竹简写的著作，多达五车，也就不足为怪了。

　　从孔子开始，兴办私学，受教育对象因此扩大。至战国，私学之风渐盛。庄子年少时有幸在当地一所私塾学校读书，并结交了比他年长几岁的同学兼朋友惠施。当老师问起他们长大了想干什么？惠施说要泽惠万国，成一国之政要。惠施后来在

---

❶ 译者注：尺，中国常用的长度单位。

❶ Translator's note: *chi* - Chinese unit of length.

said by pursuing an official career in the state of Wei and eventually became the prime minister of Wei. On the other hand, Zhuangzi's dream was to "roam and travel," preferring to act on his own whims, leaving himself time to daydream.

The instructor at the private school taught the children the history of the state of Song. In 1046 B.C., Emperor Wu of Zhou dethroned the Shang Emperor, destroying the Shang Dynasty. Emperor Wu bestowed the land of Song as a fief to the enslaved former Shang nobleman Wei Ziqi. Wei Ziqi thus became the first ruler of the State of Song. Though by the time of the Warring States Period Song was limited to northeastern Henan Province, historically it had its time of greatness, quelling a rebellion in the State of Qi and conquering the State of Cao. Duke Xiang of Song, who ruled from 650 B.C. to 637 B.C. was also recognized in the history books as one of the five great overlords of the Spring Autumn Period. At its height, Song included northeast Henan, northwest Jiangsu, northern Anhui, and southwest Shandong. However, Song was always a relatively small state, surrounded by larger countries on all sides, with Chu to the south, Wei to the north, Qi to the east and Qin to the west. In that time where the weak were devoured by the strong, Song became a target of covetous larger countries. The State of Song was forced to continuously struggle for survival; in the past it had been this way, and during Zhuangzi's youth, under the rule of Duke Huan of Song, it was still so.

Zhuangzi was very interested in history. As he listened to his teacher tell the history of the State of Song, he paid closer attention to how states maintained peaceful relations with one another than to the stories of war and bloodshed. Zhuangzi's young spirit yearned for a world of peace, full of fragrant flowers and chirping birds; a world where people had room to live and breathe, not a world of duplicity, "might makes right," and violence. He was naturally drawn towards historical events which increased the quality of life of the common people, such as the "Sunflower Hill Alliance," as well as monarchs who abided by the rules of decency and benevolence in war, such as Duke Xiang of Song in the Battle of Hongshui.

During the Spring Autumn Period in 639 B.C., against a background of ruthless territorial wars and annexations, Duke Huan of Qi who was the high king of his day, organized the Sunflower Hill Alliance (named after a hill in modern Minquan County in Henan Province). King Cheng of Chu and other powerful rulers attended the conference, where they agreed to a cease-fire treaty which brought peace and rest to the people of their countries. Duke Xiang of Song attended the conference as one of the five great lords of the

魏国谋求仕途，果然当上了魏相。而庄子的理想呢，则是"逍遥游"，喜欢一个人率性而动，有时间就留给自己发呆和遐想。

上课的先生也给他们讲解宋国的历史。公元前1046年，周武王伐纣，商朝灭亡。武王将当时沦为奴隶的商朝贵族微子启分封在宋地。微子启成了宋国的始祖。先生说，虽然现在的宋国仅局限在河南东北部一带，但在历史上也有过辉煌的时候，曾平定齐国的内乱，灭过曹国。宋襄公（前650—637在位）也曾作为春秋五霸之一彪炳史册。其疆域最大时包括河南东北部、江苏西北部、安徽北部、山东西南部。但宋国毕竟是小国，四周又与大国接壤，南有楚、北有魏、东有齐、西有秦，老师说，在当今"争于力气"、弱肉强食的时代，宋国在大国的虎视眈眈中，一直在夹缝中艰难生存。以前如此，在当今国君宋桓公时代也是如此。

庄子对历史很感兴趣。他在听先生讲述宋国历史时更加关注的是国与国之间怎样友好相处，而不是战争与杀戮。对庄子幼小的心灵来说，这个世界应成为一个和平的世界，到处花香鸟语，一个休养生息的世界，而不应充满智巧、强权、暴力。自然，在上历史课时，他对给人民带来休养生息的历史事件，如"葵丘会盟"，对战争中重仁义规则的君王，如"泓水之战"中的宋襄公，给予了特别关注。

春秋时期，针对诸侯大国争霸，兼并战争频仍这一背景，公元前639年，齐桓公以霸主身份主持了葵丘(今河南民权县)之盟，楚成王等大国诸侯均参加，并在此写下和好息战盟书，使各国人民得以休养生息，宋襄公也以春秋五霸之一的地位参加

Spring Autumn Period.

In the Battle of Hongshui, Duke Xiang of Song emphasized "benevolence and righteousness" in commanding his troops. Against the advice of his military advisors, he chose not to attack the army of Chu, twice purposefully missing perfect opportunities to attack. His delay led to the defeat of his army, and he himself suffered serious injuries from which he eventually died. From that time on, Song was relegated to a second-class state. Zhuangzi and his classmates engaged in heated debate over this event, some feeling that Duke Xiang of Song was a fool to believe in truth, morality, and benevolence in war. Zhuangzi also felt that Duke Xiang's policy of strict adherence to such rules of war as not attacking until enemy soldiers were organized into ranks and not killing elderly soldiers was not suited for the battles of the Warring States Period. However, he did not believe that bloodshed, deceit, and other "laws of the jungle" should determine victory or defeat. Zhuangzi did not agree that Duke Xiang of Song was "foolish." His classmates next asked him what the proper method of conflict resolution should be in the face of a foreign invasion, but Zhuangzi was not able to give them a good answer. The sensitive young Zhuangzi lamented over the cruelty of history, that so many bones should be buried in the battlefield after each battle. He was anguished by the indifference of the years, sorrowing that Duke Xiang of Song, one of the five great rulers of the Spring Autumn Period, should come to such an inglorious end. He ached for his own homeland of Song, repeatedly rose and fell in his quest to dominate China during the Spring Autumn Period, and brought pride and dignity as their heir of the Yin-Shang bloodline. Though the unrealistic idealism and upright but naive honesty of Duke Xiang of Song may have seemed imprudent to Zhuangzi's contemporaries who were only concerned with profit, to Zhuangzi, it was an appealing view of the world.

了这次会盟。

"泓水之战"中宋襄公强调"仁义"治军，不听谋士劝告，不进攻楚国，两次错失良机，致使全军覆没，自己也身负重伤，不治而死。从此，宋国降为二等诸侯国。当时庄子与同学们还为此事展开热烈讨论，有些认为宋襄公太傻，打仗还讲什么公理、道德、仁义。庄子也认为，宋襄公在与楚国作战时保留的"不鼓不成列"（对方不排好队列，自己不进攻）、"不杀二毛"（不杀年老的军人）等贵族战争游戏规则，确实不适合战国时代国与国之间的杀戮，但又不认同国与国之间必须通过流血、尔虞我诈、弱肉强食的丛林法则来决出胜负，他反对把宋襄公完全地看作"愚"。

同学们就问他，在外敌入侵时，那有没有更好的办法解决国与国之间的纠葛？庄子也想不出来。对于敏感的少年庄子，他感慨的是历史的残酷，一场战争让很多忠骨埋沙场；悲叹的是岁月的无情，作为春秋五霸之一的宋襄公最终竟落得如此下场；情系的是自己的国家，在逐鹿中原的春秋战国时代，几起几落，浮浮沉沉，在夹缝中生存，延续着殷商的血脉和气质，有着几分浪漫遐想，也带着几分质直憨厚，在完全注重实际利益的时人看起来有些愚笨，但在庄子看起来却有些可爱。

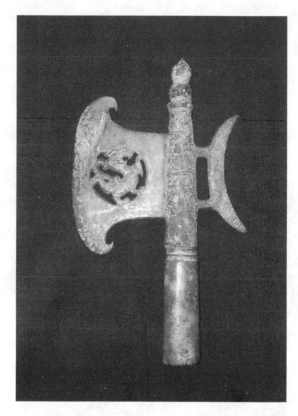

战国时期武器——青铜钺
Weapon of the Warring States Period—
Bronze Tomahawk

三 青年时期（约前350—前338）

Chapter Ⅲ Youth(About 350 B.C. to 338 B.C.)

Time flew, and in the blink of an eye, Zhuangzi was 20 years old, the year at which young men in ancient China came of age. Because of this, his family began to worry about finding him a suitable wife. Because Zhuangzi was already a well-known and gifted scholar in the town of Meng and his family was of average financial prosperity, there were quite a few families willing to marry their daughters to him. Zhuangzi, however, took exception to this, to the point that a fierce argument took place between him and his family. His family wanted him to marry as soon as possible; an early wedding would not only increase the size of the family, but also, according to the customs of the time, early weddings were believed to bring good fortune to the family. But Zhuangzi believed marriage ought to come about naturally. He was not running from marriage he viewed it as a duty which he would have to perform, no different from caring for his parents when they grew old—he was just unwilling to marry solely for the sake of marrying. Zhuangzi brought up two other objections to an early marriage: other young men who married early did so to increase the labor force of the family, to provide extra hands for helping in the fields. But as the Zhuang family lived in the county seat of Meng and not a farming village, they did not have to worry about increasing the family workforce. As for the folk tradition of early marriage to bring more sons and good fortune to the family, Zhuangzi put no stock in it. He believed that life, death, fortune, and adversity were predetermined by fate, and that it was as impossible to hide from misfortune as it was to hinder the arrival of fortune.

Zhuangzi's family was unable to persuade him to completely change his mind; however, in the face of their incessant pleas, Zhuangzi finally conceded to marriage. Soon he was engaged to the daughter of a nearby family. She was of proper age, not yet betrothed, and of elegant appearance, so Zhuangzi agreed. Before long, a simple but elegant wedding ceremony was held and his new bride joined the Zhuang family. In ancient times, the bridegroom would escort the bride from her home to his at dusk. The moment when the sun was about to set and the moon about to rise symbolized the "waning of the *yang* and the waxing of the *yin*" ❶ . Thus we can see that the origin of the character for marriage or wedding (*hun*) originated from the character for dusk (*hun*), which later had a female radical (*nü*) added to it.

Because of Zhuangzi's growing fame and the efforts of his family, he was able to find a sound job as the manager of a lacquer tree orchard not far from Meng. What made the situation even better, the orchard was operated by the

　　时光飞逝，转眼间，庄子已20岁，处于"弱冠之年"。家人开始为他操心婚事。由于庄子是蒙城有名的才子，庄子家经济实力在当地属于中等，所以上门愿意与庄家永结"秦晋之好"的女方也不少。但庄子对此不以为然，为这事，他曾与家里人发生过一次激烈冲突。家里人希望他早点结婚，一来可让家里人丁兴旺，二来按当地风俗早结婚可以给家里纳福。但庄子认为，结婚要顺其自然，他不是逃避结婚，结婚是他应尽的义务，就像他父母年老以后他孝顺和赡养他们也是应尽的义务一样，只是为结婚而结婚他有点不情愿。庄子还讲了两点理由：别的男子早娶是为了家中较早地增添劳动力，可以在干农活时有更多的人手帮忙，庄家至少目前不存在这个问题，庄家住在蒙县县城，而不是农村；对于早娶则早得子、早得福这一民俗现象，庄子不屑一顾。他认为生死祸福，自有定命，有祸躲不过，福来也挡不住。

　　家人开始拗不过庄子，但后来在家人一直地坚持下，庄子也妥协了，很快与当地不远的一户人家订了亲。这户人家"小女年方二八，待字闺中"，模样长得还端庄，庄子也就答应了。不久新娘就过了门，并举行了简单而隆重的婚礼。古人娶妻，婚礼的亲迎是在黄昏时进行的，这时太阳将要下山，月亮就要出来，含有"阳往阴来"❶的意思，因而得名"昏"，后来才加上"女"字偏旁写作"婚"。

　　经过家里人的活动，也加上庄子本身在当地小有名气，很快，庄子找到了一份体面的工作，担任漆园吏，即管理蒙城附近的一个漆树园。该园为宋国政府经营，所以庄子也好歹是在

---

❶ 译者注："阳"代表阳性事物和太阳，"阴"代表阴性事物和月亮。新郎出门迎娶代表了阳的渐消，而新娘的到来则象征阴的渐盈。

❶ Translator's note: *Yang* signifies masculinity and the sun, *yin* signifies femininity and the moon. The sentence refers to the departure of the groom (waning of the *yang*) as well as the arrival of the bride (waxing of the *yin*).

Song government, so he was now a minor official in the government.

Lacquer came into widespread production during the Warring States Period. In the *Book of Songs: Odes of Yong—ding zhi fang zhong*, we read, "... about which were planted hazel and chestnut trees, the yi, the parasol, the catalpa, and the lacquer tree." This poem describes the process by which Duke Wen of Wey, with help from Duke Huan of Qi and others, moved the capital of Wey to Chuqiu. It tells of the trees planted in the palace gardens: hazel, chestnut, *yi, tong, zi,* and lacquer. This shows that by the Spring Autumn Period, lacquer trees were already being cultivated. By the time of the Warring States, the cultivation of lacquer trees was developed even further, as evidenced by the following lines from *The Classic of History: the Tribute of Yu*: "Yanzhou brought urushi silk❶ as tribute" and "Yuzhou brought lacquer as tribute."

There were many uses for lacquer in ancient times. It was not only used to adorn furniture, household utensils, writing utensils, and art, but also to decorate instruments, burial implements, weapons, and more. To some extent lacquer implements replaced the bronze utensils which had previously been popular.

Lacquer was an expensive luxury, making it an important trading commodity. Normally, apple and orange orchards had to pay a tax of "one of every twenty golds of profit," but lacquer orchards had to pay "five of every twenty golds of profit," which shows that they were taxed very heavily. The importance of lacquer grew during the Warring States Period as the people, especially the nobility, began to demand a higher standard of living. They wanted to coat their daily-use utensils with a layer of lacquer, which both protected the utensils as well as decorated them. The great merchant Bai Gui, who lived during the middle years of the Warring States Period, used the business strategy of "buying grain during years of bumper harvests and selling silk and lacquer" to build his fortune.

In his spare time, Zhuangzi loved to read books. It was no exaggeration when his peers remarked, "there is no subject that his learning does not touch." He was especially interested in the history and culture of the surrounding states, searching for patterns in their rise and fall, and learning proper methods of governance from their experiences. For instance, though the state of Zheng (in modern Xinzheng County in Henan Province) was defeated by Han before the birth of Zhuangzi (in 375 B.C.), during the Spring Autumn Period it had been very active and powerful. This can be seen by the fact that, for a brief period in the Spring Autumn Period, even the powerful State of Qi

政府机关上班，是一个小官吏。

春秋战国时期，漆的生产渐渐普及。《诗经·鄘风·定之方中》载"树之榛栗，椅、桐、梓、漆"。这首诗反映了卫文公在齐桓公等的支持下迁卫都于楚丘时的状况。其中描写了在新建的宫庭中，栽种了榛树、栗树、椅树、桐树、梓树、漆树等树木。说明春秋中期已有漆树种植。战国时期，漆树的种植得到进一步发展，《尚书·禹贡》说兖州"贡漆丝"❶，豫州"贡漆"。

在当时，漆的用途很广，不仅用于装饰家具、器皿、文具和艺术品，而且还用于装饰乐器、丧葬用具、兵器等。漆器一定程度上已取代了先前流行的青铜器。

但漆器在当时是奢侈品，挺贵的。当然，漆在当时还是重要商品。一般如种植苹果园、橘子园，只征收"二十而一"的税，"唯有漆林之征，二十而五"，对漆林要征收四分之一的税，说明当时漆林税重。漆之所以重要，是因为战国时代的人们，尤其贵族对生活品质的要求进一步提高，他们要给日常使用的器具上漆，起保护和装饰作用。战国中期的大商人白圭就采用"岁熟取谷，予之丝、漆"，即丰年时买进谷物卖出丝、漆的办法来经商致富。

庄子在工作之余，喜欢看书。在他的同龄人当中，说得夸张一点，"其学无所不窥"。他特别关心周边国家的历史和文化，从中寻找国家兴亡的规律和为政之道。比如，郑国（今河南省新郑县一带），虽然在庄子出生前夕，即公元前375年被韩国灭掉，但在春秋时期却非常活跃，甚至一段时间之内，强大的齐

---

❶ 译者注：表面经过漆料涂抹加工的蚕丝。

❶ Translator's note:Lacquer-treated silk.

swore fealty to Zheng, following Zheng in one campaign after another.

Zhuangzi also studied Zi Chan, the renowned minister of Zheng. Confucius referred to Zi Chan as a benevolent and good man. He was well-respected by the conservative scholar-bureaucrat class as a man of accomplishment, and an intrepid and pragmatic reformer. In 536 B.C., Zi Chan had clauses from Zheng's law code engraven on a metal tripod which symbolized the authority of the nobility. He then announced this deed to the public, constituting the first written law in China. His rule was both just and strict. In terms of diplomacy, Zi Chan employed flexible strategies and was neither too humble nor too arrogant, even when dealing with great states such as Jin or Chu. One time, King Kang of Chu led troops in attacking Zheng in order to appease the King of Xu. Zi Chan firmly opposed fighting, choosing instead to allow the Chu armies to obtain some small gains and return home, in order to preserve a more lasting peace. People of Zheng did so and sure enough, this resulted in the "Peace-pursuing Alliance."

Although Zi Chan attempted to preserve the old customs and order, he was forced to adapt to the changing circumstances of his time and enact some reforms. Zi Chan said, "It is impossible to go against the anger of the masses, thus impossible to carry out the desires of a minority." By this he meant that in ruling a country, it was necessary to consider the desires and demands of many different people; single-mindedly pursuing one's own path would not bring success. He also said, "Ruling is like working in the fields. One must ponder it day and night in order to see its beginning and bring to pass its end. In ruling, one must be constant and not act without planning, just as in farming. In so doing, one reduces his mistakes." These words show that there were guidelines and a scientific approach to administration; monarchs could not base their actions on their ability to impose their personal desires on others.

Zhuangzi knew that Confucius liked and appreciated Zi Chan. When Confucius was 30, in 522 B.C., the senior official of the State of Zheng, Zi Chan, passed away after a 20 year reign. Confucius grieved his passing.

Zhuangzi took note of the improvements that Zi Chan's reforms brought to society. One of Zi Chan's opinions with which Zhuangzi disagreed was the former's belief that the only issues of importance were empowering the kingdom, enriching its people, and bringing societal, political, economic, and legal order. Zhuangzi did not readily subscribe to Zi Chan's declaration that, "Where the Way of heaven is vague and indistinct, the Way of man is clear and relevant; therefore we must concern ourselves with man and not with heaven." ❶ In Zhuangzi's opinion, there had been so much discussion of

国也对郑国俯首称臣，跟随郑国东征西讨。

庄子也注意到郑国历史上有名的执政大臣子产。他被孔子称为仁人、惠人，是守旧的士大夫景仰的人物，是一位有作为的、雷厉风行的务实改革家。公元前536年，子产将郑国的法律条文铸在象征诸侯权威的金属鼎上，向全社会公布。这是中国历史上最早的成文法。他同时执法严明，规范税制。在外交方面，子产用灵活的手腕，不卑不亢的政策，处理大国事务，哪怕对方是晋、楚这样的大国。有一次，楚康王为抚慰许国，率军伐郑。子产主张坚守不战，让楚军获取小利后满意而归，以换取较长时期的和平。郑人照此办理，果然促成了"弭兵之盟"。

子产虽力图维护传统旧制，但也不得不适应形势的变化而从事必要的改革。子产曾指出："众怒难犯，专欲难成。"意思是说，治国必须照顾多数人的愿望和要求，一意孤行则不能成功。他又说："政如农功，日夜思之，思其始而成其终。朝夕而行之，行无越思,如农之有畔。其过鲜矣。"意思是说，政事就像干农活，日夜想着它，执行中要坚持既定规划而不轻易越轨，这样，过错就会减少了。这些话说明了行政是有规律的，是有科学性的，掌权者不可以凭着权力和一己之欲去任意行事。

庄子知道孔子喜欢和欣赏子产。孔子30岁那一年，即公元前522年，执政20多年的郑国大夫子产去世了，孔子为此哀伤了一阵子。

子产的改革给社会带来的改善庄子也注意到了。庄子所不欣赏的是子产的眼里只有国富民强、社会政治、经济和法律的秩序。子产的那句话"天的道理是渺茫的，人的道理是切近的，我们是讲人不讲天的"，庄子也不敢苟同。❶ 对庄子来说，关

---

❶《庄子·德充符》篇提到了郑国大夫子产。

❶ In the chapter of *Zhuangzi* entitled "The Sign of Virtue Complete," there is mention of Zi Chan, the senior official of Zheng.

man's wisdom that it had become cliched and unoriginal. Zhuangzi longed for the wisdom of heaven.

Thus, when Zhuangzi came into contact with the culture of the State of Chu and especially the philosophy of Laozi, his spirit took heart; here was finally a culture which upheld a value system that he had always admired.

Laozi described the creator of all things in heaven and earth, calling it *Dao*, or "The Way." The *Dao* is eternal, acting among all things and yet above all things. The passage of time, the changing of the seasons, the blossoming and withering of flowers-all these are accomplished by the *Dao*. Like Laozi, Zhuangzi held the *Dao* in reverence. To him, the *Dao* is above everything because the world and the humans which inhabited it originated from the *Dao*.

But what caused Zhuangzi to revere the *Dao* even more was its manifestation of the "mysterious virtue" of "creating without possessing, achieving without pride, and leading without dominating." It was precisely this "mysterious virtue" that permitted the *Dao* to act as a moral guide for humankind. The *Dao* instructed man that he should recognize his own insignificance. In observing all that exists in the heavens and the earth, the sun, moon, and constellations of stars, we understand that they were all created by the *Dao*, and yet the *Dao* is never boastful, does not attempt to charge a "sunshine fee," an "air fee," or a "rain and dew fee." The *Dao* carries spring to the trees and snow to the fields, brings to pass "the blooming of the pear blossoms on the trees," and causes the seasons to change in an orderly fashion. Though it has all of this power, it never flaunts itself. Humans, on the other hand, are different; as soon as they achieve some small measure of success or attain some small virtue, they become arrogant and forget their true worth. "The absurd pride of the king of Yelang," "the frog at the bottom of the well," and "being lost in one's ecstasy" are all proverbs that describe the superficiality of human nature. Therefore, in the face of the eternal and all-powerful *Dao*, mankind has all the more reason to be humble.

Laozi also discussed the notion that "misfortune is the precondition of happiness, and within happiness lurks the shadow of misfortune." This is to say, happiness requires adversity in order to come to pass, but it often sows the seeds of further adversity; under certain conditions, fortune can turn to misfortune, and misfortune can turn to fortune. In later generations, this concept was developed into the story "The Old Man in the Frontier who Lost His Horse." Once upon a time, there was an old man who lived in the frontier regions of China, on the border of Hun's territory. All the travelers who passed knew and respected him. The old man always kept an open mind towards life.

于人的道理听得太多，也太俗套，他特别向往天的道理。

当庄子接触到楚国的文化，尤其是老子的思想时，他的精神为之一振，这真是他心仪的文化和修养的行为。

老子描述了天地万物的创造者"道"。道，生生不息，运行在万物之中又超越于万物之上。日月的运行，四季的变迁，花开与花落，都是道在背后承载着、维护着。对于"道"，庄子同老子一样，对其保持敬畏，因为道相对于包括人在内的这个世界有着优先性，世界是从道中产生出来的。

但更引起庄子对道敬畏的是，道在运作天地万物过程中所显示出来的"创造而不拥有，成功而不骄傲，领导而不主宰"的"玄德"。正是这种玄德，让道可以成为人们道德生活的指引者。道在告诉人们，人不应把自己看得太高。你看，天地万物、日月星辰，都是道亲自创造的，但道从来不居功自傲，向地上的百姓收什么"阳光费"、"空气呼吸费"、"雨露费"；道一夜之间让春满枝头，雪盖四野，既能让"千树万树梨花开"，也能让春夏秋冬有序运作，它有这么大的本领但却从不炫耀自己。人就不一样了，一有小成绩、小成就、小品德就往往骄傲得找不着北，也不知道自己的轻重。"夜郎自大"、"井底之蛙"、"得意忘形"形容的都是人浅薄的德性。因此，在生生不息的满有能力的大道面前，人更应该谦卑。

老子也提到"祸兮福之所倚，福兮祸之所伏"，意思是说，祸是造成福的前提，而福又含有祸的因素，一定条件下福祸相互转化。这个观点在后世演绎成"塞翁失马"的故事：从前，有位老翁住在与胡人相邻的边塞地区，来来往往的过客都尊敬他。老翁生性达观。有一天，老翁家的马不知什么原因，在放牧时竟迷了路，回不来了。邻居们得知这一消息以后，纷纷表示惋惜并对其安慰。可是老翁却不以为然，他反而释怀地劝慰

One day, for no apparent reason, the old man's horse wandered off and was lost. When his neighbors heard the news, they all expressed their sympathy and comforted him. But the old man would have none of it, and instead turned the discussion around and comforted his friends, saying, "Of course losing a horse is a bad thing, but who knows, perhaps something good will come of this?" Sure enough, a few months later, the old horse came galloping back home from across the border with another fine steed in tow. Upon hearing this, the neighbors all came back to congratulate the lucky old man and praise him for having kept a positive attitude when his horse was lost. But the old man was troubled, saying, "Who knows but what this will bring me misfortune?" His family now had a second horse, this one a beautiful Hun's steed. The old man's son was beside himself with glee, going for long rides on the horse every day. One day, the man's son was "lost in his own ecstasy" and fell from the back of the galloping horse, breaking one of his legs and crippling himself for life. When his good neighbors heard the news, they came to express their sympathy. But the old man responded with the same attitude: "Who knows, perhaps something good will come of this?" A year later, the Huns raised a great army and attacked the central plains of China. The situation in the frontier lands suddenly became extremely precarious and all the healthy young men were drafted into the army. Taking up their bows, they left for war. In the end, eight or nine out of every ten were slain. Since the old man's son was a cripple, he was exempt from fighting in the war and thus the two were able to stay together through the war.

The sensitive Zhuangzi expressed heartfelt approval of Laozi's views on the inconstancy of human life, but was even more pessimistic than his predecessor. Where Laozi saw that under certain conditions, misfortune can turn into happiness, Zhuangzi saw that everything in life changed constantly. In the passage of time, the greatest change was from birth to old age and finally to death. Zhuangzi lamented that human life was nothing but a moment, "as fleeting as a white pony's shadow flashing past a crevice." He taught that in flourishing vitality all things come into existence, and in muddled confusion all things pass away. In change we are born and in change we die. This truth brings grief to all living creatures and anguish to mankind. In addition to this, the uninvited onset of sickness and disease, as well as man's inability to control it, caused a great deal of sorrow to young Zhuangzi.

Laozi wrote that he disliked bustling commotion and desired to maintain a certain distance from worldly things. He felt that in the midst of commotion, man easily loses himself. The feeling is much like feeling lost and confused in

大伙儿："丢了马，当然是件坏事，但谁知道它会不会带来好的结果呢？"果然，没过几个月，那匹迷途的老马又从塞外跑了回来，并且还带回了一匹骏马。于是，邻居们又一齐来向老翁贺喜，并夸他在丢马时有远见。然而，这时的老翁却忧心忡忡地说："唉，谁知道这件事会不会给我带来灾祸呢？"老翁家平添了一匹胡人骑的骏马，使他的儿子喜不自禁，于是就天天骑马兜风，乐此不疲。终于有一天，儿子因得意而忘形，竟从飞驰的马背上掉了下来，摔伤了一条腿，造成了终身残疾。善良的邻居们闻讯后，赶紧前来慰问，而老翁却还是那句老话："谁知道它会不会带来好的结果呢？"又过了一年，胡人大举入侵中原，边塞形势骤然吃紧，身强力壮的青年都被征去当了兵，拿起弓箭去打仗，结果十有八、九都在战场上送了命。而老翁的儿子因为是个跛腿，免服兵役，父子二人也得以避免了这场生离死别的灾难。

对老子提及的人生无常，敏感的庄子有深切的认同感，但庄子比老子更悲观些。老子还看到，祸在一定条件下能变成福，庄子则看到人生一切都在变化中，而个人在时光流逝中变化最大的就是从生到老，再到死。庄子特别感慨，人活在天地间，就像白驹过隙，只是刹那而已。蓬蓬勃勃中，万物出生了；昏昏惛惛中，万物又死去了。既由变化而生，又由变化而死，生物为此哀伤，人类为之悲痛。除了这，疾病的不请自至，以及人在病魔前的无力抗争也让年轻的庄子唏嘘感叹了一番。

老子曾提到他不喜欢熙熙攘攘的热闹，喜欢与世俗保持距离，因为在热闹中，人容易迷失自己，就像置身于一个琳琅满目的市场，你会感到无所适从；又如一首流行歌曲所唱的，

a particularly crowded marketplace. Or, to quote a popular song, "one is extremely silent in a crowded place, where even his smile is lonely." In the end, Laozi chose a solitary and clear-headed path, rejecting the din and glamour of a worldly life and giving up his position in the court to become a hermit. Zhuangzi fully approved of this decision.

Zhuangzi considered living a hermit's life as well, feeling that there was nothing inherently wrong with it. However, he had too many worldly attachments that he was unable to give up, especially his work at the lacquer tree orchard. This was because without his job, he would be unable to provide for his wife and children. Zhuangzi was not able to be like Old Man He Diao, Chang Ju, or Jie Ni of the historically neighboring kingdoms of Chen and Cai, all of whom were scholars who had lived solitary farming lives. His family owned no lands, and as a scholar, Zhuangzi himself had no knowledge of agriculture. Zhuangzi thought to himself that if he were to be a hermit, he would not isolate himself in the mountains like Xu You, Laozi, Bo Yi, or Shu Qi. He believed that filial piety and societal roles were universal principles, that one should not retire to the mountains and avoid these human relationships.

What Zhuangzi disliked the most about Laozi was his self-righteous tone, which seemed to show Laozi's eagerness to be a teacher of monarchs. Laozi's purpose in preaching his philosophy was to help kings better rule and manage their kingdoms and subjects. This meant that Laozi assumed the role of a teacher in instructing rulers, teaching them "the monarch's art of facing south." This was another way of saying the art of ruling effectively. In ancient times, houses and palaces were all built facing south. When a ruler met with his officials, he would sit facing south and the official would stand facing north. This is the origin of the saying "he who faces south is lord, he who faces north is servant." Laozi also taught rulers how to "enact non-purposeful action and teach wordless teachings" ❶ in properly ruling the commoners and managing the affairs of state. Laozi believed that if they truly acted according to his advice, then governing a great kingdom would be as easy as cooking a small fish.

Zhuangzi was more in favor of using the *Dao* as a means of personal cultivation and refinement. "The path of the *Dao* is he who follows the *Dao*." Through abiding by the *Dao*, anybody can obtain a higher level of understanding of life and take the "higher road." From the noblest kings to the basest peddlers, all could obtain spiritual freedom through following the *Dao*. No matter the profession, as long as one was willing to go through a certain

"人多时候最沉默，笑容也寂寞"。最终，老子选择了一条孤独和清醒的人生道路，而不是喧嚣和热闹的世俗人生。他放弃了王官身份，成为了一名隐士。这也是庄子所认定的。

对于隐居的生活，庄子也动过这个念头，感觉没有什么不妥，但内心里还有很多牵挂，很多事情放不下，尤其现在若离开漆园吏的工作岗位，将来如何谋生养活妻子和小孩是个问题。庄子不可能像历史上的邻邦，陈、蔡之国的荷蓧丈人、长沮、桀溺等人过着农耕隐居生活。他家没有田地，庄子也不会耕田犁地，他是个读书人。庄子也想过，即使隐居，也不会隐到山里去，如许由、老子、伯夷、叔齐那样。对他来说，赡养父母，尽君臣之道，是天经地义的，不需要通过隐居到山里来规避这些人伦关系。

庄子对老子最不能接受的地方，就是老子身上的那种好为君王师的腔调。老子讲道的目的就是让那些君王更好地治理国家和管理百姓，也就是说，老子以帝王师的身份给他们说法，传授"君人南面之术"。"君人南面之术"，也就是统治术。古代的房屋或者宫殿，都是面南而建，君臣相见之时，君主面南而坐，臣子面北而立，所以有"南面称君，北面称臣"之说。老子教导君王们怎样"处无为之事，行不言之教"❶，以何种方式统治百姓，管理好国家。并且认为，若他们真的能按照他所说的去做，那么治理大国就像烹调小鱼一样轻而易举。

庄子更喜欢把"道"用作个人修身养性的途径。道者道路也。每个人都可以通过"道"来获得对人生更好的理解并走在某种道路上。上至王公达贵，下至贩夫走卒之辈、"引车卖浆者流"都可以在道那里获得心灵的解放。所以，只要你愿意，

❶ 意即遵循天道行事，不要试图与命运争斗。

❶ In other words, to allow nature to run its course and not try to fight against fate.

degree of training, he or she could become a master of *Dao*. It did not matter if one was a butcher, a wheel-maker, a cicada-keeper, a wash-woman, a sailor, a water-carrier, a gardener, or even one who bet on cock fights or fished for a living❶ , all could learn the ways of Dao.

Zhuangzi and Laozi both used water as a metaphor for the *Dao*, but because they interpreted the role of the *Dao* differently, the characteristics they described were also different. Laozi said, "The ultimate virtue is like water. Water benefits all things and never contends with anything." In Laozi's opinion, softness was not power, but rather an attitude. Kings were very powerful, because, "All the land under the sun belongs to the king; all the people within this country are the king's subjects." In governing a country, power was important, but attitude was more important. If the king was able to be like water and maintain a calm, free-flowing disposition, then he would be able to achieve great things. Therefore, Laozi counseled monarchs to follow the example of water and be humble, tolerant, and peaceful.

The wise and insightful Zhuangzi, on the other hand, observed that water was "peaceful, still, clear, and motionless," and was in harmony with the attributes of "tranquility, indifference to worldly gain, solitude, and inactivity" which he so strongly advocated. Zhuangzi contended that if a man's heart was able to avoid the interference of worldly things, then like still water, he would be able to see the subtleties of heaven and earth and reflect the mystery of all things. However, if the water were to become agitated, sand and mud would begin to swirl and waves would begin to splash. This was like a man's heart, because if it were full of desire for material things, abounded in conflicting thoughts, and plagued by flighty emotions and moods, it would be unable to gaze on the mysteries of the universe and the true nature of life on earth.

Zhuangzi loved oceans and rivers. Though Zhuangzi never saw the ocean, he loved to imagine it, because in so doing, his spirit would swell and broaden just like the sea. Under the blue sky and white clouds, one can imagine the majestic scene of a great mythical *roc* spreading its wings and throwing back waves for three thousand *li* then soaring ninety thousand *li* in the air. One can imagine Hebo, the once self-important river god, before the greatness of the limitless ocean, "heaving a sigh upon gazing at the sea," feeling his own narrowness and shallowness. The vastness of the ocean was enough to raise man's spiritual gaze, allowing him to pull himself out of the limits of his own self-importance, overcome the bonds of worldly desires, and travel to a land far removed from physical reality.

并通过一定的修炼，就可以在你所从事的职业和生活中成为得道高手，无论你所从事的是解牛、斫轮、承蜩、漂洗、操舟、蹈水、灌圃，甚至相狗斗鸡、钓鱼观鱼❶，都没关系。

由于对"道"的作用的认识不同，庄子和老子用水比喻道、描述道的属性时也不同。老子用水比喻道："上善若水，水利万物而不争。"在老子看来，柔不是实力，而是一种态度。帝王是很有实力的，因为"普天之下，莫非王土；率土之滨，莫非王臣"。治理国家实力很重要，但态度更重要，若帝王的态度如水"不争"、"处下"，则"有容乃大"。因此，老子向帝王提出了效法水的为人处世哲学——谦卑、宽容、无争。

独具慧眼的庄子却发现了水之"平、静、明、止"，这正与他所推崇的"虚静、恬淡、寂寞、无为"的人格修养相一致。庄子认为，一个人的心，如止水，不受任何外界因素的影响，那么就可以察天地之精微，镜万物之玄妙；而水动则泥沙俱起，浑浊浮动，如人心之物欲充斥、杂念横生、心浮气躁，当然无法洞察宇宙之奥妙、人生之真谛。

海洋和江河也是庄子所爱慕的。庄子虽然没有见过海洋，但喜欢想象海洋，因为在对海洋的体验中自己的心灵一下子广阔和浩大起来。蓝天白云下，你可以想象一只大鹏鸟"水击三千里，抟扶摇而上九万里"的磅礴气势；有了无边无际的大海，你可以想象原本骄傲自大、不可一世的河伯见了之后"望洋兴叹"，自感浅薄和有限。大海之大，足可以提升人的精神境界，让人从自我为中心的局限性中超拔出来，摆脱功名利禄等俗物的束缚，达到超越现实的逍遥境界。

---

❶《庄子》里从事这些职业的人都是得道者。

❶ All of these are characters from *Zhuangzi* who mastered the *Dao*.

In fact, before Laozi and Zhuangzi, many ancient scholars had already forged an unbreakable bond with water. Ancient scholars chose to live near water and take joy in it, a habit which gave rise to the proverb "he who is wise loves water." Such love also inspired many poets. For example, Li Bai wrote, "The torrent drops three thousand feet straight down to the valley floor/ I think it must be the Milky Way spilling to the earth from the heavens." Bai Juyi wrote, "The Bian River flows, the Si River flows / They all flow to the ancient ferry at Melon Shoal." Li Shangyin wrote, "As night rain on the mounts of Ba falls, and autumn pools are brimmed." Finally, Zhang Ruoxu wrote, "In spring the river rises as high as the sea, And with the river's rise so too rises the bright moon." There were also many stories written about water, such as "Confucius Speaks by the river," Xiang Yu's "Wu River Suicide," and the suicide of Qu Yuan in the Miluo River. These poems and stories combined to form a rich cultural heritage of respect towards water.

Zhuangzi was not content to simply read about things; he also enjoyed traveling far and wide. For instance, he once visited Shangqiu, the capital of Song. Shangqiu was located a couple dozen *li* [1] to the southwest of Zhuangzi's hometown of Meng.

Shangqiu was well-known for many things. For example, more than 10,000 years ago, one of three Huangs [2] (China's legendary "three emperors") Suirenshi discovered how to create fire at the city of Shangqiu. Because of this discovery, mankind did not have to eat raw meat any longer. In the distant past, the Shang tribe inhabited this region. The Shang were the first to engage in commerce and trade, making Shangqiu the birthplace of merchants, commerce, and trade culture. Since ancient times, armies had fought endless wars over control of Shangqiu. Shangqiu was also the capital of Zhuan Xu and Di Ku (two of five Dis—the legendary "five emperors"), as well as for the Shang Dynasty, the state of Song during the Western Zhou Dynasty, and the state of Liang during the Western Han Dynasty.

Before Zhuangzi even arrived at the gates of Shangqiu he could already see the tall, solid city walls, and the wide, deep city moat. Shangqiu's city wall was both tall and wide, between 11.5 and 12 meters high and 12 to 15 meters thick, with a base width between 25 and 27 meters. In comparison, the walls of the cities in the State of Wei during the Warring States Period were usually around 6 meters high, and only about 10 meters thick at best. The city walls used in the State of Lu were even less impressive, less than 4.5 meters high and around 20 meters wide at the base. Upon seeing the walls with his own eyes, Zhuangzi realized that their reputation was well deserved. He was not

其实，古代的文人墨客都与水结下不解之缘。古之文人择水而居，临水而咏，踏水而歌，所谓"智者乐水"，于是就有了李白的"飞流直下三千尺，疑是银河落九天"，白居易的"汴水流，泗水流，流到瓜洲古渡头"，李商隐的"巴山夜雨涨秋池"，张若虚的"春江潮水连海平，海上明月共潮生"。历史上也有很多与水有关的故事，如"子在川上曰"，项羽的乌江自刎，屈原的汨罗江自沉，都为水积淀了丰富的人文底蕴。

庄子也不满足于仅在书本上了解，他也喜欢到处走走。比如，他就去了一趟宋都商丘。商丘在庄子家乡蒙城西南方向，有几十里❶路程。

早在一万多年前，中国古代传说中的"三皇"❷之一的燧人氏，在商丘发明了人工取火，人类从此结束了茹毛饮血的历史。远古时期商部落曾在此聚居，这里的人们最早开始商业贸易，使商丘成为商人、商业、商文化的发源地。商丘自古以来为兵家必争之地。自古代传说的"五帝"中的颛顼、帝喾起，经商汤的商朝、西周时的宋国、西汉时的梁国，皆把商丘作为国都。

庄子还没到达商丘城门，远远就看见高大坚固的城墙和宽阔深广的护城河。商丘城的围墙又高又宽，高达11.5—12米，厚12—15米，底宽在25—27米之间。而战国时期的魏国城墙高度通常在6米上下，厚也不过10米左右。鲁国城墙更不怎么样，高不过4.5米，底宽20米。这次亲眼所看，果然名不虚传。难怪

---

❶ 译者注：里，中国常用的长度单位。1里合500米。
❷ 译者注：皇和帝的说法源自中国古代神话里的几位最高统治者"三皇五帝"。

❶ Translator's note: *li* - Chinese unit of length, equal to 500 metres.
Translator's note: Huang and Di—an address for the Three Sovereigns and Five Emperors, who
❷ were legendary supreme rulers in ancient China.

surprised that despite being besieged by Chu, Jin, and Lu, the walls had never fallen. The armies of Chu had approached the walls many times, once even laying siege for 9 months, but they never set foot inside the city. At that time, it was said that Shangqiu was synonymous with "impregnable."

However, this reputation was put to the test in about 445 B.C., when the walls came within a hair of being taken. After the great battle at Sishui, the kingdoms of Chu and Yue quickly raised an army and marched north in an attempt to conquer Song. In order to capture the walls of Shangqiu, King Hui of Chu employed an expert in mechanical engineering from Lu named Gongshu Ban. He undertook the construction of a mysterious new weapon—the "cloud ladder." As the ladder was designed specifically for the height of Shangqiu's city walls, it gave Chu the ability to level the fortress: the myth of Shangqiu's impregnable walls was about to come to an end. All who watched were worried for the pitiful Song defenders. There was no doubt the battle would end with the destruction of Song. Fortunately, a young man set out with haste from the State of Lu, traveling day and night to reach Ying, the capital of Chu (in what is modern-day northwest Jiangling County in Hubei Province). He used all his eloquence in a furious attempt to convince the king of Chu not to attack Song. This young man, named Mozi, would soon become renowned throughout China. Mozi also arranged for his chief disciple, Qin Huali, to take 300 choice followers and assist Song in the defense of Shangqiu. In the end, Mozi was able to convince the king of Chu not to attack Song, and the crisis was averted.

Zhuangzi's heart was full of gratitude for Mozi's aid to Song in repelling Chu. Zhuangzi also admired Mozi for rushing from state to state, sacrificing his personal pleasure and taking no thought for his own safety in order to promote his philosophy of "universal love" and "non-violence." However, Zhuangzi did not agree with the incessant quarreling between Mohists and Confucians. In Zhuangzi's opinion, both Mohists and Confucians belonged to the "major schools of thought" of their day, so for them to insult each other was only a sign of their narrow-mindedness and hypocrisy. It's just like the pot calling the kettle black. Both sides made the mistake of viewing their own philosophies as absolute and imposing their own standards and preferences on the other. For instance, in evaluating beauty and ugliness, there is no universal standard of measurement. All who saw Mao Qiang and Li Ji recognized them as beautiful women. However, if fish were to see the two women, they would flee to the depths of the pond, if birds were to see them, they would fly away into the heavens, and if deer were to see them, they would prance away into the

历史上该城多次被楚、晋、鲁国围攻，但久攻不下，固若金汤。楚国的军队曾不止一次兵临商丘城下，最长一次曾围城九个月，却从来没有踏上过这片城墙。商丘几乎成了不可攻陷的代名词。

尤其最惊险的一次，是在公元前445年前后，楚国与越国在泗水大战之后紧接着兴兵北上，准备攻打宋国。为了攻占商丘的城墙，楚惠王特地从鲁国请来了一位机械工程学专家公输般，专门制造了一种神秘的新式武器——云梯。该武器专为商丘的城墙量身打造，完全有能力将任何堡垒夷为平地，商丘城不可攻破的神话即将终结。所有人都为可怜的宋国捏了一把汗，没人会怀疑这场战争的结果，宋国一定会灭亡。幸运的是，有一位年轻人匆匆忙忙地从鲁国出发，日夜兼程赶往楚国都郢（今湖北省江陵县西北），力图用他那三寸不烂之舌说服楚王停止攻宋。这名年轻人就是后来大名鼎鼎的墨子。他同时又安排大弟子禽滑厘带领三百名精壮弟子赶赴宋国助宋守城。最终墨子说服了楚王停止攻打宋国，化解了这场危机。

对于墨子帮助宋国抵御楚国，庄子心存感激。而墨子为推广其"兼爱"、"非攻"的理念，在诸侯国间四处奔走，不顾个人安危，牺牲个人安逸和享乐，庄子也十分敬佩。不过，对于以墨子为首的墨家攻击儒家，儒家子弟又反过来非难墨家，庄子不以为然。在庄子看来，墨家与儒家都是那个时代的"显学"，两派互相说对方不好，两派的境界都高不到哪里去，只不过是五十步笑一百步。他们都犯了一个错误，把一己之见绝对化，并以自己的标准和喜好要求对方。比如美与丑，毛嫱、丽姬，是古代公认的美女，人们见了认为她们是美女，但鱼儿见了却避入水底，鸟儿见了吓得高飞，鹿见了赶快跑开，说明美丑没

woods. This goes to show that there is no universal standard of beauty.

Zhuangzi entered the city of Shangqiu and saw people, horses, and wagons everywhere, as well as shops set up on both sides of the road, selling silk, jade, porcelain, gold, silver, and leather. Zhuangzi paused for a long time in front of the shop that sold lacquer ware. As the manager of a lacquer tree orchard, Zhuangzi was relatively familiar with the process of harvesting lacquer and naturally became interested in how it was sold. Usually a small lacquer tree could be harvested five years after being planted, and would produce lacquer for about 20 years after that. Normally, lacquer could be obtained from the trees every other year, with the harvest taking place between the summer solstice and the autumnal equinox. Cuts would be made in the bark every seven days, and each tree could produce about 1 kilogram of lacquer. The better the trees grew, the more lacquer they would produce.

Zhuangzi knew that after the raw lacquer was obtained from the trees, it could be applied to the surface of various implements and utensils, creating beautiful hand-crafted art. He also knew that by making paint with lacquer, it could provide the additional functions of preventing moisture from rotting the utensils or furniture. In Shangqiu, he saw the many colors of lacquer: black, yellow, red, and white, as well as the beautiful lacquer designs made on the wooden items. There were geometric shapes, clouds and birds, depictions of hunting, dragons and phoenixes, and more.

During the Warring States Period, in other cities throughout the State of Song such as Dingtao (north of Zhuangzi's hometown), Pengcheng (south east of Shangqiu in modern Xuzhou in Jiangsu), and other counties and towns, various artisanal workshops were built which manufactured gold, leather, wood, lacquer, wagons, jade, and porcelain. These workshops were called *si* and it was said that, "All craftsmen reside in the *si*." The kingdom established a system of foremen and supervisors to manage the production and operation of the urban handicraft industry. Outside the cities, the privately operated industry handicraft was a sideline relying on farming, scattered throughout farming villages and individual families.

In addition to the little market in Zhuangzi's small town of Meng, there were seasonal markets in the small villages around Meng. On the road to Shangqiu, the capital of Song, Zhuangzi also ran into many merchants. The people of Song had a long tradition of commerce. According to historical records in Song, "Those who reap and sow are few, while those who engage in traveling commerce are many." The records also state, "The people of Yin Dynasty regard the trade as important, of whom there are many merchants."

有绝对的标准。

庄子进了商丘城，看见城内人来人往、车水马龙，街道两边摆着很多店铺，有卖蚕丝的，也有专售玉器和陶器的，也有做金银、皮革生意的。庄子在卖漆器的店铺前驻足了好久。庄子自己本身是漆园吏，相对来说，对漆的收割过程比较了解。一般一株小的漆树生长5年后就可开割，通常能采割生漆20年以上。割漆一般采用隔年割采法，每年从夏至到秋分，每刀相隔7天，每株出漆量约1公斤左右。树生长得越旺盛，出漆量也越高。

庄子只知道生漆从漆树上割取下来后，可以涂在各种器物的表面，制成工艺品和美术品；用漆作涂料有耐潮、耐腐蚀等功能。这次他亲眼所见漆器的色彩有黑、黄、朱、白，也看见木器物上用各色漆所画成的各种图案：几何纹、云鸟纹、狩猎图、龙凤图等。

在战国时代，除了宋城商丘，在宋国其他一些城市，如庄子家乡北边的定陶、商丘东南边的彭城（今江苏徐州）和一些州县城镇也出现了一些设有金、革、木、漆、车、玉、陶等多种手工业作坊。作坊称作"肆"，号称"百工居肆"。国家还专门设置工正、工师、工尹来管理城里的手工业生产和经营。而城外的民营手工业则作为副业依附于农业，分散在广大农村，一家一户进行生产。

庄子自己所在的小城蒙城就有集市，而在蒙城附近的农村则有定期的集市。在进宋都商丘的路上，庄子也碰到了许多商贾。宋人有经商的传统，据史书载，宋国"稼穑之民少，

The people of Song were talented businessmen, always searching for profit.

On the road home after this somewhat short journey, Zhuangzi felt he had learnt a lot from this trip. He now had a better understanding of the bustling, flourishing Song capital, and the skill of its artisans. He was especially interested in the work of the artisans, deciding that if he had the chance, he would have more contact with them and describe their labor in his book. This desire was to be fulfilled. Today, as we read *Zhuangzi*, we notice Zhuangzi's attention to and comprehension of the daily life of laborers, artists, and artisans. It is evident that he was very familiar with their lifestyles and habits. The following are examples of stories from Zhuangzi which describe the everyday labor of workers: "Pao Ding the Cook Cuts the Cow," "Lun Bian Cuts Wood for Wagon Wheels," "The Hunchback Catches Cicadas," "Stonecutter Shi Cuts the Dust," "Bocheng Zigao in His Fields," "The Old Gardener who Watered his Fields with a Pitcher under his Arm," and "The Man of Song who Bleached Silk Flosses." He also portrays scenes of the daily life and habits of workers, some of these stories include: "The Ferryman Steers the Boat," "The Man of Lüliang who swims in water," "The Soothsayers Read Palms," "The Anthroposcopy to Dogs and cockfight," and "Fisherman and Fish Watchers."

Zhuangzi also included the Song people's love of commerce in his book. In the chapter "Free and Easy Wandering," there are two examples of Song people doing business. The first story goes like this: a Song merchant wanted to go to the state of Yue (near modern Shaoxing in Zhejiang Province) to sell special hats which are used on ceremonial occasions. However, because the Yue people were more primitive, their custom was to cut all their hair and tattoo their bodies. They obviously had no use for his hats. The second story goes like this: a man from Song was skilled at producing a balm that prevented hands from getting dry and cracked. Generation after generation, his family had made their living by bleaching silk. A traveler heard of this medicine, and offered one hundred *liang* of gold to buy the secret of making the medicine. Thereupon the man of Song called his family together to discuss the proposition. He said, "We've been bleaching silk for generations and have made very little money, now that there is somebody willing to pay a high price for our secret, we ought to sell to him!" The first story told of a Song merchant who learned a tough lesson about "supply and demand" from an instance of commercial failure in which he didn't adequately master the information about the market. The second story showed that people from Song are adept at making the most of commercial opportunities and are always

商旅之民多"，"殷人重贾，经商者颇多"，而且善于经营，随时逐利。

经过这趟不算远的出游，庄子在回来的路上颇有感慨，他对都城的繁华和宋国的手工业水平有了更直观的了解，尤其对手工业者的生产活动产生了浓厚的兴趣，决定以后若有机会，多与他们接触，并把他们的劳动场面写进他的书里。这个愿望后来实现了。今天我们在读《庄子》一书时注意到，庄子对劳动者的日常生活、技艺和手工劳作非常了解，也深谙他们的生活习性。写到各行各业日常生产劳动的有：庖丁解牛、轮扁斫轮、痀偻承蜩、匠石运斤成风、伯成子高耕田、菜园老翁抱瓮灌圃、宋人漂洗丝絮为业；写到日常生活场景和生活习性的有：津人操舟、吕梁男子蹈水、神巫看相、相狗斗鸡、钓鱼观鱼等。

同时，庄子把宋人喜欢做生意的传统也写进了书里。《逍遥游》篇中有两处讲到宋人经商的事例。一是"宋人资章甫而适诸越，越人断发文身，无所用之！"意思是说，宋国人贩运在礼节场合使用的帽子到越国（今浙江绍兴一带）去卖，越人的生活接近原始状态，他们的习俗是剪光头发、身上刺青，根本用不着这些帽子；二是"宋人有善为不龟手之药者，世世以洴澼（漂洗丝絮）为事。客闻之，请买其方百金。聚族而谋曰：'我世世为洴澼，不过数金，今一朝鬻技百金，请与之。'"意思是说，宋国有人善于调制不让手皲裂的药物，他家世世代代都以漂洗丝絮为职业。有一位客人听说了这种药品，愿意出一百两黄金购买他的药方。于是这个宋国人召集全家来商量说："我们世世代代漂洗丝絮，赚的钱不过数金而已；现在有人愿意出高价，以百金收购这药方，我们就卖给他吧。"前一例，说明宋人在一次经营失败中得到"货不对路"的教训，因为没有很

looking for chances to make a profit.

Not long after Zhuangzi's return, Hui Shi came from the State of Wei to visit him. Hui Shi had left Song years before, journeyed widely in foreign lands, and finally traveled north to Wei to make his fortune. When Hui Shi was around 20, he began to make a name for himself on the political scene in the State of Wei and became very influential later. As he began his political career, Wei was beginning to decline from prosperity. The capital of Wei was originally at Anyi (in modern Xia County in Shanxi Province), but Anyi was too close to the State of Qin. Around 361 B.C., as Qin began to grow in power, King Hui of Wei was forced to move his capital to Daliang (modern Kaifeng in Henan) in order to protect his government from the menace of the Qin armies. In 354 B.C., the State of Zhao forced the State of Wey to surrender, arousing the dissatisfaction of the more powerful Wei kingdom. As a result, Wei led an allied army of Song and Wey troops in laying siege to the Zhao capital, Handan. This forced Zhao to call for aid from Qi the next year. The Qi armies were commanded by Tian Ji, with Sun Bin as tactical aide. At Guiling, The Qi force routed the armies of Wei, led by Pang Juan. This was the famous battle of "Annihilating Wei to Save Zhao." In the 28th year of the reign of King Hui of Wei (in 342 B.C.), Wei was again defeated by Qi at the battle of Maling, losing 100,000 men. Prince Shen, the crown heir of Wei was slain in the battle and General Pang Juan committed suicide. This was an unprecedented defeat for Wei. Qin took advantage of Wei's weakened state and gradually began to retake the land west of the Yellow River, setting the border with Wei at the Yellow River, Xiao Mountain and Han Valley.

To avenge the killing of the crown prince and the slaughter of 100,000 soldiers, King Hui of Wei summoned Hui Shi, commanding him to, "Raise an army and attack" Qi. Hui Shi felt that the plan was doomed to fail and attempted to dissuade the king, saying, "I cannot. Your humble servant has heard that kings follow certain moral standards and great kings have carefully laid plans. What your majesty has commanded me to do is neither moral nor well-planned. The country is not prepared, and I believe it is unwise to launch another war. If your majesty desires revenge, then here is a plan: change your clothes and bow down before the king of Qi. This will incite the wrath of the king of Chu. Then you can send men to Qi and Chu to stir them up against one another. This will surely result in Chu attacking Qi. When Chu, which has been building up its military strength for a long time, meets the war-devastated armies of Qi, it cannot help but defeat Qi. In this way, your majesty will have obtained revenge by using the armies of Chu." To this plan, the king of Wei

好掌握商业信息。后一例则说明宋人善于抓住商机，随时逐利。

庄子回来后不久，惠施从魏国来拜访他。惠施早年就离开宋国，远走他乡，在北边的魏国谋发展。20多岁时就在魏国政坛崭露头角，叱咤风云。惠施步入魏国政坛，正是魏国综合国力由盛转衰之际。魏国都城本在安邑（今山西夏县），安邑离秦国很近。随着秦国的日益壮大，在公元前361年，魏惠王为防范秦国兵临安邑城下，被迫迁都大梁（今河南开封）。公元前354年，赵国迫使卫国屈服，引起魏国的不满，因而魏国起兵伐赵，率宋、卫联军包围了赵都邯郸，次年，赵向齐求救。齐以田忌为将，孙膑为师，在桂陵大败庞涓所率领的魏国军队。这就是著名的"围魏救赵"的战例。魏惠王二十八年（前342年），在马陵之战中魏又大败于齐，十万之军覆灭，太子申被杀，庞涓自杀。这是魏国从未有过的惨败。秦国此时也乘机利用魏国衰弱的形势，逐渐夺回了河西故地，与三晋（即魏国）以黄河、崤函为界。

为报杀太子申和十万大军覆灭之仇，魏惠王召惠施告以"欲悉起兵而攻"齐。惠施谏阻，认为这样做乃是失策，劝其说："不可以，臣听说，王者做事有法度，霸者做事有计谋，今大王所告臣者，疏于度而远于计，现在国家没有作好准备，大王欲再次发动战争，我认为不妥。大王欲报仇，则不如改变您大王的服饰，在齐王面前卑躬屈膝，以引起楚王的愤怒，您大王再派人在齐、楚两国间游说，挑唆它们的关系，那么楚国必伐齐，以养精蓄锐的楚国攻打已被战争拖垮的齐国，则楚国必胜。这样，大王就借助楚国报了自己的仇。"魏王说："好。"

responded, "Very well." Although Kuang Zhang and other advisors were opposed to this strategy of "submitting to the king of Qi" (from *Lü Shi Chun Qiu: Ai Lei*), King Hui of Wei was adamant that the plan be put into action. Wei was a vassal state of the high king of Zhou, but now Qi forced this state to swear fealty, appearing to show contempt towards other vassal states such as Qi and Chu. In doing so, it incurred the jealousy of these two powerful states. As Hui Shi predicted, the king of Chu was enraged and sent a strong army to attack Qi. With the help of Zhao, Chu routed the armies of Qi at Xuzhou (southeast of modern Teng County in Shandong Province), indirectly bringing revenge for King Hui of Wei. Because Hui Shi's recommendation was successful, he obtained an additional measure of the king's trust and respect.

Although Zhuangzi and Hui Shi were childhood friends, Zhuangzi did not appear too enthusiastic about Hui Shi's visit. This was because of Zhuangzi's personality. Zhuangzi was very carefree; he did not like to make friends with powerful nobles or well-known officials in order to improve his own social standing. In fact, he felt a kind of natural distance between himself and those in court. Perhaps this was because as a minor official, he worked around powerful people, and had a first-hand understanding of the corrupting influence of power on human nature. Because of this, Zhuangzi was doubtful that he would still be able to have heartfelt communication with Hui Shi, the favored minister of King Hui of Wei. In addition, Zhuangzi did not have a high opinion of Wei. As all their dealings were centered on profit and there was no kindness or mercy in inter-state relations. The relationship between Wei and Song constantly oscillated between friend and enemy.

Zhuangzi remembered that in 355 B.C., the State of Wei sent General Gongsun Yan to attack Huangchi, a vassal land of the state of Song (southwest of modern Shangqiu in Henan Province). Thus, Wei and Song became enemies. But when, in the next year, Wei attacked the city of Handan of Zhao, King Hui of Wei called upon Song to help him in his campaign, viewing Song as his ally. Wei's actions put the ruler of Song in an awkward position. The ruler of Song decided to send a messenger to Zhao, imploring its king, saying, "The armies of Wei are powerful and its methods are overbearing. Now it has demanded that Song heed its call to attack Zhao together. If Song does not obey, then it endangers the state, but if it aids Wei, then it will harm Zhao. The ruler of Song cannot bear to make this decision and so we beseech you, the king of Zhao to make the final judgment." The king of Zhao replied, "I know that Song is small and weak while Wei is large and powerful. If Zhao is destroyed and Wei becomes even stronger, then it will surely annex Song, this

虽有匡章等人反对这种"王齐王"(《吕氏春秋·爱类》)的主张，但魏惠王仍即"使人报于齐，愿臣畜而朝"。齐国因让万乘之国魏称臣，显得不把秦国、楚国放在眼里，引起了秦国、楚国的嫉妒。果然，楚王大怒，主动出击攻打齐国，在赵国的配合下，大败齐于徐州（今山东滕县东南），间接地为魏惠王报了仇。惠施也因这次献策有功，进一步获得魏王的信任和重用。

虽然是儿时的朋友，庄子对惠施的来访并没有显出热情和积极。这跟庄子的性格有关。庄子比较散淡，不喜欢结交权贵显臣来增添自身地位。他实际上对官场中的人有一种天然的距离感，他自己本身就是一个小官吏，也生活在权力场内，可能对权力腐蚀人性有一定的了解。所以面对魏惠王的宠臣惠施的到来，他对两人能否进行有效、深度沟通表示怀疑。庄子对魏国印象也不怎么样：国与国之间无仁义，行事和交往一切以利益为出发点，所以魏国与宋国既不会是永远的朋友，也不会是永远的敌人。

庄子记得，公元前355年，魏国就派魏将公孙衍攻下宋国属地黄池（今河南商丘西南）。魏国成了宋国的敌人。但到了次年，魏国攻打赵国邯郸时，魏惠王却征召宋国一起去攻打，把宋国看作盟友。魏国的行径让宋君很为难。宋君于是派出使者请求赵王，说："魏国兵强而权重，现在要求宋国听从它一起攻打赵国，若不听从则危及社稷，若扶助魏国攻打赵国则害了赵国，宋国国君又不忍，请赵王定夺。"赵王说："我知道宋国弱小，魏国强大，如果削弱赵国而使魏国强大，魏必定来兼并宋，宋必不利，我也知道宋不想助魏，但实在也找不出借辞可以使宋不听从魏。"那使者说："不如这样，让宋国攻下赵国一城来敷衍魏国，其他城则佯攻，让赵国不丢失城池，仅是拖延时日，您看怎样？"赵王说："好。"果然，宋人举兵入赵境，

is not beneficial for Song. I know that Song does not wish to aid Wei, but I can think of no excuse for Song to not obey Wei." The messenger then replied, "What if Song attacked a small piece of Zhao's land to appease Wei, and abstained from attacking anything else? This will allow Zhao to not lose any cities, while at the same time postponing Wei's assault. What do you think of this plan?" The king of Zhao replied, "It is good." As planned, Song raised an army and crossed the border into Zhao, taking a city. The king of Wei was overjoyed, exclaiming, "Song has done me a great service in attacking Zhao." The King of Zhao was also overjoyed, crying, "Song has fulfilled its promise, it has taken one city and not more." Thus, both Zhao and Wei were pleased.

Unfortunately, Zhuangzi's meeting with Hui Shi went as he expected. The two men were interested in different things and unable to have heartfelt communication. Hui Shi advised Zhuangzi to apply for an official appointment, adding that he himself was in a position of no small importance in Wei and could help Zhuangzi get a post if he wanted. Zhuangzi was uninterested in official promotions and suggested that they change the subject. Hui Shi told Zhuangzi that the king of Wei had given him the seed of a giant bottle gourd[1] which Hui Shi planted and cared for. The bottle gourd which grew from it was unmatched in size, but Hui Shi was unsure how to use it. It was not strong enough to hold a lot of water, nor was it small enough to be cut up and made into a water ladle, because its diameter was greater than that of any water container. Zhuangzi replied, "You have such a large bottle gourd, why do you persist in thinking of ways to make it into a water container? Why not put it on top of rivers or oceans and use it as a life preserver. You could tie it to your waist and it could be a 'flotation device.' Thus you could swim on the waters of rivers or oceans and not sink. It appears as though your thinking is not broad enough!" Hui Shi said, "I am ashamed, this is a use of which I did not think. Unfortunately, the bottle gourd was too big, and thinking that it was useless, I smashed it."

With this conversation, Zhuangzi and Hui Shi ended their meeting.

攻下一城，魏王很高兴，说："宋人正助我攻打赵国。"赵王也很高兴，说："宋人说到做到，攻打赵国确实点到为止。"赵、魏皆悦。

庄子与惠施的会面正如庄子所预料的，两人关心的焦点不一样，也没有深度的沟通。惠施建议庄子去谋一官半职，并说自己在魏国正被魏王重用，若需要的话，可以请自己帮忙。庄子对官场晋升并不感兴趣，说，我们还是说点别的吧。惠施说，魏王曾赠送他一个大葫芦❶的种子，他把它栽植成长，结出的葫芦巨大无比，但却不知道怎么用，用它来装满水，则葫芦不够坚固，无法承载大容量的水；把它剖开做成瓢，又太大，无法放进水缸舀水，因为水缸的直径没有瓢的直径大。庄子说："你有这么大的葫芦，为什么老是想着如何在水缸里安置它？为什么不把它放在河海之上，当作游泳的救生圈来使用，把它绑在腰上，成了腰舟，你就可以浮游于河海之上，不会沉下去。看样子，你的心思还不够通达啊！"惠施说："惭愧，惭愧，这一层我还真的没想到。可惜的是，这葫芦太大，我以为没有用，已把它打碎了。"

庄子与惠施就在这样的对话中结束了他们的会面。

---

❶ 一种南瓜状的爬藤植物。

❶ A large, pumpkin-like vegetable.

云梯攻城
Invading the City by Cloud Ladders

四　中年早期（约前338—前329）

Chapter Ⅳ　Early Middle Years
(About 338 B.C. to 329 B.C.)

When Zhuangzi was about 30 years old, he had an experience which would affect him greatly and become the basis of his future life decisions.

One time, Zhuangzi went for a stroll in the chestnut orchard at Diaoling. While there, he happened to run into a strange bird that had flown in from the south. Zhuangzi observed the bird very carefully; it had a wingspan of seven *chi* and the diameter of its eye was one *cun*. It flew right past Zhuangzi's forehead and landed in the chestnut orchard. Zhuangzi held his sling in his hand and waited to one side. At that moment, a cicada found a spot in the shade where it could rest and it let down its guard, forgetting its own safety. Little did it know that a short distance away there was a praying mantis lying in wait, ready to catch it. At the same time, the strange bird was eying the mantis, preparing to swoop down on it. Meanwhile, behind the bird, Zhuangzi hid with his sling. Behind him was the caretaker of the orchard, whose suspicions had been aroused by Zhuangzi's strange behavior and was now preparing to interrogate him for appearing to be a thief.

The complexity exemplified by the story "The Mantis Stalks the Cicada, Unaware of the Oriole Lurking Behind Him" made Zhuangzi realize the difficulty involved in protecting oneself while on earth. He sensed the interconnectivity of all things. He realized that because of relationships of profit and harm, there was discord and constant scheming among all creatures. In order to protect themselves and avoid disaster, humans must spend enormous amounts of time and energy in maintaining their relationships. They must constantly consider which person or thing can bring them gain or loss, fortune or misfortune, glory or shame. Thus, the spirit is caught up and entangled in this complicated web and forced to live in bondage. Zhuangzi felt that this kind of life was not worth living, and consequently decided to search for a lifestyle of his own.

This happened to be the same year (338 B.C.) as the palace coup in which King Yan of Song, then only a lord, overthrew the king, his own brother, and usurped the throne. With this turn of events, Zhuangzi lost all hope for realizing his life goals as a court official. With this coup, the last bit of the facade of morality and benevolence covering the struggle for power and profit in court was torn away, leaving only blatant violence, cruelty, and malice in its wake. The rule became "Those who follow the strong prosper, those who oppose him are crushed" ; brotherly love, blood relations, or the bonds of friendship between lord and servant were not enough to protect those in opposition from being purged. Righteousness, justice, and peace disappeared from society. Zhuangzi's personality was honest and straightforward, and he

庄子30多岁时，经历了一件事，这件事对他触动很大，成了他以后作出人生重大抉择的一个背景。

有一次，庄子到雕陵的栗园里游玩，恰巧碰见一只怪雀从南方飞来。这只怪雀庄子观察得很仔细，翅膀张开有七尺，眼睛直径有一寸，它擦过庄子的额头直直停在栗林中，庄子则手握弹弓守候一旁。这时，一只蝉刚刚找到可以安息的树荫，放松了警惕，忘了自身的安全，不知道几步之外有只螳螂躲在隐秘的树林中，随时准备捕捉它。而此时，那只怪雀也盯着螳螂准备下手。怪鹊的背后则偷偷站着手持弹弓的庄子，而在庄子的不远处，则有守园人怀疑着这一园中可疑的人物，随时准备把庄子当小偷盘问……

"螳螂捕蝉，黄雀在后"的生物链让庄子意识到，人处在世上保全自己是何等的艰难，万物互相牵累，因利害关系相互倾轧和算计。为了保全自己，躲避灾祸，就要花大量时间和精力谨慎处理各种人际关系，并随时盘算哪人、何事会给自己带来得失、福祸、荣辱。这样，心灵就被这些所牵挂和缠累，活在不自由当中。这样的生活，庄子觉得不值得，他决定去寻找真正属于自己的生活。

此时，适逢宋国发生宋君偃逐兄篡位的宫廷政变（前338年），庄子对在仕途中实现自身的理想不再抱有希望。当今，仕途中的利益权势之争，连最后的一块遮羞布，即仁义道德的旗号，也撕下了，仅剩下赤裸裸的暴力、残忍和冷酷。所谓"顺我者昌，逆我者亡"，哪怕是兄弟之情、骨肉之亲、君臣之义，若挡我者，照样给予肃清。社会的正义、公平、和平不复

was not willing to bow and scrape to those in power. Therefore, he decided not to be dependent on the despotic court, and instead elected to resign as manager of the lacquer orchard.

The years Zhuangzi spent managing the lacquer tree orchard helped him realize that if a person was too useful, he would arouse the attention of worldly things, be used by them, and gradually be forced to live according to their standards and demands. Living this way would cause loss of personal freedom, and was detrimental to personal growth. In the chapter "The World of Men" he wrote, "Osmanthus can be eaten, hence it is cut down; lacquer can be used, hence it is extracted. Men know all the benefits of usefulness, and are yet unfamiliar with the benefits of uselessness." By this he meant that the reason that osmanthus trees were cut down was because of their edible bark; the reason that lacquer trees were cut open was because the lacquer they produced was useful. Only in being useless could one avoid being used and exploited by worldly things, leaving room to grow.

Zhuangzi also understood that if one were too useful, it could lead to the outcomes depicted in proverbs such as, "the arrow pierces the lead bird in the flock," "the wind blows hardest upon the tallest tree in the forest," or "he whose actions are nobler than man's peers is censured by the masses." In other words, if a man rises above the crowd, people will become jealous of him, and it will cause him to be the target of false accusations, condemnations, reproaches, and in some cases even threats upon his life.

Zhuangzi left his position as manager of the lacquer orchard because he was uninterested by worldly things, unwilling to live by worldly standards, and did not wish to be exploited like one of his trees.

At that time, wars between states were frequent. This helped Zhuangzi gain a better understanding of the world around him. For instance, Song's stronger neighbors Chu, Qi, Wei, and Qin all avidly desired to conquer the smaller Song. Qi, Qin, and Zhao had all attempted to invade Dingtao, one of Song's cities. At the time, Dingtao was one of the most prosperous cities in China's central plains region. Song's geographic position was not only economically strategic, but also militarily important. Of all the various states, Chu understood this fact most clearly. As Chu gradually annexed the smaller kingdoms surrounding it, it fixed its sights on Song, attacking them from the north. Not only did Chu send its own soldiers to attack Song, but it would often also incite Song's other neighbors, such as Zheng, to attack it. In *Zuo Zhuan*, the greatest number of recorded wars are between Song and Chu.

Zhuangzi did not wish to be involved with the carnage of war. Although

存在。庄子个性率真，不愿曲阿奉迎，于是决定不愿再依附专制庙堂，辞掉漆园小吏。

管理漆园的这几年生涯也让庄子意识到，一个人若过于有用，容易受世俗关注，被世俗占用，并按世俗的标准和要求生活，这样反而失去了个人的自由，不利于自己个性的成长。他在《人间世》篇中写道："桂可食，故伐之；漆可用，故割之。人皆知有用之用，而莫知无用之用也。"意思是说，桂树皮可以吃，所以被砍伐；漆可以用，所以漆树被切割。世人都知道有用的好处，而不知道无用的好处。因为无用，也就不被世俗征用和占用，所以可以给自己留更多的生长空间。

庄子也意识到，过于有用，也易导致"枪打出头鸟"，因为"木秀于林，风必摧之"，"行高于人，众必非之"。人若超于群，众必妒之，会招致他人对你的诬陷、非难、责罚，严重的甚至会危及自身性命。

由于庄子不愿像漆树那样听任宰割，对俗世中的利益之争也不感兴趣，也不愿以社会标准要求自己委屈活着，遂弃漆园之职。

当时，国与国之间战争频繁，这让庄子对周遭世界有了更深刻的认识。以宋国为例，宋国是小国，成了周边大国楚、齐、魏、秦觊觎的对象。齐、秦、赵三大强国都曾想夺取宋国的定陶。定陶是当时中原最繁荣的城市之一。宋国地理位置的重要性不仅在经济上，也在军事上。这一点楚国最深知其利害。楚在逐步吞并周围小国后，将重要目标锁定在宋国，故楚北举必攻宋。它不仅自己出兵不断攻打宋国，而且还经常指使郑国等宋周边国家攻宋。《左传》中关于宋楚之战的次数最多。

庄子不想卷入战争的杀戮当中，虽然他佩服他的朋友惠施

he respected his friend Hui Shi for being a diplomat and negotiating among different kingdoms, he realized that once the wheels of war began to turn, not even Hui Shi had the power to stop them. Ultimately, Zhuangzi believed that profit and lust are the driving forces of war. They cause contention, competition, and death. Unless the hearts of men became penitent, there would be no end to war.

Because Zhuangzi had such a clear understanding of the cruelty and viciousness of human nature, he felt that Confucianism was a little naive, saying that, "they are clear on rites and rituals but neglect to understand the human heart."

In Zhuangzi's opinion, the human heart could be more treacherous and rough than mountains or rivers. It was impossible to rely on Confucianism's teachings to suppress the ugliness of human nature and encourage the ruling class to do good instead of evil. He described the system established by Confucianism to bridle human evil as being like a safe, which a man bought, believing his possessions to be safe from thieves. But upon finding the safe, a resourceful thief stole it along with the precious things inside. The men who stole the kingdom had become the ruling class. Such as in 481 B.C., Tian Chengzi, the Left Prime Minister of Qi, had Duke Jian of Qi and the Right Prime Minister, Jian Zhi, arrested and killed, usurping the political power of the state and creating an authoritarian Qi government. In 387 B.C., King Wu of Wei sent a messenger to the high king of Zhou and the other nobility, asking for the Tian family to be recognized as the hereditary king of Qi. The next year, the Tian family was recognized as part of the royal family. Comparing this to the plight of the impoverished people who stole hooks because they were hungry, were found guilty of robbery and then sentenced to death, we can see the injustice of the world at that time. This was the origin of the proverb "those who steal hooks are executed and those who steal kingdoms are made kings." What cruel irony! Even more ironic, the former were tried and sentenced by the latter. In fact, dishonest nobles were responsible for stealing the most wealth and profit from the state, eventually gaining control of the whole government.

Of course, the fact that Zhuangzi found Confucians naive did not mean that he had no use for Confucian concepts such as benevolence. However, he felt that the concept of benevolence in Confucianism had internal divisions, complex stratagems, ritualistic behaviors of love, and constraining boundaries; he believed in something greater than benevolence, something which was not limited by Confucian parameters. For instance, according to the Confucian definition of benevolence, if one were to step on somebody's foot in the street,

作为一名外交家周旋于各国之间，但发现，战争的机器一旦发动，就不能停止，即使惠施也无能为力。说到底，是人的利益和欲望驱动着战争，导致人世间那么多的是非、竞争、杀戮。如果人心不归正，战争永不会停止。

正因为对现实的残酷和人性的丑恶有着深刻的认识，庄子感觉儒家思想有些天真，他们"明乎礼义而陋于知人心"。

在庄子看来，人心险于山川，靠儒家那一套来抑制人性中的丑恶，让统治阶级不作恶、向善，实际上不太可能。儒家所建制的一套防范人性丑恶的制度犹如发明了一个保险箱，自以为有了这个保险箱，就可以拒盗贼于门外，但高明的小偷最终连保险箱及保险箱内的东西一起偷走了。那些窃取了国家的人成为了诸侯，如公元前481年，齐国的左丞相田成子把齐简公和右丞相监止杀死，窃取了齐国的国家政权，实现了"专齐之政"。到了公元前387年，由魏武侯派使者请求周天子和诸侯们承认田氏为侯。于是次年，田氏被列为诸侯。而那些因饥饿贫穷而盗窃钩子的人却被宣判犯盗窃罪而被诛杀。真是"窃钩者诛，窃国者为诸侯"！多么绝妙的讽刺！而对前者的审判却是由后者作出的。实际上，后者盗取社会的财富和国家的权利最多，整个国家都被他们窃为己有了。

庄子也不是不需要"仁"的道德。但庄子认为儒家的"仁"有区分、有谋略、露爱迹、讲规范，不算"仁"的最上乘。在现实生活中，如果在街上踩了别人的脚，需要赔礼道歉；若是

he would need to offer a formal apology; if an older brother stepped on his younger brother's foot, he would only have to comfort his brother a little; if a father stepped on his child's foot, then no apology would be necessary. But in Zhuangzi's opinion, one should not differentiate between friends and others in showing respect, nor between strangers and friends in treating with honesty. A truly wise man employs his wisdom instead of schemes. True love is beyond any expression and great kindnesses needs no spoken thanks.

It was not in Zhuangzi's nature to establish a societal standard of morality and require all people to follow it. He believed that so doing was like "cutting the feet to fit the shoes." This was a proverb that suggested that forcing people to conform to a certain set of rules without consideration for individual differences could actually do more harm than good. To a large extent, this was exactly what Confucianism did. It used all sorts of incentives, restraints, rules, and instructions to correct the behavior of those who did not conform, forcing the people to measure themselves against one single standard. In reality, life is extremely diverse and there are an infinite number of differences between people. One cannot say that something which is longer is better or that something which is shorter is not good enough. Though a duck's feet are short, if they were any longer, they would cease to function properly. Though a crane's feet are long, if they were cut short, it would cause pain. Therefore, those things which are naturally long should not be shortened and those things which are naturally short should not be lengthened; thus nothing will be vexed. Confucians, on the other hand, insist upon measuring duck feet and crane feet according to the same scale, resulting in sadness and anguish. Both ducks and cranes lose the true meaning of life, and both are prevented from naturally growing into their potential.

After Zhuangzi resigned as manager of the lacquer tree orchard, he wove straw sandals to make a living. Word of his noble and pure aspirations, his learning and talent, as well as the profoundness of his personality began to spread far and wide. His name became respected, and people began to emulate his behavior, desiring to be his disciples.

During the Warring States Period, it was customary to establish private schools, recruit disciples, and pass on one's philosophy to students. At that time, disciples of Confucius and Mozi were "everywhere under heaven," and even Xu Xing of Chu, the leading philosopher of the Agriculturists, had several dozen disciples.

Zhuangzi took a laissez-faire approach to recruiting students. He did not want to flaunt his talent because doing so was not in his personality. He also

哥哥踩了弟弟的脚，只需安慰一下弟弟；若是父亲踩了自己儿子的脚就毋须更多礼仪。但是，在庄子看来，至礼是没有人我之分的，至义是没有物我之分的，至知是不用谋略的，至仁是不表露爱迹的，大恩是不用言谢的。

从本性上说，庄子不喜欢通过制订某一道德和社会标准，并要求所有人的思想都统一到某一立场、某一标准和规则上来。庄子认为这样做是削足适履。而儒家在某些方面做的就是这样的工作，用各种钩、绳、规、矩来矫正那些不符合标准的行为，强迫百姓来共同遵守某一尺度。实际上，生活千姿百态，个体千差万别，长的不算有余，短的不算不足。所以，鸭脚虽短，接长了它就会烦恼；鹤脚虽长，折断了它就会悲伤。因此，本来长的不要折断，本来短的不要接长，这样就没有什么可忧愁的。而儒家非要将鸭脚、鹤脚的长度按统一标准裁定，结果扰攘多事，让鸭、鹤失去了生命的真实，妨碍了它们自然地成长。

庄子不再担任漆园之吏后，靠编织草鞋为生。他高洁的志向、博学的才华、深思的品格渐渐传开。有人仰其名，慕其为人，愿成为他的门徒。

在战国时代，开设私学，招收门徒，把自己的思想传授给学生成了时代的风气。当时，儒、墨的门徒已经“充满天下”，就连同时代的农家代表楚人许行也有门徒数十人。

庄子对招收门徒持顺其自然的态度。他不想太虚张声势，这不符合他的性格。他也知道跟随他的人不会很多。很多人之

knew that there would be few willing to follow him. The reason that so many were willing to become Confucian or Mohist disciples was because the reputation of Confucianism and Mohism was as great as the sun at midday. By learning from these schools of thought, one could easily carve out an official career for himself. Zhuangzi, unlike Confucius or Mozi, did not maintain close ties with high class society. The latter two men were able to provide their disciples with inside information and relationships that would help them in their careers. For instance, Confucius promised an official position to one of his students, Qidiao Kai. Mozi also encouraged his disciples, saying, "Learn well now, and I will make you officials." By this he meant, "If you study hard now, when the time comes, I will recommend you to be a minister." Zhuangzi could make no such promises. He was removed from the court and had not built relationships with the officials. Thus, those students in search of ways to further their careers usually did not come to Zhuangzi.

Zhuangzi had his own opinion about recruiting students and establishing his school of thought. The establishment of Confucius' private school had already broken the old custom of "all learning takes place in the palace." He had effectively moved the concept of schools from palaces to the people, broadening education to include not only the nobility but also commoners. However, Confucius' understanding of education conformed to the official government position. The education that Confucius provided focused on developing the moral character of his students and was designed to provide the ruling class with the officials and functionaries that it needed, hence the saying "He who excels in learning can be an official." This saying implied that not learning or learning poorly meant one was not qualified to work in government. Confucius used this technique to train more qualified personnel and strengthen the existing system of hereditary rule. "Hereditary rule" meant that titles, noble rank, official positions, and wealth were all passed on according to blood relations from one generation to the next. During the Spring Autumn and Warring States Periods, no matter if the education was in the palace or among the people, its purpose was still to train the personnel that the rulers needed. Additional insight into this process can come by examining the Chinese characters for education, *jiao yu*. *Jiao* is an associative compound character; the character for jiao in oracle script❶ depicts a hand holding a stick and beating a child. The original meaning of *jiao* was to discipline children with a stick to cause them to bend to the will of their elders. In conjunction with this, we read in *An Explanation of Words and Characters*: "*Jiao* is administered by those above and carried out by those below." *Yu* is a

所以愿意成为儒、墨之门徒，是因为儒、墨名声很大，如日中天，通过在那里的学习，可以更方便地进入仕途。而庄子不像孔子、墨子那样与上层社会常有密切的联系。他们有能力为门徒提供各种仕途消息和官场人脉关系。如孔子答应一个叫漆雕开的学生，提供仕途。墨子也对弟子说过："姑学乎，吾将仕子。"意思是说，好好努力学习吧，等有出息了，我推荐你去做官。庄子这方面没有，也疏于在官场积累人脉关系，所以奔着仕途而来的求学者一般不会投在他的门下。

　　庄子对招徒设教也有自己的看法。孔子开办的私学冲破了"学在王官"的旧传统，学校从宫廷移到民间，教育对象由贵族扩大到平民，但孔子对教育的理解跟官方基本一致，也就是说，孔子开创的教育基本上侧重于学生的道德培养，主要为统治阶级培养所需的各级官吏，这就是所谓的"学而优则仕"。"学而优则仕"包涵着这样的意思，即不学，或者虽学而不优，就没有做官的资格。孔子只不过用这种途径培养人才，补充当时的世袭制。世袭制就是指名号、爵位、官职以及财产等按照血统关系世代传承。所以，在春秋战国，无论学在民间，还是"学在王官"，教育的目的是培养官方所需的人才。这也可从"教育"的词义上窥其端倪。"教"是会意字，它的甲骨文❶写作：一手拿一根棍棒打一个孩子。说明"教"的本意是以棍棒训子，令其遵循长辈的意志。所以《说文解字》说："教，上

---

❶ 译者注：甲骨文是刻在龟甲或兽骨上的中国古代文字，使用于商朝（公元前16世纪—前11世纪）。

❶ Translator's note: Oracle script is the ancient Chinese script discovered on oracle bones, used in the Shang Dynasty, between the 16ᵗʰ and 11ᵗʰ centuries B.C.

phonogram or picto-phonetic character; in seal script❶ it is written as an upside-down *zi* (child) character. The ancients believed an upside-down *zi* character was symbolic of a disobedient, unfilial child. Such a child had to be moved with emotional appeal and enlightened with logical appeal. He or she had to be persuaded to return to the right way. This process of returning to the right way came to be defined as yu. We read in *An Explanation of Words and Characters:* "*Yu* is to raise a child and cause him to do what is good." Thus, we see that in ancient times, *jiao yu*, or education, implied training and developing positive virtues in people.

Zhuangzi was dubious towards the moral indoctrination that was popular in worldly education. Because of this, he was not very active in recruiting students.

On the other hand, Confucius enjoyed being a teacher. Confucius said that as long as a student brought 10 pieces of cured meat as an entrance fee, he would accept any and all who came, regardless of their social class. In fact, if a student could not afford to pay the fee because his family was poor but had a good attitude towards learning, Confucius would still accept him as a student. Zhuangzi, on the contrary, did not enjoy being a teacher. Because of this, he did not care about the number of disciples he had. He felt that having two or three followers with whom he could have heartfelt communication was enough.

Zhuangzi had a few disciples who loved to travel high and low and enjoy the sights of mountains and rivers with their teacher.

Once as Zhuangzi was walking through the mountains, he saw a large tree with dense, lush foliage. Nearby in the shade of the tree lay a woodcutter who was resting rather than cutting the tree. Zhuangzi inquired as to why he was not cutting, and the woodcutter replied, "This tree is useless." Zhuangzi turned to his disciples and said, "Because this tree is not useful timber, it can enjoy a long life." After Zhuangzi and his disciples left the mountain, they called on one of Zhuangzi's friends, who was overjoyed to see him. In order to properly show hospitality for his guests, Zhuangzi's friend called his children to butcher a goose to cook. The children asked if they should butcher the goose that honked, or the one that did not honk. His friend replied, "The one that does not honk." The next day, Zhuangzi's disciples questioned him, asking, "If you please, teacher, yesterday that tree in the mountains was not chopped down because it was useless, and so it will be able to live out its natural life. However, that goose was slaughtered because it was useless. So in applying this lesson to us, should we try to be useful or useless?" Zhuangzi replied, "It

所施，下所效也。""育"是个形声字，它的篆书❶字形是个颠倒的"子"字。古人认为，颠倒之子即不顺、不孝之子，需要动之以情、晓之以理，劝其入正途，故谓之"育"。所以《说文解字》说"育，养子使作善也。""教育"二字的古意就是培养人的良好品德。

庄子对世俗流行的、侧重于道德培养的教育内容持怀疑态度，因此他对招徒设教也就不很积极了。

孔子好为人师。对孔子来说，只要有人交纳十块腊肉，作为履行入学的礼节，他就不问来者出身贵贱，一律施教。如果学生当中有人因家贫交不起学费，但却有良好的学习态度，孔子也会收他为学生。庄子却不好为人师，所以也不在乎弟子人数，只要从者三二人，能与其心有戚戚焉，足矣。

庄子也有几个弟子，喜欢跟在老师后面游山玩水。

有一次，庄子在山中行走，看见一棵大树，枝叶茂盛，伐木的人在树旁休息，却不加砍伐。庄子问其故，答曰："此树没什么用处。"庄子转过身来对弟子说："这棵树因为不成材，所以能颐享天年。"一行人出了山，借住在庄子的一个朋友家里。难得庄子出来走动走动，朋友非常高兴，吆喝家童赶紧杀鹅款待客人。家童请示，是杀会叫的，还是不会叫的？答曰："不会叫的。"第二天，弟子向庄子请教："请问老师，昨天，山中那棵树因没有用，不遭砍伐，得以过完自然的寿命；而那只鹅却因没有用，就被杀了。那我们处在这个世上，究竟该采用有用的方式，还是无用的方式？"庄子说："我很难回答，

---

❶ 译者注：篆书是古代书体之一，曾用于官方文书，后来成为秦朝时官方文书的通用字体。

❶ Translator's note: Seal script is a form of Chinese script that was used on official seals and eventually became the official form of script during the Qin Dynasty.

is difficult for me to answer your question. Because human life is ever-changing, there is no hard and fast answer. If you insist on me giving you an answer, I would say that if one were too useful, he would be used and exploited by society. However, if one were too useless, he would be bullied. Perhaps one needs to consider each situation when deciding whether to advance or retreat, to show strength or feign weakness, or to reveal one's talent or hold one's peace." Upon hearing this, his disciples pretended to understand, though in reality they did not. They still hoped that there could be definitive answers in life.

In 334 B.C., the State of Wei was bitterly defeated in successive battles to Qi and Qin. King Hui of Wei, along with the king of Han and the rulers of other small kingdoms, was forced to travel to Xuzhou to pay homage to King Wei of Qi. In what was called the "Xuzhou Meeting of Kings," King Hui acknowledged Qi's hegemony and King Wei of Qi as his lord. In return, King Wei of Qi allowed King Hui of Wei to keep his title as king. By this time, Hui Shi had already been promoted to prime minister of Wei. Zhuangzi decided to take this chance to travel to Wei and pay him a visit.

Zhuangzi did not know that his trip to Wei to see Hui Shi would result in a great misunderstanding. There were people who told Hui Shi, "Zhuangzi has come to replace you as prime minister of Wei!" Hui Shi was very alarmed, for he knew that Zhuangzi's talent and learning were no less than his own. Hui Shi decided that whether the rumors were true or false, it would be best to place Zhuangzi in custody first. In an attempt to find Zhuangzi, Hui Shi ordered all the inns and major highways to be searched for three days, but nothing was found. Just as Hui Shi was feeling bewildered at being unable to capture Zhuangzi, a messenger came to report that Zhuangzi had arrived at his front door. Zhuangzi told Hui Shi, "Allow me to tell you a story. In the south there was a great, phoenix-like bird, called a *yuan*. As it flew from the south to the north, it was only willing to perch in phoenix trees, eat bamboo fruit, and drink sweet spring water. In its flight, it happened to cross an owl clutching a rotten mouse in its claws. The owl glimpsed the *yuan* as it passed, and for fear that the *yuan* coveted its mouse, the owl tried to scare off *yuan* by giving a loud cry 'Hah!' Now, my friend, are you trying to scare me off with your position as prime minister of Wei?" On hearing this, Hui Shi did not know how to respond, but his face betrayed his embarrassment.

This story does not end here. The following year, on the eve of the battle between Chu and Qi, which took place in Xuzhou, the king of Wei accepted Gongsun Yan's plan to publicly ally with Qi and secretly ally with Chu. The

人生千变万化，没有一成不变的标准答案。如果真的要说几句，我认为，有用会被社会征用和利用，而太无用确实也会被欺负。也许要看时机和环境来选择人生某个时刻的进或退，逞强还是示弱，显山露水还是默默无闻。"弟子们听了，似懂非懂，他们希望人生还是有明确答案为好。

公元前334年，魏国在接连惨败于齐、秦之后，惠王被迫协同韩国及其他小国诸侯赴徐州朝见齐威王，承认齐国的霸主地位，即所谓"徐州相王"，尊齐威王为王，同时齐威王也承认魏惠王的王号。那时惠施已是魏相。庄子决定在这一时刻去魏国造访惠施。

庄子没想到，这次去魏国给惠施造成了很大的误会。有人对惠施说："庄子来这里，想取代你魏相的位置。"惠施大为惊慌，他知道庄子的才华和博学不在自己之下。惠施决定不管传言是真是假，先找着庄子并把他限制起来再说。于是，连着三天在全国各地旅馆和交通要道搜寻庄子，但一无所获。正在纳闷之际，有人报庄子找上门来了。庄子对惠子说："给你讲个故事吧。南方有一种凤凰之类的鸟，叫鹓，从南海出发，飞往北海，途中非梧桐树不栖息，非竹子果实不吃，非甘美泉水不喝。这时有一只猫头鹰抓着腐烂的老鼠，瞥见鹓飞过，就抬头望着对方大叫一声：'吓！'现在，你也想为了你的魏相职位来吓我吗？"惠施听了，一时间不知如何作答，一脸窘相。

上边的故事还有个后续，在这里交代一下。说的是次年，楚、齐徐州之役前夕，魏王采纳公孙衍计谋，公开与齐结交，

king ordered Hui Shi to the State of Chu to make the negotiations. After completing the mission, as Hui Shi was traveling from Chu back to Song, he passed Zhuangzi, who was fishing in the Mengzhu Marsh to the north of their hometown. Zhuangzi looked up at Hui Shi, pompously riding past in his lavish carriage with a hundred retainers following after him. Zhuangzi thought of that time a year before, when Hui Shi had doubted his character, and his heart filled with indignation and disappointment. Zhuangzi took the fish that he had caught and flung them back into the lake, showing his contempt for Hui Shi, who had become dependent on the royal court in his efforts to obtain wealth. Zhuangzi was about 35 that year.

Hui Shi knew that he had misunderstood Zhuangzi. To show Zhuangzi his sincerity and trust, Hui Shi decided to introduce Zhuangzi to King Hui of Wei.

Thus, wearing patched-up clothes and shoes tied together with hemp rope, Zhuangzi went in to meet with the king. The king of Wei said, "Good sir, why are you dressed so? You seem morose and sickly!" Zhuangzi replied, "Tattered clothes and broken shoes are the clothes of a poor man, not a morose and sickly man. A scholar often appears fatigued and sickly because his righteous ideals cause him great anxiety over the current state of affairs. This is such an unfortunate time for people with noble ideals to be born! Have you ever witnessed the joy of leaping monkeys? When they play in great trees such as catalpa, *yu*, or camphor, they can climb freely among the branches. But when they are in thorny hedges they have to move very carefully and keep watch both forward and behind, afraid even to shiver. Our time is one of fatuous monarchs and treacherous ministers; the whole land is sick. In looking at all the tragedy in the world, it would be strange if I did not appear distressed and quiver with fear."

During the days that Zhuangzi spent in the State of Wei, he gained a deeper understanding of the Yang Zhu school of thought. Yang Zhu of Wei taught, "Look after the wholeness of your 'self' to keep it true, do not allow material things to burden your body." (from *Huainanzi: A Compendious Essay*) By this he meant that one must preserve his or her inherent nature and not allow it to become weighed down by material things. Zhuangzi heartily agreed with this viewpoint. In his later years, he wrote the chapter "The Secret of Caring for Life" in tribute to Yang Zhu's philosophy: "An accordance with the central element of our nature is the regular way to preserve your body, keep yourself alive, maintain your energy, and live out your years." This meant that in submitting to the natural principle of fate, one could save one's life, preserve one's nature, protect one's body, and peacefully live a full life.

暗地里与楚结交，派惠施到楚国进行外交。惠施完成外交由楚归宋途中，庄子正在家乡北边孟诸泽钓鱼。庄子看见惠施从车百乘，浩浩荡荡从他身边经过，想起一年前惠施对他人格的怀疑，心生不平和失望，遂把多钓的鱼扔进湖里，以此表示对依附庙堂以谋取钱财的惠施之不屑。时年庄子35岁左右。

惠施知道自己误会庄子了，为了显示自己的诚意，也为了表明自己对庄子不存戒心，决定把庄子引荐给魏惠王。

于是，庄子去见魏王，身披一件打了补丁的粗布衣服，脚穿用麻绳拴住的破鞋。魏王说："先生为什么这副打扮，看起来病快快的？"庄子说："衣服破旧，鞋子穿孔，这副打扮是贫穷，而不是病快快。读书人因为怀着正直的理想，对时势忧虑而现出疲惫的神情，甚至有些生病的样子，所以才病快快。对怀着正直理想的人来说，现在正是生不逢时啊！您难道没有见到跳跃的猿猴吗？当他们处在梓、豫、樟这些大树上的时候，可以攀缘树枝，往来自如。等到它身处枳、棘、枸这些多刺的树丛中时，就要小心行动，瞻前顾后，还会害怕发抖。现在正处于昏君乱臣时代，整个时代病了，人们因为对时代悲戚而显得忧心疲乏，不战战兢兢才怪呢？"

在魏国逗留的几天里，庄子对杨朱学派有了更深切的了解。魏人杨朱强调"全性保真，不以物累形"（《淮南子·氾论》），着重自身修养，保全原有天性，不致为外物所累。这一点庄子很认同。他在晚年写《养生主》篇时向杨朱思想致敬。庄子说："缘督以为经。可以保身，可以全生，可以养亲，可以尽年。"意思是说，顺着自然之理，以此为法则，将可以保护生命，保全天性，可以养护身体，安享天年。

Zhuangzi appreciated the fact that Yang Zhu was a profound, pensive man. He also admired the personality and elegance with which he lived his daily life. "Yang Zhu acted more like a poet than a philosopher." It is said that one time he went on a walk, and upon arriving at a fork in the road, he suddenly began to cry. This was because the fork in the road caused him to reflect on the divergences in the road of life. If a person were to walk just a few degrees off course, it might take him a long time before he realized his mistake, and he could be thousands of *li* off his destination by that time. This is the predicament that caused Yang Zhu such sorrow. Another time, Yang Zhu's little brother left the house, wearing a white robe. As he was on the way home, he changed into a black robe because it had rained that day. Because the family dog did not recognize the brother, it began to bark furiously at him, prompting the brother to be so angry he wanted to kick it. Yang Zhu restrained him, saying, "Imagine that this dog left in the morning with white fur and came back later with black fur, would you not also think it strange?

One time, Yang Zhu's neighbor lost a sheep, so he took a group of people out to look for it. He invited Yang Zhu's young servant to assist him in finding the sheep. Yang Zhu objected, saying, "You've lost one sheep, there's no need to stir up all the neighbors! Do you really need all these people to help you find the sheep?" His neighbor explained, "You see, there are many diverging roads out in the mountains!" The neighbor led the group of men along the main sheep path, and whenever they came to a fork in the road, he would send one man along the other path to search there. It did not take very long before all the men he brought were all spread out. The neighbor continued along the path, and soon came to yet another fork in the road. He stood at the fork mulling over what to do, and finally had to pick a path at random and walk along it. Again, he soon came to another fork in the road. With the sky darkening, the neighbor had no choice but to return home. As he walked, he ran into the men who had come with him, who reported that the same thing had happened to them. There was nothing to do but come home empty-handed. Yang Zhu saw them as they returned to the village, and asked, "Have you found your sheep?" The neighbor responded, "It is lost." Yang Zhu then asked, "With so many people searching, how could it be that the sheep was lost?" The neighbor said, "The forks in the road only led to more forks. I stood at one fork, and didn't know which path to take, so I just came home."

As time passed, the people gradually forgot about the lost sheep. But Yang Zhu's servant discovered that his master was still feeling depressed about the missing sheep, as he did not speak or laugh all day long. Feeling that this was

庄子喜欢杨朱深思的品格，也喜欢他日常生活行为中所流露出来的个性和气质。杨朱行事不像个思想家，倒像个诗人。据说，有一次他外出到了一个岔路口，竟然哭了起来。因为他联想到人生的歧路，如果一个人处在人生十字路口，错走半步，省悟过来时有可能已差之千里，所以杨朱为之悲戚。又有一次，他的弟弟出门时穿了一袭白衣，回来时因为天下雨就换了一身黑衣，结果家里的狗没有认出来，朝他狂吠不止，弟弟气得要踢打它。杨朱制止他，说："假设这狗出去时为白色，回来时却变成了黑色，难道你不同样感到奇怪吗？"

杨朱的邻居跑丢了一只羊，邻居带着众人去寻找，也请杨朱的年轻仆人帮忙。杨朱不以为然地说："嘻！跑丢一只羊，何必兴师动众，要这么多人去寻找呢？"邻居解释说："您不知道，山野岔路太多！"邻人带领大家先沿着赶羊的大路找，一遇到岔路就分派一个人去寻找。如此，没过多久，带去的人分派完毕。那邻人只身继续走大路，没走多远，前面又出现了岔路。他站在岔路口左右为难，只得任选了一条路向前找，走不远，又有岔路，邻人无可奈何，看看天色已晚，只好往回走。沿途碰到路上回来的人，也说遇到同样的情况。他们只好空手而归。回到家，杨子问："羊找到了吗？"邻居说："跑丢了。"杨朱又问："这么多人找，羊怎么还能跑丢呢？"邻人回答道："岔路之中又有岔路，我站在岔路口，不知道该选择哪一条路去找，所以就回来了。"

这事过去了，找羊的事也被大家遗忘了，但杨朱的仆人发现，这件事后杨朱神情郁闷，整天不言不笑。仆人奇怪，问道：

strange, the servant asked Yang Zhu, "The sheep was worthless livestock, and anyway, it didn't belong to you, so why are you so depressed?" Yang Zhu did not respond, and no one could figure out what he was thinking.

Zhuangzi thought that it must be as impossible for worldly people to understand Yang Zhu, as it would be for a sparrow to understand the aspirations of a roc ❶ . As a matter of fact, the meaning of the story "The Sheep Becomes Lost Among the Forks in the Road" is quite profound. To a figurative "sheep" who is accustomed to a simple lifestyle, the multiplicity of forks in the road can cause it to lose its way. When faced with situations in which there are many choices, the sheep becomes confused and doesn't know what to do, finally becoming lost. To a figurative "sheep searcher," the large number of paths will bewilder him, causing him to wander back and forth at the crossroads and be unable to continue his search.

After returning from Wei, Zhuangzi's fame grew by the day. Hearing that Zhuangzi could be a useful official, King Wei of Chu sent two ministers to inform Zhuangzi that the king desired him to be an administrative official and manage the great affairs of state. At the time, Zhuangzi was fishing in the Pu River, northwest of his hometown. Holding his fishing pole and without turning his head, he said to the ministers, "I heard that there is a magical turtle in Chu that has been dead for 3,000 years. The king of Chu had it placed in a bamboo box, wrapped in a piece of cloth, and then enshrined in a temple. May I ask, if this turtle had the choice, do you think it would rather die and be revered and enshrined, or live and crawl about in the pond muck?" The two ministers replied, "It would rather live and crawl about in the muck." Zhuangzi then said, "Then please return to your lord. I too would like to crawl about in the muck." The two ministers did not know how to convince Zhuangzi, so they said, "If it is not too much trouble, why not first visit Chu and then decide?" So Zhuangzi replied, "Okay."

Zhuangzi decided to travel to Chu, not to obtain an official position, but rather to expand his knowledge and see the world. Chu, after all, was the birthplace of Daoism!

On his way to Chu, Zhuangzi saw a farmer using a shadoof, or water pump, to irrigate his fields. These shadoofs replaced the old practice of "watering the fields with an urn under one arm." In Zhuangzi's time, the standards of labor and production improved for farmers. This can be seen in two ways: First, irrigation techniques were improved and new irrigation tools wcrc invcntcd. Winchcs, pullcys, and pumps camc into widcsprcad usc during this time period. The shadoof employed lever principles in watering the fields.

"羊是不值钱的牲畜，况非夫子所有，您为何闷闷不乐呢？"
杨朱也不回答，大家都弄不清杨朱到底在想什么。

庄子想，要世俗之人理解杨朱，难啊！正如麻雀难知大鹏❶之志。实际上，"歧路亡羊"所包含的意思相当深刻：对过惯简单生活方式的"羊"来说，道路的繁杂会使它迷失方向，有多种选择的环境将使它无所适从，最终迷失自己；对于"寻羊者"来说，多条道路，会对他们造成迷惑，同样他们也将徘徊在岔路口而无法选择继续前进的方向。

从魏国回来后，庄子声誉日隆。楚威王听说庄子是个人才，就派两位大夫去转达他的心意，希望庄子来楚国做执政之臣，处理国家大事。当时，庄子正在家乡西北边的濮水钓鱼。他手持鱼竿，头也不回地说："我听说楚国有一只神龟，已经死了三千年；楚王特地把它盛放在竹盒里并用布巾包裹，供奉在庙堂之上。请问，如果让这只乌龟重新选择生活的话，它是会选择死了让人尊敬地供奉，还是活着拖着尾巴在泥塘里爬来爬去呢？"两个大夫说："宁愿活着拖着尾巴在泥塘里爬来爬去。"庄子说："那就请回吧。我希望自己拖着尾巴在泥塘里爬来爬去。"两个大夫不知道怎样才能说服庄子，就说："有机会去楚国看看，然后再作决定，好吗？"庄子说："好。"

庄子决定去楚国一趟，不是为讨得一官半职，而是增广见闻。楚国毕竟是道家思想的发源地呀！

庄子去楚国的路上，遇见过农民采用桔槔来灌溉，代替过去"抱瓮而出灌"的原始方法。在庄子时代，农民的生产劳动条件有所改善。首先，水利条件优越，灌溉工具得到改进，这时，辘轳、桔槔已被普遍使用。桔槔灌田是利用杠杆原理灌田

---

❶ 译者注：神话中的一种巨大的鸟。

❶ Translator's note: A large mythical bird.

The shadoof, also called *qiao* (bridge), was composed of two lengths of straight wood. One length was placed vertically on a river bank or next to a well. The other was attached horizontally to the end of the vertical length of wood. A rope was tied to one end of the horizontal piece of wood from which hung a water bucket, and a large stone was attached to the other end. In this manner, the *shadoof* employed a lever to pump water. One could release the rope, allowing the water bucket to dip into the river or well, and with the help of the rock, one could gently pull the bucket back up.❶ Second, farming tools were improved. Stone farming implements had already evolved to copper, then from copper to iron. These iron tools facilitated plowing and made it possible to plow deeper furrows. Finally, farmers began using farm cattle to plow their fields. This dramatically increased the production of labor. Because of all these innovations, one *mu*❷ of land could now produce 70 kilograms of food, more than ever before.

On his travels to Chu, Zhuangzi also saw for himself the prosperity of Ying, the capital of Chu. In describing the affluence of Ying, someone once said, "The wagons entering and leaving the city are lined up wheel to wheel and the pedestrians are shoulder to shoulder. In the streets of the city, people push each other because it is so crowded; the new clothes you wear in the morning are torn by evening because of all the shoving." For all the hustle and bustle of Ying, it was still not the most prosperous of the various kingdoms. At the time, the largest, most thriving capital was the Qi capital, Zi (just north of modern city of Lin Zi in Shandong Province). There were 70,000 households living in Zi. It was said that if everyone in the city held up the hems of their robes, it would form a tent, that if they all lifted their sleeves, it would form a curtain, and if everybody started to wipe off his sweat at the same time, the sweat drops would seem like rain.

Zhuangzi also made a trip to the State of Lu to visit Duke Jing of Lu. Duke Jing of Lu said to him, "In Lu, there are many who adhere to Confucianism, but those who follow your teachings are very few." Zhuangzi said, "Actually, those who adhere to Confucianism are also very few." Duke Jing of Lu said, "All the people of the kingdom wear Confucian garments, how can you say there are few Confucians?" Zhuangzi said, "An upright man does not necessarily need to wear a certain style of clothing in order to understand a certain style of self-cultivation; likewise, just because a man wears a certain style of clothing does not mean he is trained in its corresponding school of thought. If you do not agree with me, why not order all those who wear Confucian clothes but don't have Confucian accomplishment to be put to death

的一种方法。桔槔也称为"桥",是用两根直木组织而成,一根直木竖立在河边或井边;另一根直木用绳横挂在竖立直木的顶端。在这根横挂的木条上,一端系着长绳,绳上挂着水桶或汲瓶,另一端系着大石块,利用杠杆原理来汲水。汲水时,把绳一放,让水桶或汲瓶浸入河中或井中,在大石块的帮助下,轻轻一拉,水桶或汲瓶就升上来了。❶其次,农业工具有了改进,耕地的主要工具,已由石制改为铜制,又由铜制改为铁制。这种铁制农具轻便犀利,易于深耕。再者,也开始使用牛耕,劳动生产力有了显著提高。所以,当时有了粮食亩❷产70公斤的记录。

庄子也亲眼目睹了楚都郢的繁华。有人这样描写郢的繁华:"来往的车辆是车轮抵着车轮,行人是肩碰着肩,在市区的道路上你推着我,我推着你,早上穿的新衣服到了晚上就被挤破了。"在各国的国都中,郢不是最繁华的。当时最繁华、规模最大的要数齐都淄(今山东省临淄北)。淄有七万户人家,听说,人们的衣襟连起来可以合成围帐,人们的衣袖举起来可以合成幕,大家一挥汗就好像下雨一般。

庄子后来也去了一趟鲁国,见到了鲁景公。鲁景公说:"鲁国的儒者很多,而学习先生这一套学说的人很少。"庄子说:"鲁国的儒者也很少。"鲁景公说:"全鲁国的人都穿着儒服,怎么能说少呢?"庄子说:"君子有某种修养的,未必穿某种服装;穿某种服装的,未必了解某种修养。如果您认为我说的不对,何不下命令给国人说:'不具备儒者修养而穿儒服的,

---

❶ 见《庄子·天运》《庄子·天地》篇。
❷ 译者注:亩,中国常用的土地面积单位,1亩合667平方米或1/15公顷。

❶ Refer to the chapters "The Revolution of Heaven" and "Heaven and Earth" for instances where *Zhuangzi* makes mention of the shadoof.
❷ Translator's note: *mu* - Chinese unit of area, approximately equal to 667 sq. kms or 1/15 of a hectare.

and see what happens?" Duke Jing of Lu issued the order, and five days later no one wore Confucian clothes anymore, with the exception of a few men standing outside the front gate of Duke Jing's Palace. After a careful inspection, it turned out that they were real Confucians. Zhuangzi said, "In all of Lu, there are only a few real Confucians, how can you say there are many?" ❶

Zhuangzi greatly admired true Confucians, even though their philosophy and interests were different from his. He admired them because they lived in the real world, not in rigid rituals and rules. For instance, it was written that Confucius had admired the senior official Qu Boyu of Wey. Zhuangzi also admired Qu Boyu, not just because Confucius did but because Qu Boyu was truly deserving of his respect. Qu Boyu was a man of noble character, who was straightforward and open, had a sympathetic heart, and was adept at seeing the weaknesses in human nature. When Confucius met with difficulties in his journeys and had nowhere to turn, he would often flee to the protection of Qu Boyu, which showed Qu Boyu's kindness and generosity. One day, Qu Boyu sent a servant to visit Confucius and Confucius asked the messenger how Qu Boyu was doing lately. The man replied, "He is trying to overcome his weaknesses, but suffers because he is unable to." When the servant left, Confucius said to his disciples, "That man truly understands Qu Boyu." Each day, Qu Boyu would reflect on the mistakes he had made the day before and do his best to make sure every day he was better than the day before. Every year, he would reflect on his imperfections of the year before. Even when he was fifty, he still reflected on his past faults. This is the origin of the saying, "Fifty years old and forty-nine years of mistakes."

As Zhuangzi traveled extensively and saw more of the world, his philosophy became more and more mature.

都处以死罪。'看他们敢不敢穿？"于是，鲁景公颁发这项命令，五天以后，鲁国没人敢再穿儒服。只有若干个男子除外，他们穿着儒服，站在景公府邸的大门外。经过仔细盘查，那些人确实是真正的儒者。庄子说："全鲁国只有若干个真正的儒者，可以算多吗？"❶

庄子对真正的儒者是佩服的，因为他们活在真诚和真实中，而不是活在僵化的教义和规条里，即使他们跟自己的思想和趣味不一样。比如，孔子曾很敬佩同时代的卫国大夫蘧伯玉，庄子也很敬佩蘧伯玉，不是因为孔子敬佩而敬佩，而是蘧伯玉这个人值得敬佩。因为蘧伯玉品德高尚，光明磊落，具有同情心，也善于察觉人性的弱点。孔子周游列国走投无路之际，曾数次投奔蘧伯玉。有一天，蘧伯玉派人来拜望孔子，孔子向来人询问蘧伯玉的近况，来人回答说："他正设法减少自己的缺点，可却苦于做不到。"来人走后，孔子对弟子说："这是了解蘧伯玉的人啊。"蘧伯玉每一天都思考前一天所犯的错误，力求使今日之我胜于昨日之我；他每一年都要思考前一年的不足，到了五十岁那年，仍然在思考之前所犯的过错。所谓"年五十，而有四十九年非"。

经过以上游历与博见，庄子思想更成熟了。

---

❶ 见《庄子·田子方》篇。原文是鲁哀公，实乃鲁景公；原文中说真正的儒者只有一个，因考虑到是寓言，不能太坐实，故改为若干个。

---

❶ Refer to the chapter "Tian Zifang" for the whole story. Though in the original text the story the Duke was Duke Ai of Lu, in reality, he was actually Duke Jing of Lu. In addition, in the original text it is written that there was only one true Confucian, but because it was a parable, it should not be taken too literally. That is why in this version there are "a few" true Confucians.

战国帛画，中国现存最早的绘画作品，
画面左侧一只名为"夔"的怪兽被打败
Painting on Silk of the Warring States Period—
the Earliest Painting Currently Preserved in China
A Beaten Monster(*Kui*) on the Left of the Painting

五　中年晚期　（约前329—前319）

Chapter V　Late Middle Years
(About 329 B.C. to 319 B.C.)

Confucius once said, "At forty, a man began to understand the world," a saying which also describes Zhuangzi. As Zhuangzi's understanding of the evil in human nature deepened, he gradually lost what little optimism and illusions he once had for human society.

In the couple dozen years that Zhuangzi had been on earth, he saw that no matter what reforms were made by the various kingdoms or how many times the government changed in a kingdom, the social system devised by mankind was unable to bring human nature under control. It was especially ineffectual at checking the ambition of rulers. On the contrary, the reforms and government changes made by the various kingdoms exposed mankind's wretchedness even more.

To understand the ambition of rulers, let us first examine the history of how the rulers of the various kingdoms came to be called "kings." In the beginning of the Warring States Period when the high king of Zhou Dynasty was still in power, the rulers of the various feudal states were called *jun* (lord), to show their subordination to the Zhou Dynasty. No matter how strong a feudal state became, it would never dare call itself a "kingdom," because only the high king of Zhou could be called *wang* (king). However, as the political power of the high king of Zhou began to wane, the lords of the various feudal states rushed to call themselves *wang* (king), revealing their ambition and obsession with power, as well as their disobedience to and independence from Zhou.

In 353 B.C., the ruler of Qi was the first in the Central Plains region to take the title of *wang*. At that time, Zhuangzi was not yet twenty. Nine years later, Duke Xiao of Qin, then Lord Xiao of Qin, sent Wei Yang to persuade Lord Hui of Wei into accepting his suggestion. Wei Yang told Lord Hui of Wei that since the small states of Song, Wey, Zou and Lu were under the control of Wei, the state of Wei could then ally with Yan to the north and Qin to the west. Thus when the ruler of Qin made himself king, the lord of Wei could also make himself king, and no one could prevent them from doing so. Ten years later, in 334 B.C., after losing consecutive battles to Qi and Qin, King Hui of Wei was forced to go with the ruler of Han and the rulers of other smaller states to Xuzhou to see King Wei of Qi. King Hui had to acknowledge the hegemony of Qi in what was called the "Xuzhou Meeting of Kings." At the same meeting, Qi allowed King Hui of Wei to retain his title of king. In 325 B.C., Lord Huiwen of Qin proclaimed himself king, and in the same year, the ruler of Han also declared himself king. In 323 B.C., Wei called a meeting of five states, during which rulers of Zhao, Yan, and Zhongshan also declared themselves

孔子说，"四十而不惑"。这句话用在庄子身上也是合适的。随着对人性丑恶的认识越来越深刻，他对人类设计的社会制度的作用也少了些浅薄的乐观和幻想。

庄子在生活的数十年间看到，不管诸侯国如何改制，本国政权如何更迭，人类设计的社会制度很难制伏人类，尤其是统治者的野心；相反，诸侯的改制和国内政权的更迭更加暴露了人性中欲壑难填、人心不足蛇吞象的弱点。

先看看各国称"王"的历史。本来，战国时期，周天子还在，各诸侯间应以"君"相称，表明附属于周朝，诸侯国就是再强盛也不敢以"王"相称，因为只有周室才是"王"。但对权力的崇拜和野心，使各国诸侯迫不及待地宣称自己为王，蔑视周天子的统治，以示不附属、不听从于周。

公元前353年，齐国率先在中原称王。那时庄子不到20岁。过了9年，秦孝公派卫鞅去向魏惠王游说，劝说他除了号令宋、卫、邹、鲁等小国之外，北面争取燕国，西面争取秦国，秦自己称王，魏也称王。再过了10年，即公元前334年，魏国在接连惨败于齐、秦之后，魏惠王被迫协同韩及其他小国诸侯赴徐州朝见齐威王，承认齐国的霸主地位，即所谓"徐州相王"，尊齐威王为王，同时齐威王也承认魏惠王的王号。公元前325年，秦惠文君自称为王，同年，韩也称王。公元前323年，魏

kings. Thus, Qi, Wei, Qin, Han, Zhao, Yan, etc. had all declared themselves kingdoms. Added to these the state of Chu, which had been a kingdom since the Spring Autumn Period, and one can see the formation of the seven great kingdoms of the Warring States Period.

It was not enough for the rulers to simply go from being called *jun* to being called *wang* (king); they also desired to be called *di*, or emperor. In 288 B.C., King Zhao of Qin took the title of "Western Emperor," offering the title of "Eastern Emperor" to the ruler of Qi.

Let us turn our attention to the State of Song. The reason that Song, being a small land, was able to survive so long was not because its neighbors were overly kind, but rather because its neighbors were unable to agree on how to divide Song territory up amongst themselves. That all changed when in 286 B.C., Song was invaded and ravaged by Qi.

Zhuangzi was disappointed with the way the Song was ruled. First, in 338 B.C., Song Yan instigated a palace coup by ousting his older brother and seizing the throne, becoming the ruler of Song. 10 years later, Song Yan's thirst for power was again made manifest when he changed his title from *jun* to *wang*. From that time on, he lost himself in riotous living and tyrannical rule. This was evident especially in his later years, when he believed he was the greatest in the world. He shot an arrow in the air and struck the ground with his whip in challenge to the gods of heaven and earth. He destroyed the altars to the ancestors of heaven and earth, showing that he was not even afraid of ghosts. To show his bravery, he berated the honest ministers of state in public, cut open a hunchback man's back, and hacked off the legs, from the knees down, of people who fearlessly ventured into cold water in the morning. He even raised armies and marched them around to threaten surrounding states. Because of these actions, his people were terrified and other states were horrified. They all thought of him as a tyrant, referring to him as *jie* ❶ .

The following story can be found in *Zhuangzi*: a man came to pay his respects to the king of Song and was given ten carriages. The man went to Zhuangzi and boasted of the carriages he had received. Zhuangzi replied, "A poor family that makes its living by weaving reeds lives on the riverbank over there. The family's son dove into the deep ocean abyss and found a pearl worth a thousand gold pieces. The father said to him, 'Quick, take a stone and smash it! The pearl must have been lying under the chin of the great black dragon of the deep abyss. The fact that you have obtained that pearl is not a testament to your skill, but rather means that the black dragon must have been asleep at the time. If it awakens, how will you be able to stay alive?' The current situation in

又发起五国相王，除魏、韩已称王外，赵、燕、中山也相继称王。至此，齐、魏、秦，韩、赵、燕等前后称王，再加上在春秋时已称王的楚国，战国七雄真正形成。

从"君"的称号到"王"的称号还不够，还要从"王"的称号到"帝"的称号。公元前288年，秦昭王称"西帝"，并向齐国送"东帝"的称号。

再看宋国。宋国作为小国之所以能撑到现在，不是邻国太友好，而是各国对瓜分宋国不能达成一致意见，直至公元前286年被齐国攻灭。

宋国的统治同样让庄子失望。先是在公元前338年宋偃发动宫廷政变，逐兄篡位，成为宋国的国君。过了10年，宋偃权力野心进一步彰显，改君称王，从此沉湎享乐，暴政不断。尤其在晚年，自认为老子天下第一，用弓箭射天，长鞭扑地，表示敢向天地神祇挑战。把祭祀天地祖先的祭坛摧毁，表示他连鬼也不在乎。又当面训斥国中谏臣，切开驼子的背，砍断早晨不畏寒冷涉水人的小腿，以示勇。还对外挥军出击，四面扬威。于是，国人惊骇，诸侯惊愕，皆称之为"桀"❶，认为宋偃是暴君。

《庄子》中曾记载这样一个故事：有人拜见宋王，获赐十辆马车。他就以这十辆马车向庄子夸耀。庄子说："河边有一家穷人，靠编织芦苇为生，做儿子的潜入深渊，得到千金之珠。做父亲的对他说'拿石头来敲碎它！'千金之珠一定藏在九重深渊黑龙的颔下，你能取得宝珠，不是你水平高，而是适逢黑龙在睡觉。如果它是醒的，你还能保住小命吗？现在宋国的形

---

❶ 译者注：桀，夏朝（约公元前2070年—前1600年）最后一位君王，以残暴著称。

❶ Translator's note: The last emperor of the Xia Dynasty (about 2070 B.C. to 1600B.C.) who was known for his cruelty.

Song is worse than the deep abyss; the ferocious cruelty of the king of Song is greater than that of the black dragon. The fact that you have obtained ten carriages means he must have been asleep. If he awakens, your bones will be crushed to powder!" In this parable, the father wanted his son to destroy the pearl in hopes that he would abandon his avarice, and also to prevent him from risking his life by trying to enter the dragon's lair again. Similarly, Zhuangzi hoped to teach the lesson that one should not have any illusions about the ruler of the State of Song.

The government did not care for social justice or proper human relations. It pursued only its own selfish desires, and was indifferent to whether the commoners lived or died. In this chaotic world where proper rituals were universally violated, was it possible to counter human evil with a system devised by humans? Zhuangzi's attitude toward this question was depressed and pessimistic, because he saw human evil more clearly.

History proved Zhuangzi correct. About 60 years after Zhuangzi passed away, in 221 B.C., the armies of Qin marched into the prosperous eastern city Linzi. This ended the resistance of Qi, the last of the six states to oppose Qin, and Ying Zheng, the king of Qin, became the ruler of all of China. He felt that the title of *wang* was not grand enough; after all, he had defeated the kings of the six other states, and now he needed something to differentiate himself from them. *Di* and *huang*❶ had already been used, and neither of them felt magnificent enough. Therefore, the Ying Zheng combined the two ancient words together, making a new word: *huangdi*❷ . When Ying Zheng declared himself *huangdi*, we see that man's worship of power and fame was amplified even more.

In his youth, Zhuangzi spoke passionately about bringing righteousness to the world and was only a little cynical and pessimistic about the world. The middle-aged Zhuangzi, however, was filled with pity and remorse for mankind.

Zhuangzi realized that life on earth was not easy. In the space of a short life, humans have to face the long farewell of death, the withering of life's brief springtime, and the anguish of sickness and pain. The human condition is full of unpredictable and uncontrollable changes, such as diseases which may befall one at any time.

Zhuangzi taught that when confronted with the vast, eternal universe that possesses the power to create and destroy, all that man can do is try to remove the negative effects of all that happens around him. Removal does not mean "escape from," but rather to pass through the essence of the experience. This means that while we cannot control what has happened in the

势，更胜过九重深渊；宋王的凶猛，更胜过黑龙。你能得到马车，一定是碰到他正在睡觉。如果宋王是醒的，你就要粉身碎骨了！"此寓言中父亲要儿子敲碎宝珠，是期望他弃绝贪念，防止他再入龙潭冒险。庄子实际上在传达这样一个信息，不要对宋国的统治者抱有幻想。

是啊，执政的不顾社会正义和人间正道，只是一味满足一己之私，罔顾百姓死活，在这一"礼崩乐坏"的乱世，用人自身设计的制度来对付人性中的丑陋和邪恶，可能吗？庄子有些消极和悲观。说到底，是因为他对人性的丑陋和邪恶看得更清楚了！

历史也证明了庄子这一观点。庄子去世60余年后，即公元前221年，秦国的军队开进了繁华的东方城市临淄，六国最后一个抵抗者齐国灭亡，嬴政宣布天下统一于秦。他要给自己起一个封号，感觉王不够，因为六国的王都被他干掉了，再称王不能与他们区别开。帝，以前也被用过，皇❶也用过（所谓三皇五帝）。嬴政觉得皇不够，帝也不够，于是就把两个称号凑一起：皇帝❷。人对权力、名声、地位的膜拜在嬴政称皇帝事件中再次被放大。

如果说青年时期，庄子还一腔热血，有点愤世嫉俗，对社会悲愤，对人生悲观。那么，中年庄子的心境，则是对人类充满悲凉与悲悯。

庄子意识到，人活在世上不容易。人生太短暂，人生还要面临生死的离别、青春韶华的逝去、病痛的折磨。世事多变幻，

---

❶ 译者注：古代君王的尊称。
❷ 译者注：最高封建统治者的称号。在中国皇帝的称号始于秦始皇。
❶ Translator's note: An ancient term of respect for the emperor.
❷ Translator's note: Modern word for emperor.

past, we can control our attitudes towards what has happened and maintain a certain distance between our hearts and outside events. This will prevent us from being controlled, bound down, or restrained by the circumstances of life.

However, man is often unable to properly cope with things that have happened to him. For instance, people often compare themselves to others, with the result being either arrogant or self-loathing. Most often, people fall into painful self-loathing because when they measure themselves to the standard of others, they discover their many weaknesses. They are unable to meet the demands and standards of society because there is always somebody who has more or who is better than them. This causes them to hate themselves and forget that there is no need to copy others. They don't realize that in copying others, they lose their innate uniqueness and become somebody else. It is not necessary to become perfect in someone else's eyes; it is enough simply to live truthfully and simply.

In relation to this principle, Zhuangzi once told the following parable: The *kui* ❶ , who walks on one leg, was once very jealous of the many-legged millipede. The millipede, on the other hand, was jealous of the snake, because though he walked with so many legs, he was unable to catch up to the snake who did not have any. The snake was jealous of the wind, because while he had to wiggle his back and chest in order to move as if he had legs, the wind blew unhindered from the Northern Sea to the Southern Sea, without leaving the slightest trace. The wind was jealous of eyes, because no matter how gracefully the wind blew, it was unable to compare with the way that eyes could smoothly and effortlessly turn in all directions. The eyes were jealous of the heart, because even though the eyes could turn and change directions effortlessly, it could not compare with the speed and smoothness of a man changing his mind, which takes place in the space of an instant.

人不能控制事情的发生，譬如生病，要来就来，不是自己所能预料和控制的。

人在生生不息的宇宙面前，在带来成与毁的造化面前，唯一所能做的是消除所发生的事件对自身的影响。消除不是为了逃避，而是在经历事件中穿越事件本身，也就是说，已发生的事件我们不能改变，因为它已发生了。我们所能改变的就是对事件的态度，让事件在融入我们内心乃至生命当中有个恰当的距离和位置，而不是因事件的发生，我们的心思意念被外在事件控制、捆绑和羁绊。

可世人常常不能恰当处理生活中已发生的事情。比如，世人常有一种比较的思维，常把自己跟别人比较，结果是要么过分自大，要么过分自卑。更多的时候，人们陷入痛苦自卑当中，因为当他用别人的标准丈量自己时，总发现自身有缺陷，达不到社会和他人制定的要求和标准，总有人比自己多、比自己好。于是他开始自卑起来，忘记了他不需要去复制别人，他若复制了别人那一套，那他就不是他，他就是别人了，他自身存在的独特性也就找不到了。每个人不需要成为别人眼中标准的、完美的人，他需要的是真实而平凡地活着。

庄子曾讲过一个寓言：夔❶用一只脚走路，它羡慕多脚的蚿，因为蚿有那么多的脚；蚿羡慕没有脚的蛇，因为自己用这么多的脚走路，却赶不上没有脚的蛇；蛇羡慕风，蛇走路需要鼓动背与胸，还是像有脚一样，而风呼地从北海吹到南海，却好像一点痕迹都没有；风羡慕眼睛，因为风再怎么吹，也比不上眼波流转，任意向四面八方看；眼睛羡慕心，因为眼睛再怎么转，也比不上心思意念转得快，心思意念发生在一瞬间。

---

❶ 译者注：传说中的一条腿的怪物。

❶ Translator's note: A mythical, one-legged monster.

In the end, each of the creatures in the story was filled with pain and a sense of inferiority. None of them realized that they all had their own unique ways of living, and that there was no need for them to spend their lives comparing themselves to others. All they had to do was listen to their own hearts in order to develop into the kind of being that they wanted to be. This is similar to how an oak seed desires to grow into an oak tree; it doesn't measure itself against the standards set by the apple tree, even if apple trees are the standard by which society measures success.

Zhuangzi also told another story. There was once a young man from the state of Yan who went to Handan in the state of Zhao to learn how to walk like Zhao people. In the end, he was not only unable to learn the gait of Zhao people, but he also forgot his old walk, and was left with no choice but to crawl home.

Unfortunately, most people do not learn from these stories and do not even realize that they are miserable. They chase after fashions, measure themselves against standards set by others, and finally lose their way in life, forgetting themselves and their true quest in life.

Because Zhuangzi did not have a stable income, he began to taste the bitterness of poverty. One time, Zhuangzi went to see a nearby official who was in charge of managing ditches and canals and asked to borrow some rice from him. The official replied, "Yes, of course you may. In fact, just wait until I have collected the taxes from my lands and I will lend you 300 pieces of gold, how is that?" Zhuangzi was so angry that his face turned purple, retorting, "Allow me to tell you a story. Yesterday as I journeyed here, I heard a voice cry out to me. I turned back and saw that it was a crucian trapped in a puddle made by a wheel rut in the road. The crucian was gasping for breath because it did not have enough water. I asked what the crucian wanted, to which it answered that it was thirsty and needed a little water to save its life. It claimed to be a servant of the water people of the Eastern Sea. I told the crucian not to worry, that I was traveling south to meet with the rulers of Wu and Yue, where I would persuade them to carry the water of the West River to rescue it. The crucian was so angry its face turned purple, and it exclaimed, 'I don't have the water I need to survive, there is no room for me to move about, and all I need is a little bit of water to save my life. If you insist on bringing the water of the western rivers, then you might as well look for me at the dried fish store when you return!' "

As a poor person, Zhuangzi came across people like the official who treated him with disrespect, contempt and indifference. Though Zhuangzi

结果，它们各自都陷入了痛苦和自卑中，而没有发现，它们都有它们自己的存在方式，不需要通过比较他人来活着。它们唯一需要的是学会倾听自己内心深处的召唤，让自己长成为想要长成的那个样子，就如橡树的种子渴望长成橡树那样，不需要用苹果树的标准来要求自己，即使整个社会以苹果树为评估体系和衡量标准。

庄子也讲过另外一个故事：有一个燕国的少年，到赵国邯郸去学走路，结果，他不但没有学会赵国人的走法，反而把自己原来的步法也忘了，最后只好爬着回家。

可惜，大多数世人不觉得自己悲哀，跟着社会潮流跑，用他人的标准来要求自己，结果人生迷失了方向，忘记了自己是谁，自己真正所要追求的是什么。

由于没有稳定的收入，庄子体验到了贫穷的滋味。庄子曾向附近管理河道水情的官吏监河侯借米。监河侯说："好的。等我收到封地的赋税之后，就借给你三百金，可以吗？"庄子气得脸色都变了，说："给你讲一个故事吧。我昨天来的时候，半路上有人在喊我，回头一看，原来是一尾鲫鱼，正伏在车轮压凹的地方，因没水而直喘气。我问它有什么事？它说它现在太渴了，需要有一升一斗的水来救它，它自称是东海的水族之臣。我说，好的，我将到南方游说吴国、越国的君主，说服他们引西江的水来迎接你。鲫鱼气得脸色都变了，说：'我现在失去了日常必需的水，没有了容身之地，只需要一升一斗水就可以活命，你竟然这样说，那你不如早一点到卖干鱼的地方找我吧！'"

因着贫穷，你会遇到像监河侯这样的人，在生活中对你不

knew such a life of poverty very well, he still did not want to change the original intentions of his heart to lead a poor life.

During the Warring States Period, there were many intellectuals who, like Zhuangzi, were impoverished but unwilling to pursue careers in government. Some well-known examples include Chen Zhong and Xu Xing. Chen Zhong was born into the noble, ruling class. Though his older brothers and parents were incredibly wealthy, he rejected the life of a nobleman. Unwilling to become an official in the government, he insisted on providing for himself, and made his livelihood by weaving straw sandals, like Zhuangzi. As the representative philosopher of the Agriculturists, Xu Xing was more famous than Chen Zhong, but he was still not dependent on any nobleman. Instead, he led his several dozen disciples in agricultural work, providing for himself by "weaving straw sandals and mats."

Zhuangzi believed that material poverty mattered little. The important thing was for one to be understood on an intellectual level. This, however, was often not easy to do.

It was very difficult for the people of Zhuangzi's time to understand him, because they often used commonly accepted practice and well established social norms to judge people living outside the bounds of worldly standards. This naturally meant that it was impossible for them to understand these "other people." In "Free and Easy Wandering," Zhuangzi used the parable of a roc and sparrow to explain this phenomenon: In the far north where grass and trees do not grow, there was an endless expanse of ocean. In the ocean there lived a great fish, named *kun*, that was several thousand *li* wide, though no one really knew how long it was for certain. One day, the fish changed into a great roc. Its back stretched into the distance like the Mount Taishan and was many thousands of *li* wide, though again, no one really knew exactly how wide it was. When the roc stretched out its wings, they looked like clouds hanging from the sky. It flapped its wings and rose into the sky, flying straight up for ninety thousand *li*. It soared above the clouds with its back to the heavens, and then turned and flew south. A sparrow perched near a pool of water laughed mockingly at the roc, saying, "Where does he think he's flying? In a short hop I can take off into the air, I can fly up a short distance and then come down, what is the point of flying ninety thousand *li* into the sky and then going south? Is it not enough to dart and dive among the bushes and fields? Besides, this is the way that everyone has agreed is proper to fly, what does that big roc think he's doing?"

Zhuangzi knew that to be understood by others was too much for him to

尊敬，甚至歧视、怠慢。庄子何尝不知道这一点，但他是不会改变选择贫穷生活这一初衷的。

在战国时期，像庄子那样贫穷但不肯出仕的知识分子不少，著名的例子还有陈仲和许行。陈仲出身于当权的贵族家庭，兄长和父母都非常有钱，但他鄙弃贵族生活，也不愿出仕，坚持自食其力，与庄子一样以编织草鞋为生。作为农家代表的许行虽比较有名，但也不依附于某一权贵，他带领的数十门徒，都参加农业劳动，以"捆屦织席"维持生活。

庄子认为，物质上贫穷一点，并没有什么，关键是精神上能否有人理解你，但事实上这一点也很难做到。

世人很难理解庄子这样的人，是因为世人常用流行的习见、惯用的社会标准来衡量那些不在世俗规范和框架内的人，自然，他们理解不了这些"另类"。庄子在《逍遥游》中用鹏与学鸠的故事作了形象说明：在草木不生的北方，有一片广阔无际的大海，那里有一条大鱼，鱼身之宽几千里，没有人知道它有多长。它的名字叫鲲。它变化为鸟，名字叫鹏。鹏的背部宽阔，不知有几千里，犹如泰山之绵延，双翅展开时犹如垂挂在天边的云朵。它拍翅盘旋上升，直飞到九万里的高空，凌越云气，背靠青天，然后飞向南方。水泽边的麻雀讥笑大鹏说："它要飞到哪里去呢？我一跳跃就飞起来，不到几丈高就落下，何必要飞到九万里的高空，再往南飞呢？在蓬蒿草丛中扑腾，不是挺好的吗？这也是我们大家所认同的飞行绝技呀！这大鹏鸟要干什么呢？"

其实，庄子也知道，要世俗之人理解自己也太难为他们了，

ask, just like it was impossible for the sparrow to understand the will of the great roc. The people around him lived their whole lives within the box of worldly standards. They had been trained to conform. They had lost their imaginations. All they could do was take their small fishing rods and thin fishing lines to fish for small guppies and carp in shallow ditches. On the other hand, those who had thrown off the fetters of conformist thinking and had the courage to venture into the unknown caught the big fish. They were the ones who invented great hooks and thick black fishing lines, who used fifty bullocks as lures, and who fished in the vast ocean. Even if they were often unable to catch fish, they never lost faith. They believed that nothing that was easily attainable was worth obtaining because, "The fruit that is easily picked is the first to rot." Just as Zhuangzi wrote, after a long period of waiting, when a great fish finally swallowed the lure, it dived and jumped, writhed and churned. When it flapped its fins, the waves of the sea were thrown into the sky, the whole ocean was shaken, people a thousand *li* away heard the noise like howling wolves and moaning ghosts, and they shook with fright.

The people of Zhuangzi's time had also lost the ability to think. They only desired accepted answers and existing limits. They were unable to see or think about anything outside the narrow scope of their established limits, and did not want to think about anything else. Doing so was unbearable and surpassed their imaginations. Though their physical eyes were healthy, their spiritual eyes were blind; though their bodies were healthy, their minds were handicapped. Just like blind men, these people were unable to see the beauty of the world around them; like deaf men, they were unable to hear the beauty of music.

Zhuangzi hoped to find a bosom friend, somebody to comfort his lonely heart and keep him company on the path of life.

Zhuangzi thought of his compatriot Song Rongzi. For an ordinary person, either to be talented enough to hold an official position and capable enough to serve the people in a certain place, or to be well appreciated by one ruler and thereby obtain the love and respect of the people of that region, would be a wonderful and amazing thing. But for Song Rongzi, even if all the people of the world complimented him, he would still not be very excited. Similarly, even if all the people of the world criticized him, he would not be very depressed. This was because he did not seek after worldly achievements. This compatriot was had very similar aspirations to Zhuangzi in many respects, but unfortunately he was in the state of Qi, not in Song at that time.

就如小麻雀很难理解大鹏鸟的志向一样。世俗之人长期生活在俗世的标准和条条框框内，已被驯化，丧失了想象力，只能拿着小鱼竿、细钓绳，走到小水沟旁边，钓小泥鳅、小鲫鱼之类，很难钓到大鱼。而那些摆脱时代观念桎梏，敢于冒险勇于探索人类未知的人，才能钓到大鱼。他们打造了大钓钩与粗黑的长绳，用五十头阉牛作钓饵，在大海边钓鱼。也许常常钓不到鱼，但他们却一直没有失去信心。他们相信，太容易得到的东西都不是好东西，"速得的果子必然朽坏"。果然，在漫长的等待中，终于迎来了大丰收，钓到了一条大鱼，当大鱼吞饵，牵动大钩沉入大海又急速跳跃、翻腾，摆动鱼鳍时，整个大海波浪滔天，海水震动不已，在千里之外都能听到这声音，如鬼哭狼嚎，让人听了心里害怕。

世俗之人也失去了思考的能力，只求规范的答案和现成的标准，标准之外的往往看不见，也思考不了，也不想思考，因为这超出了他们的想象力和承受力。他们肉体上的眼睛虽然健全，但心灵上的眼睛已瞎了；他们身体虽然健康，但心智上有残缺。这样的人，就如瞎子，没办法给他看五彩的美景；如聋子，没办法给他听优美的乐声。

庄子多么想找到一个知音，以安慰自己孤寂的心，在自己前行的路上有人陪伴，相互说说话。

庄子想起他的同胞宋荣子。对于一般的人来说，如果自己的才智可以担任一个官职，行事可以造福一个乡里，德行可以投合一位国君，以至得到一国之民的爱戴，那肯定风光无比，是了不得的事情。但对宋荣子而言，即使全世界的人都称赞他，他也不会特别兴奋，即使全世界的人都责备他，他也不会特别沮丧，他不会汲汲追求世间的成就。这位同胞在某些精神方面与庄子投合，可惜人不在宋国，而在齐国的稷下。

Zhuangzi had once thought highly of Hui Shi, but Hui Shi's only passion was for participating in court affairs and developing his debating skills. One particular story illustrates Hui Shi's eloquence. Someone once insinuated to the king of Wei that Hui Shi spoke only in parables and that there was nothing he spoke that was not in parable. The next day, the king of Wei called Hui Shi into his presence and commanded him, saying, "Speak clearly and directly... without parables." Hui Shi responded, "If there were a person here who did not know what a sling was or how it was shaped, could you tell him that it is shaped just like a sling?" The king replied, "No, you could not." Hui Shi continued, "If you tell him that it is shaped like a bow and that its string is made of slips of bamboo, then will he not know what a sling is and how it is shaped?" The king responded, "Yes, of course he will know." Hui Shi concluded, "This is the principle of using the listener's knowledge about the shape of a bow to help him understand the shape of a sling, and this is the usefulness of parables. Therefore, when I speak, I cannot refrain from using parables." Upon hearing this, the king was convinced that Hui Shi should be allowed to use parables.

Zhuangzi admitted that Hui Shi was very eloquent. He learned from Hui Shi how to train his mind to think logically and analyze problems like a debater. In spite of all this, what Zhuangzi really wanted was somebody who could understand him without having to speak. At least for the moment, he felt that the two of them were completely different kinds of people: one of them used his eloquence and intelligence to forge a successful official career, while the other took his wisdom and learning and hid himself among the common folk. One of them focused on the honor and glory of man as well as personal position and power, while the other sought to mold his spirit out in the wilderness, traveling leisurely over the whole land, and enjoying the beauty of nature and the inner freedom that comes from not being burdened by worldly cares.

　　庄子曾看好惠施，但惠施又过于热衷于官场和雄辩。有一则故事说明惠施的辩才。有人曾暗中对魏王说，惠施言事必用比喻，若没有比喻，就不能言事。第二天，魏王就把惠施叫到面前，要求他"言事则直言"而"无譬"。惠施说："现在有人在此，不知道'弹'是什么，'弹'的形状是怎样的？是否可以对他说：'弹'的形状就像'弹'？"魏王说："不可以。"惠施接着说，如果改为这样说："弹的形状像弓，而用竹片做弦。这样对方知道'弹'了吧？"魏王说："知道了。"惠施说："这就是用听者所知道的弓的形状，来让他明白还不知道的弹的形状，这就是比喻的作用。因此，说话不能没有比喻。"惠王听了心里折服。

　　庄子承认惠施口才很好，也从与他的辩论中学习思辨，锻炼自己的思维能力。但他要的是心灵深处的默契。至少在目前，他感觉他们两个人骨子里是不同类型的人：一个藉口才和聪明为自己仕途拼搏，一个带着智慧和博学藏身于民间；一个目光聚焦于个人的风光和体面、地位和权势，一个在山水中陶冶心情、在天地中遨游，享受自然美景和内心精神的自由，不为俗累。

战国漆器
Lacquer Ware of the Warring States Period

六　晚年（前319—前286）

Chapter VI　Later Years(319 B.C. to 286 B.C.)

In 305 B.C., the state of Qin conferred an enormous sum of money to Chu. Having received this bribe from Qin, Chu betrayed its alliance with Qi. To strengthen its union with Chu, the king of Qin also married a girl from Chu. That same year, Qi, Han, and Wei united to attack Chu, because, "Chu has abandoned the allies of its vertical alliance and allied with Qin." King Huai of Chu sent his son, Heng, the crown prince of Chu, to Qin as a hostage to supplicate Qin for aid. Qin sent a strong army led by a man named Tong to reinforce Chu, and the armies of the three allied kingdoms were forced to retreat. In 302 B.C., Wei and Han renewed their ties to Qin. When Qin had secured its diplomatic ties to Wei and Han, a senior Qin official dueled with Heng, the crown prince of Chu, and in the ensuing fight, "The prince slew the official, fled from Qin, and returned to his own state." Once again, Qin and Chu broke off diplomatic relations.

In 301 B.C., Qin, Han, Wei, and Qi all attacked Chu. In the face of the combined assault of four kingdoms, Chu was forced to divide its forces, sending Zhao Sui and his army to block Qin's advance, while deploying Tang Mie and his troops to defend against Qi, Han, and Wei. Because of Zhao Sui's cautious attitude, his troops blocked Qin's route but did not engage them in open battle. On the other hand, Qi, Wei, and Han were able to capture Chu's "Square City." In the Battle of Falling Sands, the allied army dealt a heavy blow to the Chu forces, causing the defenders to lose the initiative in the war. The State of Chu faced difficulties both within and without—in the border regions, it had to furiously raise troops to fight and die for the kingdom, while in the hinterland the people were subjected to heavy taxes and forced labor. Finally, after the Battle of Falling Sands, the people of Chu could take no more, and with Zhuang Qiao as their leader, they rose in massive revolt. The rebel army, made up of slaves, impoverished peasants, penniless freemen, and fallen noblemen, rampaged all over the State of Chu and began to establish illegitimate local governments. This turn of events rocked Chu society to its core.

At this time, the foreign affairs of the State of Chu were as complex as thousands of intertwining roots and as unpredictable as clouds blown in the wind. In addition, domestic affairs were filled with the commoners' cries of dissent. If the rulers did not proceed carefully, there would be outright civil unrest and the government would be shaken. The predicament faced by the State of Chu not only escaped the control of its leaders and diplomats, but also proved impossible for the Confucians, Mohists, or even Zhuangzi to solve.

In these perilous circumstances, Zhuangzi traveled to Chu to pay a visit to

公元前305年，秦"厚赂于楚"，楚于是"背齐而合秦"，秦、楚"合婚而欢"。同年，齐、韩、魏因"楚负其纵亲而合于秦"，三国联合攻楚。楚怀王以太子横为人质，向秦求救。秦遣客卿通率兵救楚，三国军队退去。公元前302年，魏、韩又转而亲秦，当魏、韩与秦关系和好时，秦一大夫与楚太子横斗殴，"楚太子杀之而亡归"。秦、楚关系又告破裂。

公元前301年，秦、韩、魏、齐共攻楚。面对四国的攻伐，楚国分头抗之，一方面派昭睢率军抵抗秦国，另一方面又派唐蔑率军抗击齐、韩、魏三国军队。拒秦一路，因昭睢持慎重态度，双方陈兵对峙，并未发生激战。齐、魏、韩三国则联合攻打到楚国的"方城"，尤其垂沙之役，大胜楚军，楚国处于被动挨打的局面。在外要服兵役，为国家当炮灰，战死在沙场；在内又有沉重的苛捐杂税和繁重的徭役，终于，楚国的百姓们忍无可忍，在垂沙之役后，爆发了以庄蹻为首的大起义。这些由奴隶、贫苦民众、破产自由民、没落贵族组成的起义军，在楚国境内东征西战，进行地方割据，给当时社会以很大的震动。

此时，对于楚国来说，国与国之间关系错综复杂，盘根纠结，外交上风云突变；国内百姓怨声载道，对社会心怀不满。当政者稍微处理不慎，就会引发社会动荡，政局不稳。时势的发展已远超出楚国当政者所能掌控的范围，也超出外交家所能左右的范围，当然也超出儒家、墨家包括庄子本人所能轻易提供答案就能解决的范围。

就在这一背景下，庄子去了一趟楚国，朝见了楚威王的儿

King Huai of Chu, the son of King Wei, the ruler of Chu. In his conversation with the king, Zhuangzi spoke of nothing but the rebellion. He told the king that Zhuang Qiao and his followers had become "robbers and thieves" and rebelled against the government, and the local governments could do nothing to stop them. The reason for them doing so was not because they were really robbers and thieves at heart, but because they were intent on changing their miserable living conditions. They thought that they could use war and unrest to force society to pay attention to them. Zhuangzi hoped that the king of Chu could sympathize with the plight of his people. ❶

In his later years, the only consolation that Zhuangzi had was being able to spend more time with Hui Shi. In 322 B.C., Qin attacked Wei, annexing part of its territory. King Hui of Wei believed that his strategy of using Hui Shi to maintain alliances with Qi and Chu to fight Qin had already failed. He chose instead to use the plan proposed by Zhang Yi, a minister from Qin, and ally with Qin and Han against Qi and Chu. The king appointed Zhang Yi as prime minister of Wei and expelled Hui Shi from his court. From that moment on, Hui Shi slowly retreated from the political scene in Wei. He was no longer prime minister of Wei, though he would occasionally travel to the palace to help with important national affairs. In 319 B.C., when King Hui of Wei passed away, was one instance where Hui Shi returned to the palace. As the appointed day for the funeral approached, heavy snows blocked the intended path of the funeral procession. The court ministers tried to convince the crown prince to change the date of the funeral, but he refused. They dared not continue their attempts to convince the prince, and turned instead to Xi Shou, the senior official in the court. Xi Shou told them he would be of little help, and that the only one who could convince the crown prince was Hui Shi. In the end, Hui Shi did not disappoint and succeeded in persuading the prince to change the date. Hui Shi said to the prince, "Have you decided on a date for the funeral?" The prince replied, "It is already set." Hui Shi then said, "In the ancient times, King Ji of Zhou had his tomb built on Chu Mountain where it was washed over by mountain torrents, exposing both the inner and outer coffins. His successor, King Wen, said, 'It must be that my predecessor wished to look upon the faces of his people, and so he allowed the water to break open his coffin.' Thereupon King Wen had the coffin placed in the entryway to the palace and allowed the commoners to look into it, waiting three days before he had it reburied. This was a manifestation of the benevolence of King Wen. Now the date of the funeral has already been set, but heavy snows have fallen for over half a month and the roads are blocked. I humbly ask you to change the date of the funeral. I

子楚怀王。庄子没有提到别的事情，只提及百姓造反的事情。他跟楚王说，庄蹻及其逃亡的民众，之所以沦为"盗贼"，并起义造反，而地方政府禁止也禁止不了，不是他们天生就是盗贼和暴民，而是他们想改善做牛做马似的处境，通过抗争，发出一些声音，让社会注意到他们的存在，希望楚王多体恤民生之多艰。❶

晚年能让庄子慰藉的事就是惠施与他在一起的时间多了。公元前322年，秦攻打魏，夺得了一些土地。魏惠王认为用魏相惠施合齐、楚抗秦的策略已失败，转而采用秦相张仪提出的合秦、韩抗齐、楚的策略；并起用张仪为魏相，把惠施逐走。于是，惠施从魏国的政治舞台中渐渐退出，不再担任魏相，只是偶尔魏国一些重要国事需要他帮忙时，他才去客串一下。如，公元前319年，魏惠王死。临近预定的惠王葬期，天下大雪，道路阻断。群臣多谏太子改期，不从。群臣不敢继续劝谏转而求告朝廷中的元老犀首；犀首亦表示无可奈何，认为只有惠施或能劝谏太子。惠施果然不负众望，说服了太子。惠施对太子说："下葬时间定了？"太子答曰："已定。"惠施说："昔者周王季的坟墓在楚山，墓地被流水冲击，棺椁露了出来。文王说：'是先君想见一见群臣百姓，所以让流水把它露了出来。'于是，把棺椁设置在朝见之所，让百姓瞻仰，三天后再下葬。这是文王的仁义。现在，下葬时间已定，但大雪已下了半月之久，交

❶ 见《韩非子·喻老》。

❶ Refer to *Han Fei: Explaining Aging*.

imagine that your father is not in a hurry to be buried, but rather that he wishes to linger and comfort the grieving ministers and commoners and so has caused heavy snows to fall." To this, the prince responded, "Your words are wise and well-reasoned. We'll set another day for the king's funeral."

In 316 B.C., Tian Xu became prime minister of Wei. Hui Shi advised Tian Xu to build relationships with the people around the king. He said, "You must be like the poplar tree, which can survive even if planted horizontally or upside-down or if broken as a sapling. However, even if ten men plant it, all it takes is one man to pull it out of the ground and end its life. Thus a hardy tree, planted by ten men and which can grow in adverse conditions, is powerless to withstand the damage done by even one man. Why is this so? Planting is hard, but pulling out is easy. You enjoy the favor of the king at present: this is like being planted by the king. But there are many who will desire to pull you out of the ground. You must be prepared for this danger."

Even after Hui Shi stepped down from politics in Wei, his passion for debate remained. He enjoyed placing his chair beneath a tree and arguing loudly about different subjects to himself. When he was tired, he would lie down next to the zither. Zhuangzi would often find himself dragged by Hui Shi beneath the parasol tree to discuss philosophical questions. The two men sometimes enjoyed going for strolls together; one well-known debate took place between them while they were strolling one day:

> Zhuangzi and Hui Shi were walking across the bridge over the Hao River. Zhuangzi exclaimed, "The white fish swim so leisurely in the water, how happy they must be!" Hui Shi responded, "You are not a fish, how do you know if the fish is happy or not?" Zhuangzi then said, "You are not me, how do you know that I don't know whether or not the fish is happy?" Hui Shi responded, "I am not you, of course I don't know what you are thinking. Using this same logic, the fact that you are not a fish means that you do not know whether or not the fish is happy, this should be obvious." Zhuangzi would not give up, saying, "Let us return to what we said in the beginning. As soon as you said, 'How do you know if the fish is happy', you already knew that I knew whether or not the fish was happy, that's why you asked me. I knew it by standing on the bridge over the Hao River!"

The two of them were unparalleled debaters; they were both very learned and were interested in acquiring new knowledge.

Hui Shi once asked Zhuangzi, "Is not the man who has attained the

通阻断，难以成行，请太子改日而行。想必先王不急着下葬，也是为了多停留片刻以安抚社稷和百姓，所以才使雪下得这么大。"太子说："说得甚有道理，先王择日下葬。"

公元前316年，田需相魏。惠施告诫田需，一定要与魏王左右的关系搞好，比如杨树，生命力很强，横栽能活，倒栽能活，折断了栽种，也能生长。然而，即使十个人去栽种它，只要有一个人把栽种的拔出来，它都无法生长。因而，以十人之众，种植容易生长的植物，都不能胜过一人搞破坏的，为什么呢？种植难，拔去易。如今，田需虽得魏王赏识，获魏王栽培，可欲拔去者多，这样他一定会遇到危险。

惠施从魏国政坛退下来后，对雄辩的热衷还是丝毫不改。他喜欢倚在树底下高谈阔论，疲倦的时候，就挨着琴而卧。庄子也常被惠施拉去梧桐树下谈学问，或一起出去游玩。一个历史上有名的辩论，便是在他们游玩时引起的：

> 庄子和惠施在濠水的桥上游玩。庄子说："白鱼在水中从容地游来游去，这是鱼的快乐啊！"惠施说："你不是鱼，怎么知道鱼是快乐的？"庄子说："你不是我，怎么知道我不知道鱼的快乐呢？"惠子说："我不是你，当然不知道你的情况。以此类推，你不是鱼，那么，你不知道鱼的快乐，这是明显的。"庄子说："还是回到我们开头所谈的，你说'你怎么知道鱼快乐'这句话时，你已经知道我知道鱼的快乐才来问我。我是在濠水的桥上知道的啊！"

他们都好辩论，辩才犀利无比；他们亦很博学，对于探讨知识有浓厚的兴趣。他们曾探讨过得道的人有情还是无情：

> 惠施对庄子说："得道的人难道是无情的吗？"庄子

Dao without emotion?" Zhuangzi replied, "Yes." Hui Zi then asked, "If a person be without emotion, how then can he be called a person?" Zhuangzi said, "If the *Dao* gives to man his appearance and the heavens and earth give him his form, how can he not be called a person?" Hui Shi answered, "Man is different from the grass and the trees. Since this is so, how can he not have emotion?" Zhuangzi said, "The emotionless state of which you speak is different from what I mean by 'without emotion'. I do not mean that a person be truly emotionless, but rather that people should not harm their original natures with notions of good and evil, that they should not add unnecessary worldly things, and especially that they should not damage the pure emotions of their original natures." Hui Shi then inquired, "How can this be done?" Zhuangzi answered, "The answer is to accept and follow the natural course of things. What you try to do is control and use emotions. In my opinion, in some matters you are too emotional. This is apparent in your obsession with such riddles as, "The South has no limit and yet has a limit." You lean against your tree, indulging yourself in this empty and useless talk. This obsession prevents your heart from feeling at peace and expends your vital energy, to the point that you are unable to live according to the natural way that the *Dao* has laid out for you."

Though Zhuangzi and Hui Shi often found each other at odds when debating and though Zhuangzi occasionally criticized Hui Shi, their relationship got progressively better. This was because Hui Shi left the political scene and became a scholar, undergoing quite a large change himself. It was also because the more time they spent together, the closer they came to understanding the depths of each other's hearts. Thus, a deep friendship began to be born.

Sometimes Hui Shi was also outspoken in his criticism of Zhuangzi's idea.

When Zhuangzi's wife passed away, Hui Shi came to offer Zhuangzi his condolences. He saw Zhuangzi squatting on the ground, banging on a pot and singing to himself as if nothing had happened. Hui Shi criticized him, reminding him of the many years he had spent with his wife, of the painful hardships she endured raising their children, and of the fact that as his wife she had never enjoyed a well-off life. Now that she had died, Hui Shi argued, if Zhuangzi did not want to cry, that was his own business; but singing and banging on a pot was too much, even for him.

说："是的。"惠子说："人如果没有情感，怎么能叫做人呢？"庄子说："道赋予了人容貌，天地自然赋予了人形体，怎么可以不叫做人？"惠施说："人非草木，孰能无情，既然叫做人，又怎么可以说没有情感的呢？"庄子说："你说的没有情感不是我正在谈的无情，我所说的无情不是说人真的没有情，而是说，人不以好恶损害自己的本性，不去人为地增加一些不必要的，尤其是损害了人的本性的情绪，如一些超过了度的好恶之情。"惠子说："那怎样能做到呢？"庄子说："那就是顺其自然。你所要做的就是对情的自然生发和运用。在我看来，你在一些事情上就处在过度的'情绪'反应中，如执迷于'南方无穷而有穷'而不能自拔，倚着树干高谈阔论，这种沉溺之情不能让自己的心神安宁，损耗了自身的精力，以至于没有按照道所给予人的自然的方式生活。"

虽然在辩论中庄子经常与惠施观点不一致，甚至批评他，但他们的关系却越来越好，一方面惠施离开政治从事学术自身有了改变，另一方面，他们在朝夕相处过程中彼此走进对方内心深处，生长出了友谊。

惠施也有直言批评庄子的时候：

庄子妻子死了，惠施前去吊唁，见庄子随便地蹲在地上，一面敲盆一面唱歌，好像没事似的。惠施就批评他，毕竟妻子与他一起生活了多年，含辛茹苦把孩子抚养大，跟他在一起也没沾什么光，如今她年老身死，庄子不哭也就罢了，还要敲着盆子唱着歌，有些过分了吧。

Perhaps Zhuangzi could have argued in his own defense, saying that he had already seen the nature of human life and death, and then used flowery philosophical rhetoric to explain life and death. He could have said that human birth was nothing but a gathering and formation of *qi*(vital energy), that death was nothing but the dissolving of the human form, and that the *qi* would return to the universe. Arguing in this vein, he could have said that she was not dead, but that she was sleeping soundly in her heavenly home. But after all, that would have only been a philosophical explanation.

In later generations, there are records of Zhuangzi considering Hui Shi to be a personal confidant.

One time Zhuangzi went to attend a funeral and as he passed Hui Shi's grave, he turned to those in the procession, saying, "In the land of Ying there is a man who smeared some lime on the tip of his nose, a layer as thin as the wings of a fly, then asked a stonemason to raze the lime away with his axe. The stonemason took up his axe and brandished it forcefully. He chopped down the thin layer of lime, leaving the nose whole and unharmed. The man from Ying stood there and his face exhibited no emotion whatsoever. When Lord Yuan of Song❶ heard this, he asked the stonemason to come and perform the same feat for him. The stonemason replied, I am able to scatter the lime with my axe. But the man from Ying who was my partner died a long time ago.' Ever since Hui Shi passed away, I am unable to find anybody to talk with me anymore."

After Hui Shi passed away, Zhuangzi could find no one to debate with, so in *Huai Nan Zi: Necessity of Training* we read, "When Zhong Ziqi was on his deathbed, Bo Ya snapped the strings of his zither, knowing that there was nobody else who could appreciate his music; when Hui Shi died, Zhuangzi refused to speak, knowing that there was nobody else with whom he could truly communicate." This means that after the death of Zhong Ziqi, Bo Ya destroyed his zither because there was no longer anybody who could be his bosom friend. When Hui Shi died, Zhuangzi actually stopped debating altogether, because there was no longer anybody on earth who could debate with him. In their later years, Hui Shi had become Zhuangzi's only debating rival.

In Zhuangzi's later years, he also came to a new understanding about Confucius. In one of his discussions with Hui Shi, Zhuangzi praised Confucius. Zhuangzi told Hui Shi, "Confucius lived to be sixty, and throughout all those sixty years, he was constantly adapting. Those things he agreed with in the

也许庄子会自我辩解，说自己已看破人的生与死，然后用一套气化哲学解释人的生与死，说人的出生是"气"凝聚成形，死则是形的解散，气重归于天地，所以她没死，她是安静地睡在天地大房间里。但那毕竟是哲学解释。

在后世的书里，还有庄子视惠施为莫逆的记载：

庄子送葬时，经过惠施的墓，他回头对跟随的人说："郢地有个人把石灰抹在鼻尖上，薄得像苍蝇翅膀，再请石匠替他削去，石匠运起斧来轮转生风，顺手砍下，把石灰完全削去，而鼻子毫无损伤，郢地那个人站在那里也面不改色。宋元君❶听说这件事后，召石匠来表演。石匠说：'我还是能用斧头削去石灰的。不过，与我配合的对手，即郢地那个人已经死去很久了。'自从惠施去世以后，我也找不到对手可以与我谈话了。"

惠施死了，庄子再也找不到谈话的对手了，所以，《淮南子·修务》云："钟子期死而伯牙绝弦破琴，知世莫赏也；惠施死而庄子寝说，言世莫可为语者也。"意思是说，钟子期死后，伯牙因世上已无另外的知音，就毁掉了他的琴；惠施死了，庄子竟至于停止谈说，因为世上再没有可以与之谈辩的人。言下之意，惠施成了他晚年唯一的谈辩对手。

晚年的庄子对孔子也有新的理解。庄子在一次跟惠施谈话时赞扬了孔子。庄子对惠子说："孔子生年六十，而六十年中与时俱化，起初认为对的，终又否定掉了，而现在认为对的，

---

❶ 宋元君，宋王偃的儿子，公元前298—288年在位。

❶ Lord Yuan of Song, the son of King Yan of Song, and his reign was between 298 B.C. and 288 B.C.

beginning were repudiated by him in the end, and those things he disagreed with at fifty-nine were the things he agreed with at sixty. This is the wisdom of his life! Wisdom never ceases to open new horizons and dig deeper depths. If a man stubbornly refuses to change, then for him it is as though life were already over." Hui Shi asked, "Was Confucius not diligent in pursuing his dreams and of superior intelligence, eloquence, and tactical planning?" Zhuangzi said, "Confucius has already forsaken all these things. He said himself, 'Man obtains his essentiality from nature. Though the *qi* which descends to earth as a living spirit may speak in rhymes and with great eloquence, restraint, and wisdom, though he is able to discern between right and wrong and good and evil, yet these things can only cause people to profess to be convinced without truly being convinced. Only he who can convince the hearts of his listeners will be able to bring peace to the earth.' Confucius spent his life in learning. The best example was his diligent reading of *The Book of Changes*; he read it so much that the cord holding the book together snapped repeatedly. He also said that with a few more years of study, his understanding of *The Book of Changes* would be even more profound. Confucius once mentioned that if he had started learning *The Book of Changes* when he was fifty, then he would have been able to avoid making any big mistakes. After living to be sixty, Confucius' experiences were plentiful, as were the hardships he survived. Because of this, anytime Confucius heard something that made him unhappy, he was able to analyze it calmly, without anger and without being influenced by the outside world."

Zhuangzi admired Confucius for having maintained his personal integrity throughout his life. Zhuangzi remembered learning that once, when Confucius was 60, he narrowly escaped losing his life as he passed through the state of Song. As Confucius passed through Song, he ran into Sima Huantui of Song, who was assistant to the highest military commander in Song at the time. Sima Huantui was a very profligate, evil man. For instance, after three years of hard work, the stonemason who was building Huantui's stone inner and outer coffins fell ill from overwork, and the coffins were still not finished. Upon hearing this, Confucius harshly criticized him. Because of Confucius' criticisms, Sima Huantui bore a deep grudge against him. Once when Confucius was teaching his disciples and resting under a tree, Huantui gathered some men together to harass him. Huantui cut down the tree under which Confucius and his disciples had been resting and screamed that he wanted to kill Confucius. Confucius' disciples worriedly cried, "Master, let's leave quickly!" Confucius replied, "I still have to finish my life's work, with the

正是在五十九岁时认为不对的。这是他人生的智慧啊！智慧永远是在展现更开阔、更高深的领域。一个人若顽固不化，则无异于人生已经结束。"惠子问："孔子是勤于立志、善于智力、口才、权谋的吧？"庄子说："孔子已经放弃这些了。他自己说过：'人从自然中获得本性，含灵气降生于世，即使讲话声音也合乎韵律，口才出众，说话合乎法度，智力超群，面对利与义能分辨好恶是非，但这些仅仅让人口服而已。只有让众人心服的人，才能使天下安定。'孔子一生是活到老，学到老。最典型的例子是他勤读《易》，致使编联简书的皮绳多次断裂。他还说，如果多给他几年功夫，那么，他对于《易》的知识会更加丰富的。他也谈到，他如果五十岁就开始学习《周易》，那么就可以不犯大错误了。孔子到了60岁，阅历多了，受到的磨练也多了，所以耳朵里听到任何不如意的话，他也能冷静地分析，犯不上生气，不为外界所影响。"

孔子一生一直坚持自己的操守，让庄子很敬佩。庄子记得，也就是孔子60岁那一年，孔子曾路过自己的国家，性命险遭不测。孔子过宋的时候，遇到了本国的司马桓魋(tuí)，这人当时是宋国最高军政长官的助手，是一个很奢侈的人，也是一个大恶人。他为自己造一个石的棺椁，造了三年都没造好，干活的工匠累得都病倒了。孔子曾就这事狠狠地批评过他。他记恨在心，当孔子和弟子们歇在一棵大树底下，孔子正对弟子进行讲学时，桓魋带了一些人来扰乱，把孔子和弟子纳凉休息的那棵大树砍掉了，还嚷嚷着要杀孔子。弟子们说："老师，我们快走吧！"孔子说："我有我追求的事业，老天爷会保佑我，

protection of Heaven, what can Huantui do to harm me?"

In his later years, Zhuangzi summarized the wisdom he had accumulated during his life into three broad categories: first, the way of observation, second, the omnipresence of the *Dao*, and third, how to walk with the *Dao*.

Zhuangzi taught that the *Dao* is everywhere, in the walls, in ants, in excrement and urine—in the *Dao*, both the base and the noble have the same worth. The *Dao* is all around you—as long as you are willing to let go of your outside worries, to accept that which cannot be changed, to endure that which must be endured, and to change that which can be changed, you will be able to feel it. By working fairly, enduring patiently, and living happily, you will be walking with the *Dao* and in the *Dao*. To see the *Dao* is to live with one's heart open, to look at the world without preconceived notions, to understand the subtleties of abstract ideas, and to seize upon the essence of life from amidst this complicated, bustling world. Hegel, the German philosopher, once expressed this same notion in the following words: "If a man can see obvious differences, such as the difference between a pen and a camel, we do not say that he possesses exceptional intelligence. Likewise, we do not say that a man who can compare two similar things, such as an oak tree and a pagoda tree, or a monastery and a cathedral, and who knows that they are similar has great powers of comparison. We require that a man be able to see differences among similarities and similarities among differences." ❶

Before long, Zhuangzi's death drew near. As he approached death, his disciples told him they wanted to give him a lavish funeral. They wanted to use the finest catalpa, cedar, and mulberry woods to make his inner and outer coffins, and then pile layers of stones and charcoal on and around the coffin. Zhuangzi said, "Heaven and earth shall be my inner and outer coffins, as burial offerings I shall have the sun and the moon, like two pieces of round jade, and as precious jewels I shall have the stars. Thus all that is shall be buried with me. Is not my offering complete? What could be better than this?" His disciples responded, "Without a coffin, we worry that the crows and eagles will come and devour your body." Zhuangzi said, "On the earth there are crows and eagles which come and eat, but under the earth are there not ants and worms which come and eat? How biased you are to steal me away from the birds and give me to the insects!"

Zhuangzi's was the life of a wise man.

桓魋能把我怎么样！"

晚年的庄子用智者的眼光看这个世界，总结出几点人生智慧：一、观看之道，二、人生处处都是道，三、与道同行。

道是无所不在的，在瓦壁、在蝼蚁、在屎溺之中，低贱和尊贵的在道中都具同等价值。道也在身边，只要你放下一切对外在的执着，去接受不可改变的，去承受需要承受的，去改变那可以改变的，去享受所拥有的，平和地工作、旷达地忍耐、幸福地生活，那么你已经与道同行，在道中生活了。用一种开放的胸怀，尽可能不带成见去看这个世界，跳出表象中的比较与分别，在世界纷繁与喧嚣的背后抓住人生最本质的东西，那就是观看之道。德国哲学家黑格尔说："假如一个人能看出当前即显而易见的差别，譬如，能区别一枝笔与一头骆驼，我们不会说这人有了不起的聪明。同样，一个人能比较两个近似的东西，如橡树与槐树，或寺院与教堂，而知其相似，我们也不能说他有很高的比较能力。我们所要求的，是要能看出异中之同和同中之异。" ❶

庄子要死了。临终的时候，弟子们想要厚葬他，准备选用上好的楸、柏、桑来制作棺椁，棺椁外再用一层层石块、木炭堆积。庄子说："我把天地当作棺椁，把日月当作双璧，把星辰当作珠玑，把万物当作殉葬。我陪葬的物品难道还不齐备吗？有什么比这更好的呢！"弟子们说："不用棺椁，我们担心乌鸦与老鹰会把先生吃掉。"庄子说："在地上有乌鸦和老鹰来吃，在地下棺椁里不是照样有蝼蚁过来吃吗？你们把我从乌鸦和老鹰嘴里抢出来，送给蝼蚁吃，真是偏心啊！"

庄子的一生是智者的一生。

❶ 黑格尔：《小逻辑》，商务印书馆，1980年版，第253页。

❶ Refer to *Science of Logic* by Georg Wilhelm Friedrich Hegel.

庄周梦蝶图
Painting of Zhuangzi Who Dreams of a Butterfly

七　文学庄子

Chapter Ⅶ　Zhuangzi　and Literature

Zhuangzi's Imagination

Mr. Wen Yiduo, in *New Interpretations of the Classics: Zhuangzi*, acclaims *Zhuangzi* as a literary masterpiece: "[This book] is so full of beautiful literary decorations that one cannot possibly finish them all—colorful descriptions, poems, odes, legends, stories, and all kinds of source material combine for the enjoyment of the reader."

In the world of Zhuangzi's writing, plants and animals could speak and think like humans. In his stories, we read of a narrow-minded sparrow, a skeleton who penetrated life and death, an arrogant frog at the bottom of the well, an robur tree who proclaimed the usefulness of uselessness, a snake who was jealous of the wind, a *yuan* who spoke with the clouds, and two shadows who could speak to each other. Because Zhuangzi portrayed his own life in the universe that he described, in his writing, anything that had form became his dwelling place. Zhuangzi's life was full of the universe, and there was no place in the universe that was not teeming with life. Zhuangzi could debate with skeletons, talk to the fall rain, play with fishes, fly with butterflies, and soar with great mythical birds. In describing the roc, Zhuangzi wrote, "When it journeys to the southern darkness, the waters are roiled for three thousand li. He beats the whirlwind and rises ninety thousand li, setting off on the sixth month gale." He wrote, "When we make an effort and fly up, we can get as far as the elm or the sapanwood tree, but sometimes we don't make it and just fall down on the ground" to describe the cicada and the sparrow, contrasting them to the great roc. He described the Great Chinese toon, writing that it "lived for eight thousand years in spring and eight thousand years in autumn." He wrote of the morning mushroom and cicada which "do not know twilight or dawn . . . spring or autumn," to describe the differences in lengths of time.

Zhuangzi's writing tended to be fantastic and fictional rather than realistic.

We can compare the imaginations of Zhuangzi and Mencius. Mencius' writing was more realistic. This can be seen from the subject material of Mencius' parables, which were most often based on historical legends or folk stories. Though he did add original elements, the bulk of his stories were realistic, focusing on historical people and events. Even the fictional parts of his parables were still not far from reality. For instance, the man in the story "The Man who Tried to Help the Shoots Grow By Pulling them Up" (found in *Mencius: Gongsun Chou Part One*), as well as the soldier in the story "The Soldier who Fled Fifty Paces Laughs at the One who Fled a Hundred" (found in *Mencius: King Hui of Liang part one*), are both examples of realistic characters from Mencius' writing. In "The Man who Tried to Help the Shoots

（一）　庄子的想象力

闻一多先生在《古典新义·庄子》中对《庄子》评价很高："（这书中）有着你看不完的花团锦簇的点缀——断素、零纨、珠光、剑气、鸟语、花香——诗、赋、传奇、小说，种种的原料，尽够你欣赏的，采撷的"。

在庄子笔下，动植物像人一样会说话和思考，如目光短浅的学鸠、参破生死的骷髅、自高自大的坎井之蛙、鼓吹无用之用的社栎，蛇可以艳羡风的自由，云雾与鹤纵横议论，影子与影子相互之间可以进行对话。由于庄子把他自己的生命熔铸到他所描写的自然宇宙之中，所以凡是有物的地方，也是他生命存在的地方。生命充满了宇宙，宇宙无一处不洋溢着生命。他可以与骷髅论辩，与秋水共语，与鱼同乐，与蝴蝶齐飞，与大鹏一起展翼；他用"水击三千里，抟扶摇而上者九万里，去以六月息者"形容大鹏，以"决起而飞，抢榆枋，时则不至而控于地"的蜩与学鸠表现事物的大与小，用"以八千岁为春，八千岁为秋"的大椿，"不知晦朔"、"不知春秋"的朝菌、蟪蛄来说明时间的长与短。

庄子的写作偏于想象，而不是写实。

我们可以比较庄子与孟子的想象力。孟子写作偏于写实，这从孟子寓言取材的内容上可以看出来。孟子寓言多取材于历史传说和民间故事，虽有本人创作的成分，但大多侧重于现实和历史中的人和事，即使有虚构的也跟生活贴得很近。如取材于民间故事《揠苗助长》（《孟子·公孙丑上》）中的宋人，取材于现实生活《五十步笑百步》（《孟子·梁惠王上》）中的士

Grow By Pulling them Up," we read of a farmer who lived in ancient Song. After planting his rice seedlings, he grew impatient and hoped to be able to harvest earlier. Every day he would go into his fields and think to himself about how slow the shoots were growing. Finally, he could wait no longer, saying to himself, "How can I make those shoots grow higher and faster?" He thought about it repeatedly before concocting the perfect plan—he would pull the shoots up by just a few inches. After a long day's work, he happily shouldered his hoe and went home to rest. At home, he told his family, "Today I am exhausted! I spent all day helping those shoots grow faster!" His son hurried out to the fields, only to find that the shoots had all withered and died. "The Soldier who Fled Fifty Paces Laughs at the One who Fled a Hundred" is a story which took place on a battlefield. During battle, the war drums sounded and the soldiers of both armies fought sword to sword, spear to spear. Realizing that they had lost, the soldiers of the losing side threw off their helmets and armor, dropped their swords and spears, and fled the battlefield in disarray. Among the losing soldiers, there was one who had fled a hundred paces before another soldier had made it fifty paces. At that moment, the soldier who had only fled fifty paces laughed mockingly to himself at the soldier who had run a hundred paces, calling him a coward. In reality, the soldier who ran fifty paces had no right to mock the one who fled a hundred, because even if he had not made it a hundred paces, he still ran!

In contrast to Mencius, the material for Zhuangzi's parables often originated outside of history and folklore. Rather, Zhuangzi often used material from ancient myths, such as the *kun* who became a roc (which originated from monster stories found in books such as Universal Harmony), the Yellow Emperor (which originated from myths from the Kunlun Mountain region of China), and the "primordial chaos" (which is related to stories found in *The Classic of Mountains and Rivers*), etc.

There are many mythical stories found in *Zhuangzi*. Of these, "The Kun who Became a Roc" became an archetype of story-writing for future authors. Stories which are based on this one include "An Essay on the *Kun* who Became a Roc" by Gao Mai, and "An Ode to the Great Roc" by Li Bai. According to Swiss psychologist Carl Jung, an archetype is a universal mental construct which originates from the collective unconscious. The collective unconscious manifests itself in myths, stories, and all other imaginative works. As the basis for man's consciousness, the collective unconscious carries with it healing and saving power, encapsulating the secrets of mankind's growth and

兵。《揠苗助长》讲述的是古时宋国有个农夫，在种了禾苗后，希望能早点收获。每天他到稻田，都发觉那些禾苗长得非常慢。他等得不耐烦，心想："怎样才能使禾苗长得高，又长很快呢？"想了又想，终于想出一个妙计，就是将禾苗拔高几分。经过一番辛苦劳作后，他满意地扛着锄头回家去休息。回去后对家里的人说："今天可把我累坏了，我帮助禾苗长高了一大截！"他儿子赶快跑到田里，一看，禾苗全都枯死了。《五十步笑百步》讲述的是发生在战场上的一个故事。战场上，战鼓一响，双方士兵就刀对刀、枪对枪地对打起来。打败的一方，丢盔卸甲，拖着刀枪，赶紧逃命。其中，有一个士兵逃了一百步，另一个士兵逃了五十步。这时，那个逃了五十步的竟嘲笑那个逃了一百步的胆小怕死。实际上，那个逃了五十步的没有资格嘲笑那个逃了一百步的，他虽然没有逃到一百步，但他同样也是逃啊！

与孟子相比较，庄子的寓言除取材于历史和民间之外，更多源于古代神话，如鲲化为鹏（来源于《齐谐》之类的"志怪"神话）、黄帝（来源于昆仑神话）、混沌（与《山海经》神话有关），等等。

《庄子》中的神话故事很多。其中鲲鹏神话成了庄子以后的作家写作的原型。如，高迈的《鲲化为鹏赋》，李白的《大鹏赋》等都受了这方面的影响。按瑞士心理学家荣格的说法，原型是一种来源于集体无意识的普遍的心理结构，这种集体无意识出现在神话、故事及所有的想象的作品中，作为意识基础的集体无意识本身带有治愈和拯救的力量，包含了人成长和智慧的一切秘密，艺术家受这些力量支配并在作品中发挥了这些

wisdom. Artists are controlled by this force and give form to it in their works.

Zhuangzi possessed incomparable and boundless imaginative power which enabled him to take everything as the subject of his writing such as "The vast universe, the miniscule fly, and everything in between."

In the chapter "External Things," Zhuangzi wrote of a great fish which threw up "white waves like mountains and sea waters that lashed and churned. Its noise was like that of gods and demons and it spread terror for a thousand *li*." Of course to catch such a large fish, the fisher, the childe from the state of Ren, would have to forge a giant hook and prepare a thick cord, then use fifty bullocks as bait. After making these preparations and casting his line, the fish carried the hook deep into the sea, then leaped out of the water and wriggled its fins, throwing up white waves as tall as mountains. The sound made by the ocean was as loud as crying ghosts and howling wolves, so that even people a thousand *li* away heard it and were frightened. When the childe finally caught the fish and had it cut and dried, people from east of Zhejiang to north of Cangwu Mountain were able to eat their fill.

In "Ze Yang," Zhuangzi wrote of two clans of tiny creatures who established kingdoms on the left and right horns of a snail, called Chu and Man. "On top of its left horn is a kingdom called Chu, and on top of its right horn is a kingdom called Man. At times they quarrel over territory and go to war, strewing the field with corpses by tens of thousands."

In his book *On Qu Yuan's Spirit of Literature*, Wang Guowei expressed heartfelt affirmation and appreciation of Zhuangzi's imagination, exclaiming that the imagination of this southern author was even greater and more abundant than that of northerners. He wrote, "Zhuangzi depicted things as large as the fish in the northen ocean, as small as the kingdoms on the horns of the snail. He wrote of things as ancient as the Great Chinese toon, as ephemeral as the morning mushroom or cicada. His description of the Seven Sages getting lost in the wilderness around Xiang City and his portrayal of the confusion of the subjects who lived on the north bank of the Fen River when their king left them to meet the Four Scholars are examples of his unusual imagination. This kind of imagination is incomparable in northern literature. Hence we may say that there are some parts of the books of *Zhuangzi* and *Liezi* that can be called 'prose poetry' ."

Zhuangzi's imagination was not filled with irrelevant nonsense, but rather provides a liberating power to our spirits that awakens in our dreams.

From a psychoanalytic standpoint, the story "The *Kun* who Became a Roc" in *Zhuangzi* symbolizes a person's active expansion of his or her

力量。

庄子的想象力无与伦比，真正做到了想象没有边际，"宇宙之大，苍蝇之微，皆可取材"。

《外物》篇写到"白波若山，海水震荡，声侔鬼神，惮赫千里"的大鱼，这条大鱼这么大，垂钓的任公子当然要打造大钓钩与粗大的长绳，用五十头牛做钓饵，结果这条大鱼上钩了。它牵动大钓钩沉入海中，又急速跃起摆动鱼鳍，掀起的白浪如山，海水所发出的响声如鬼哭狼嚎，千里之外的人听了都害怕。任公子钓到这条大鱼后，把它剥开风干，从浙江以东到苍梧山以北的人，都饱餐了一顿。

《则阳》篇提到在蜗牛的左、右角里分别立国的触氏与蛮氏。"有国于蜗之左角者，曰触氏；有国于蜗之右角者，曰蛮氏。时相与争地而战，伏尸数万。"意思是说，有一个国家在蜗牛的左角上，叫做触氏；另一个国家在蜗牛的右角上，叫做蛮氏。这两个国家为了争夺土地，经常发生战争，死亡数万。

王国维在《屈子文学之精神》中对庄子的想象无比肯定和赞赏，认为南方作家庄子想象力伟大丰富，远胜于北人，"言大则有若北溟之鱼，语小则有若蜗角之国，语久则大椿冥灵，语短则蟪蛄朝菌；至于襄城之野，七圣皆迷；汾水之阳，四子独往；此种想象，决不能于北方文学中发见之。故《庄》、《列》书中之某部分，即谓之散文诗，无不可也。"

庄子的想象不是胡思乱想，它给予我们心灵解放的力量，让我们的感官在梦想中苏醒。

《庄子》中鲲化为鹏的故事在心理治疗中可表述为，一个人如何积极拓展自身的生命空间并渴望成长。鲲如同一个人，

comprehension of the world, as well as a desire for further growth. The *kun* is like a person who dreams of flying and wishes to employ the active part of himself in expanding his comprehension of the world. His earlier life was limited to the space below the surface of the sea, and as the inner-most desires of his heart were unable to be satisfied, the imagination of the *kun* was piqued repeatedly by the possibilities and open spaces before him. Under the impetus of his dreams, the *kun's* living space had the possibility of expansion, until finally, the freedom of the *kun* was no longer restricted by the surface of the ocean. The progress in its life was enough to step beyond the sea and enter the immenseness of the skies.

"The *Kun* who Became a Roc" teaches us that within each of us is a force driving us to grow into the form that we were always destined to have. The Swiss psychologist Carl Jung was especially concerned with the active imaginations of patients in therapy. In his opinion, his work was less therapy than it was unleashing the potential, creative power of his patients. Therefore, the purpose of imagination is to allow life to learn to fly, to arouse man's vital energy, to free the stiff, frozen, and enslaved life. In Jung's words, many of those who came to him for help felt as though their lives were "stuck." A good psychotherapist could analyze the images in the patient's dreams to reveal a multitude of hidden possibilities as well as those things in development which had caused the personality to lose balance or forget its potential. One of Jung's methods was to stimulate the active imagination, as mentioned above. He would use techniques such as this to release the hidden creative power of his patients.

In addition to "The *Kun* who Became a Roc," there are other stories in *Zhuangzi* which expand our overly limited vision, help us escape from the dangers of conformist limitations, and draw us into poetic reveries. In "Zhuangzi Dreams of a Butterfly," Zhuangzi is unsure whether he is dreaming of himself having turned into a butterfly, or whether a butterfly has dreamed that it turned into Zhuangzi. In later generations, frequent poetic allusions are made to this story, which can be seen in such phrases as "Zhuangzi's dream," "butterfly dream," "dreaming of a butterfly," etc. Often, these poems refer to "Zhuangzi Dreams of a Butterfly" in order to create a dreamy, misty, or fantastic mood. Other times, poems allude to the story to establish the illusory nature of human life as well as the state of "forgetting one's self and external things." Examples of such poems include "The Inlaid Harp" by Li Shangyin: "The sage Zhuangzi daydreamt and was enchanted by a butterfly / And Emperor Wang set the yearning of his youthful heart on a cuckoo." Li

它梦想飞翔，希望通过自身中积极的部分来拓展生命的空间，它以前的生活仅局限在海平面以下，其内心深处的渴望未得到满足，于是面对生存的可能和空隙，鲲的梦想一次次被驱动。有了梦想的驱动，鲲的生命空间就有了拓展的可能，终于有一天，鲲的生命的自由度不再局限于海平面以下，它的生命成长足以跨越海平线并进入广阔的天空。

鲲化为鹏的故事告诉我们，每个人生命中都有成长的动力，并希望长成本应成为的那个样子。瑞士心理学家荣格特别重视治疗中病人的积极想象力。在他看来，与其说他的工作是治疗，还不如说是发挥病人身上的创造性潜能。因此，想象的目的是让生命学会飞翔，激发人的生命活力，消解和重整已僵化、冰冻和被奴役的生命。用荣格的话说，很多求助者感到自己在生活中"被卡住了"，动弹不得，而心理咨询师通过对他的梦和梦中形象的分析，揭示被隐藏起来的种种可能性，揭示个性中曾导致片面发展、被遗忘或者丢失的东西。荣格的方法之一就是上述提到的积极的想象，用这种方法释放病人身上未被发掘出来的创造力。

除了鲲鹏故事，《庄子》中其他的想象和形象同样扩大了我们过于狭小、局促的视界，使我们摆脱沉重、僵化、羁绊自我的各种危险因素，也使我们注意到某些充满诗意的遐想。在庄周梦蝶中，庄子不知道是自己梦见自己变成了蝴蝶，还是蝴蝶梦见自己变成了庄子。后世诗文中常见的"庄周梦"、"蝴蝶梦"、"梦蝴蝶"等用典均本此而来，所言即指庄周梦蝶这件事及其在梦中所变成的那只蝴蝶，诗文中的引用，多用作虚幻、睡梦及迷蒙之态，或用来表示人生原属虚幻的思想，也用来形容物我两忘的境界，凡此种种用意均随引文而异。如，"庄生

Shangyin modified the image of the "butterfly dream" to describe the hollow feeling he experienced after pursuing an official career and failing. The word "daydream" conveys the ephemeral nature of the dream state, while the word "enchant" suggests the obsession of the dreamer. These feelings of intoxicating obsession and hollow disappointment, in addition to the butterfly image, were what the poet wanted to convey. Another example of such a poem can be found in "Ancient Poetry Number Nine" by Li Bai. He wrote, "Zhuangzi dreamt of the butterfly, the butterfly dreamt of Zhuangzi / Form can change so easily, this is true for all things." Li Bai used Zhuangzi's image of a butterfly to discuss the transitory nature of human life and to encourage his readers to not care too much about gaining or losing things in life.

In *Zhuangzi*, we read the description of Pao Ding, the ox butcher, whose movements and sounds as he cut the ox were mirrored in the dance of "the Mulberry Forest." We also find the story about the joyful freedom of the fish in the Hao River, and the story of the holy man who lived on the remote Gushe mountain who, "sucked the wind and drank the dew, who climbed upon the air and mist, rode upon a dragon, and wandered beyond the four seas." In reading these stories, we are transported to a state of poetic reverie and receive additional faith in the future.

Zhuangzi was not an ordinary poet, but rather a philosopher-poet. Furthermore, he was also not just an ordinary philosopher-poet, but rather one whose imagination was extraordinarily rich. This can be seen from his vivid descriptions of masters of the *Dao*, some of whom were ugly, some foolish, some crazy, some dull, and some stupid. An example of an ugly person who mastered the *Dao* is Aitai Ta, around whom men and women flocked (found in the chapter "The Sign of Virtue Complete"). An example of a foolish person who mastered the *Dao* is Kuang Qu, who, "wanted to speak but forgot what he wanted to say." (found in "Knowledge Wandered North"). An example of a crazy person is Meng Zifan who sang to a dead body (found in "The Great and Venerable Teacher"). An example of a dull person is Nie Que, who had no thoughts or ambitions (found in "Knowledge Wandered North"). An example of a stupid person is Bo Ju, who cried in the market (found in "Ze Yang"). Other notable characters include the old hunchback who concentrated single-mindedly on his tasks, the man of Lüliang who was a skilled swimmer, and the talented carpenter Zi Qing (found in the chapter "Mastering Life").

Zhuangzi's descriptions of the *Dao* masters can be illustrated with a specific example of the insanity of Meng Zifan and his transcendence over worldly things. Meng Zifan, Zi Sanghu, and Zi Qinzhang became friends with

晓梦迷蝴蝶，望帝春心托杜鹃"（李商隐《锦瑟》）。李商隐借"蝶梦"之形象为自己所用，抒写了自己对于仕宦之途的追求梦想以及此梦想失败落空后的无尽感慨。"晓"字暗示了梦境的短暂，"迷"字暗示了梦者的痴迷。这种痴迷沉醉、怅然若失的情意是诗人所欲表达的。再如，"庄周梦胡蝶，胡蝶梦庄周，一体更变易，万事良悠悠"（李白《古风》其九）。李白借用庄子梦见了蝴蝶还是蝴蝶梦见了庄子这一事件，展示人生虚实的转换，认为对人生的得失不必太在乎。

《庄子》中，庖丁解牛时的合于桑林之舞，在濠梁之上自由快乐的濠梁之鱼，藐姑射之山上"吸风饮露，乘云气，御飞龙，而游乎四海之外"的神人……都给我们带来了诗意的遐想，并使我们对生活和未来充满信心。

庄子不是一般的诗人，而是诗人哲学家，也不是一般的诗人哲学家，而是一个内心世界非常丰富、充满想象力的诗人哲学家。这可从他塑造的得道高人，或丑，或愚，或狂，或钝，或痴的情状中看出来：或丑，丑如"雌雄合乎前"的哀骀它（《德充符》）；或愚，愚如"欲言而忘其所欲言"的狂屈（《知北游》）；或狂，狂如临尸而歌的孟子反（《大宗师》）；或钝，钝如无心无谋的齧缺（《知北游》）；或痴，痴如当市痛哭的柏矩（《则阳》）。另外还有凝神用志的佝偻丈人、蹈水有道的吕梁丈夫、巧夺天工的木匠梓庆（《达生》），等等。

这里举一具体例子，说说孟子反的狂与超凡脱俗。孟子反、子桑户、子琴张，三人结交为朋友，常相视而笑，心心相印。有一天，子桑户死了，尚未下葬。孔子听说了这件事，就派子

one another. When they saw each other, they would often laugh because their hearts were so close one to another. One day, Zi Sanghu died, but had not yet been buried. When Confucius heard of this, he sent his student Zi Gong to help arrange the burial. Zi Gong went to visit Meng Zifan and Zi Qinzhang, but found that they were not mourning, but rather were playing the zither and singing, "Oh Sanghu! Oh Sanghu! You came from the *Dao* and now you've returned to the *Dao* to rest, but we are still on earth!" Zi Gong went up to them and asked, "According to the rites, is it proper to sing songs to the dead body?" The two friends looked at each other and laughed, saying, "What do you know of the true meaning of the rites?" Upon saying this, the two of them paid Zi Gong no more heed. Zi Gong finally left, telling everything he had seen and heard to Confucius, saying, "What kind of people are they? They don't seem to care at all for the man's life or death, and they even sang songs to the dead body without mournful expressions. They didn't seem to feel any grief for the dead. What kind of people are they?" Confucius replied, "They are people who live outside the realm of worldly things while we are people who are confined by worldly things and defined by them. We are different from them. I did not think ahead when I sent you to mourn with them. They are together with the creator of heaven and earth, the *Dao*, and travel with the great *qi* that exists between heaven and earth. In their minds, the beginning and end of life are inextricably connected. They believe that when the *qi* of the *yin* and *yang* coalesces, it forms man—when it disperses, man dies. Human life and death are just manifestations of different stages of *yin* and *yang*, and as such, one should not fear death. Therefore, why would Meng Zifan and Zi Qinzhang care about worldly rites and rituals, which are merely things to perform for others to see!"

II. Zhuangzi's Rhetorical and Linguistic Style

In order to avoid being killed for his honesty and to prevent his book from being destroyed for not conforming to mainstream thought, when Zhuangzi wrote, he had to be fanciful, exaggerated, and even a little crazy.

However, much of the levity and nonsensical nature of Zhuangzi's writing was also because he was a poet. His disposition was profoundly romantic. As such, he hoped that human life might be interesting and full of imagination rather than full of rigid ethical rules and regulations. Mr. Wen Yiduo in *New Interpretations of the Classics: Zhuangzi* had this to say about Zhuangzi: "In truth, his thinking was not reserved, harsh, or cold like the dominant philosophies of his time; it was not something that caused people to frown or

贡去帮忙料理丧事。子贡去时看见孟子反与子琴张没有在哀悼，而是在弹着琴，唱着歌说："哎呀，桑户啊！哎呀，桑户啊！你从大道来，现又回去，已归回大道安息，可我们还在世上为人！"子贡上前说："请问对着尸体唱歌，合乎礼节吗？"二人相视而笑，说："你哪里知道礼节的真正意思？"说完就不理睬他。子贡回去后，把所见所闻告诉孔子，说："他们是什么人呢？竟然把人的生与死置之度外，还对着尸体唱歌，脸色平静，看不出对死去的人的哀痛。他们是什么样的人呢？"孔子说："他们是遨游于世俗之外的人，我们是拘泥于世俗之内的人，被世俗的礼节所规范。我们与他们是不同的，我太缺乏充分考虑了，竟然派你去吊丧。他们与创造天地的大道同在，遨游于天地大气之中。在他们看来，生命的开始与结束是相接的，阴阳之气凝聚成形，就成了人，当阴阳之气散掉，人就死了，所以人的生与死是阴阳之气在不同阶段的表现，死亡对他们来说也就没什么可怕了。这样，他们又怎能在乎一些世俗的礼节，并表演给众人观看呢！"

（二） 庄子的言语与言说方式

庄子著书，既要避免生前其书太直白而招来杀身之祸，又要预防身后其书因不合主流思想被剿灭，所以说话有些疯疯癫癫，虚虚实实，不正儿八经。

庄子著书不庄重、不正经，也因他是诗人。他具有浓厚的浪漫主义气质，希望人生有趣而不是乏味，希望生活高迈且富有想象，而不是在刻板的程序和教条式的伦理中度过一生。闻一多先生在《古典新义·庄子》中对庄子这样评价："实在连他的哲学都不像寻常那一种矜严的，峻刻的，料峭的，一味皱

rack their brains trying to figure out. His thinking was, in essence, nothing but a beautiful poem... his naivety, like a child that cries when it cannot grasp the moon, his mysterious melancholy, the wisdom of his yearning, the limitlessness of his aspirations, the boundlessness of his admiration, all combine to make him the truest of all poets."

With the romantic disposition of a poet, Zhuangzi wrote poems which did not follow the rules of rhyme and meter. This can be seen in four main ways: first, the use of enormous descriptive words which were inappropriate for the size of the things they modified; second, the use of strange and eccentric diction; third, the adept use of modifiers; fourth, the use of extraordinary rhetorical devices. The following section will discuss these in greater detail.

In *Zhuangzi*, the word "grand" (or "great") appeared more than 140 times, and there are more than 200 compounds containing "grand." In comparison, in *Laozi*, we only find around twenty uses of the word "grand," and about 30 compounds containing "grand." From this fact we can see how much Zhuangzi enjoyed using this word.

The relation between the grandness of Zhuangzi's diction and the scope of his spiritual gaze is reflected in the chapter "Free and Easy Wandering." In this chapter, Zhuangzi employs disproportionately grand words to describe his ideal world, in order to better highlight his transcendence over worldly things. In the beginning of the chapter, he writes of the immensity of the *kun* and roc, in the middle he describes the greatest of all human beings—the holy men and sages, and in the end he depicts enormous gourds and trees. Liu Fengbao of the Qing Dynasty wrote, "Zhuangzi's spirit is barely discernable and impossible to grasp, in this sense he is singular in all of China." The sections and layers of

眉头、绞脑子的东西；他的思想的本身便是一首绝妙的诗。"
"他那婴儿哭着要捉月亮似的天真，那神秘的惆怅，圣睿的憧
憬，无边际的企慕，无涯岸的丽羡，便使他成为最真实的诗人。"

　　具有浪漫诗人气质的庄子，他写作不循规蹈矩，主要体现
在以下四个方面：一、用大而无当的辞；二、用稀奇古怪的
辞；三、擅长各种修辞技巧；四、别出心裁的言说方式。下
分述之。

　　据统计，"大"字在《庄子》中出现次数达140多次，与
"大"组合的词汇达200多个，而在《老子》中"大"字仅出现
20多次，与"大"组合的词汇仅30多个。足见庄子对"大"的
喜好程度。

　　《逍遥游》篇集中反映了庄子文辞之大与其精神境界高远
之关系。庄子在该篇中为了衬托出他超尘脱俗的逍遥境界，处
处用"大而无当"之言来描述他理想的世界，以及在这一世界
中的逍遥。在篇首，叙鲲鹏之大，中腹，叙人中之最大的至人、
神人、圣人，于篇末，叙大瓠、大樗。清代刘凤苞说："缥缈
空灵，则推南华为独步也。其中逐段逐层，皆有逍遥境界，如
游武夷山九曲，万壑千岩，应接不暇。起手特揭出一大字。乃
是通篇眼目。大则能化，鲲化为鹏，引起至人、神人、圣人，
皆具大知本领，变化无穷。至大瓠、大树，几于大而无用，而
能以无用为有用，游行自适，又安往而不见逍遥哉！"意思是
说，写作的缥缈空灵，庄子可算为独步天下。《逍遥游》中逐
段逐层的描写，都指向一种逍遥的境界，读该篇，就如同游武
夷山九曲溪，万壑千岩，应接不暇。开篇就写鹏之大，这"大"
成了整篇的文眼。大，意味着有足够的空间让生命成长和转化。
鲲转化为鹏，紧接着引出至人、神人、圣人，这些人都具有大
知的本领。再接下来写到大瓠、大树，它们大到近乎无用，而

"Free and Easy Wandering" all exhibit a free and easy state of mind.

The reaction of worldly people to the greatness of Zhuangzi's writing can be captured by the following sentiment: "I read with surprise and fear the immensity of his diction. It is as boundless as the Milky Way, both exaggerated and removed from human life." This means that Zhuangzi's words were as broad and sweeping as the Milky Way. They had no limits, were exaggerated, separated from normal human emotion, and both surprising and frightening to those who read them.

Zhuangzi's writing style was expansive and all-inclusive, while his "understanding exceeded the physical world and his writing was of the supernatural." Zhuangzi loved to write of supernatural things. In his writings we see strange people, animals, and landscapes. From ancient to modern times, writers have exclaimed over Zhuangzi's ability to describe the supernatural. Li Bai wrote that, "Zhuangzi spoke of lofty theories in swelling and fantastic language." Tu Long of the Ming Dynasty felt that *The Book of Songs* was, "broad, sweeping, distinct, and clear; the wind and sun are both made lucid." He wrote that in reading *The Book of Songs*, one was left with a graceful, peaceful, simple, and solemn feeling, whereas "*Zhuangzi* and Lie Yukou were free and unrestrained, as energizing as lightning, as unpredictable as flashing light, making readers thrilling. This is why they are extraordinary books."

In addition, Zhuangzi used bizarre things as metaphors for his philosophy, in order to show his rebellion against worldly things. Zhuangzi's was a dark time, and consequently many of the characters in his allegories were people handicapped by cruel punishment. Such characters include Wang Tai, Shentu Jia, the toeless Shu Shan, etc. The specific reason why these characters were without feet or toes is not clear, but it seems as though they had all had their feet cut off as punishment, likely because they did not cooperate with the rulers ❶ .

In Zhuangzi's dark time, he employed strange words and bizarre rhetorical devices to express his dissatisfaction with reality. For example, when making the names of countries or people, he used rare characters and strange words. Characters from his stories with strange names include "Zhi" (meaning knowledge),"Shaozhi" (meaning ignorance), "Nieque" (meaning cutting edge broken),"Wuzu" (meaning footless), "Hundun" (meaning chaos), "Zhili Shu" (meaning fragmented), "Wuweiwei" (meaning indescribable), "Hongmeng" (meaning primordial world), "Tiangen" (meaning roots of Heaven), "Guang Chengzi," etc. Countries from his stories with strange names include Zong, Xu, the Chu Clan, the Man Clan, etc. These names had

能以无用为有用。庄子写作变化无穷，随心所欲，真是逍遥啊！

俗世之人对庄子表现精神境界之高的大辞的反映是，"惊怖其言犹河汉而无极也，大有径庭，不近人情焉。"意思是说，庄子的言论像银河一样辽阔无穷，不着边际，过分夸张，不近人之常情，听了既惊讶又害怕。

庄子文辞风云开阖，"意出尘外，怪生笔端"。庄子好用奇笔，笔下有奇人、奇物、奇山、奇水。古今文士，每每奇之。李白说庄子"吐峥嵘之高论，开浩荡之奇言。"明代屠隆认为，《诗经》"廖廓清旷，风日熙明"，读之能给人"庄雅"、"和婉"、"简严"之感，而"庄、列之文，播弄恣肆，鼓舞六合，如列缺乘蹻焉，光怪变幻，能使人骨惊神悚，亦天下之奇作矣。"

庄子用"奇"辞表达他的思想，直接源于他对世俗的反叛。庄子时代是一个昏暗的时代，庄子笔下很多寓言人物都是刑残之人，如王骀、申徒嘉、叔山无趾等。这些断足或断趾之人具体致残原因不明，但他们受的都是刖刑❶，估计与他们不与当局者合作，遭到当局者惩罚有关。

在那个昏暗的时代，庄子用奇辞、怪语来表达他对现实的不满，如他用稀奇古怪的字眼造人名、国名。人名如知、少知、齧缺、无足、浑沌、支离疏、无为谓、鸿蒙、天根、广成子等，国名如宗、脍、触氏、蛮氏等。这些名字闻所未闻，然而在这些表面离奇的名字背后隐藏着庄子的深意，如丑人哀骀

---

❶ 译者注：中国古代一种砍断脚的酷刑。

❶ Translator's note: A cruel punishment in ancient China.

never been heard before, but behind the superficially strange names was hidden the deeper meaning of Zhuangzi's philosophy. For example, though Aitai Ta (meaning mournful, tired horse) was extremely ugly, both men and women really liked him. When men were around him, they would be drawn to him and unwilling to leave. When women saw him, they would beg their parents to allow them to marry him, even if they could only be his concubine. When the rulers of nations saw him and spent one month with him, they would appreciate his way of handling affairs and hand over the affairs of state to him. All of this was because he was of impeccable moral character.

Though Nie Que and Wang Tai were deformed, they were both morally irreproachable. Characters with such silly names as Chaos, Indescribable, and Primordial World were masters of the *Dao* in Zhuangzi's stories, while characters with intelligent names such as Shu(Sudden) or Hu(Swift) were used by Zhuangzi to criticize those who did not understand the way of *Dao*. Characters like Roots of Heaven and Guang Chengzi were used as metaphors for boundless, all-knowing men, while Ignorance and Footless were used to describe foolish, worldly men.

Zhuangzi's use of bizarre language was a "twisting" of language as it is commonly used. Through transforming and exaggerating words, he broke the normal rules of language use, thereby criticizing and mocking societies, worldly notions, cultural order, and value measurement.

Behind Zhuangzi's use of bizarre language, one can also find Zhuangzi's care for worldly people. Zhuangzi found it difficult to communicate with such people, so he used bizarre words and language to establish distance between himself and them, presenting his superiority and pride. At the same time, he expressed his compassion and commiseration for worldly people. He regretted that they were unable to cease in their quest to fulfill their carnal desires. He saw that they slaved away their whole lives only to find themselves still very distant from their goals. They were utterly exhausted at the end of life and yet still without a spiritual resting place.

Worldly people had long since fallen into the trap of selfish ego-centricism. Though the poison ran deep, they had no idea they were even sick. Zhuangzi hoped to use bizarre words and phrases to highlight this problem and break through to them as they read his words. This would help awaken them and cause them to reflect on their lives. Lin Yunming of the Qing Dynasty captured Zhuangzi's sentiment when he wrote, "Zhuangzi sometimes seems indiscriminate in his criticism. When he deems it neccessay, he will criticize anyone relentlessly, whether the object of his criticism be a sage, a holy man or a king. However, other times he seems sensible and intimate; his world was

它，长相虽很丑陋，但却很受男女的喜欢。男人与他相处，会被他吸引而不愿离开。女人见了他，便恳求父母把自己嫁他为妻，哪怕做妾也行。国君见了他，与他相处了一个月，就很欣赏他的为人，决定把国事交托给他。原因在于哀骀它的品德高尚。

同样，齧缺、王骀虽然残疾，也都是品德高尚之人；浑沌、无为谓、鸿蒙名为懵懂愚钝，庄子却认为是得道者，而行动敏捷快速的"倏"和"忽"却被庄子用来指斥无道之人；"天根"、"广成子"比喻为广大无边、全知全能之人，"少知"、"无足"比喻为世俗愚昧之人。

庄子上述的奇辞、怪语是对日常语言的"扭曲"。他通过变形、夸张等手段来打破日常语言的常规，从而完成对奠基于日常语言之上的世俗社会观念、文化秩序以及价值尺度的抨击和嘲弄。

在庄子"奇"辞的背后也隐藏着他对俗世的一份关怀。对俗世之人，庄子感觉很难沟通，他用奇文、怪辞标其高识，划清与他们的界线，显示自身的清高和高傲；同时他对俗世之人也抱着同情和悲悯的态度，认为他们在这个世上追逐自身的欲望而不能停止，终生劳苦忙碌却离成功很远，一生疲惫不堪却不知心归何处。

世人陷于"我执"已久，中毒已深，对自身这一症状已不觉知，庄子希望用奇字、怪辞表述这些问题，让他们在阅读时有突兀之感，以此"警醒"自身，从而引起对自身生存情境的反思。清代林云铭捕捉到了庄子这一情怀："庄子似个绝不近情的人，任他贤圣帝王，矢口便骂，眼大如许；又似个最近情

contained in alleys, living rooms, workrooms, and butchers' shops. With every stroke of his pen, he revealed his understanding of the multitude of human emotions and the profundity of his heart."

This discussion of Zhuangzi's language summarizes Zhuangzi's complex, even paradoxical inner heart.

This was Zhuangzi: he took all that was great, distant, and bizarre, in order to help his readers escape the base, familiar, ordinary, and secular.

Zhuangzi was also proficient at all kinds of rhetorical devices. He was good at employing words that expressed form and state and at the end of these words he liked to add the empty word "ran" (the character "然") to make his writing fresh and full of imagery. For example, in the story "Zhuangzi Dreams of a Butterfly," he used the expression "xuxuran" (meaning "lifelike"), to depict the nimbleness and airiness of the butterfly's flight. He used the expression "ququran" (meaning "astonishment"), to describe the suddenness with which he awakened from his dream, sitting up straight and stiff. The airiness of the butterfly and the rigidity of his awakening form a stark contrast. In the story of Song Rongzi and Liezi in "Free and Easy Wandering," he used the expression "youran" (meaning "in a natural way") to describe Song Rongzi's cheerful smile and happy disposition. He used the expression "weishuoshuoran" (meaning "not to run after hastely and desperately") to express his nonchalance and casual manner towards life. In addition, he used the word "lingran" (meaning "light and graceful"), to describe Liezi's carefree disposition and lighthearted disposition. Zhuangzi also excelled at dingzhen, a rhetorical device by which the first character of a phrase is the same as the last character of the previous phrase. For example, "The Way doesn't want things mixed in with it. When it becomes a mixture, it becomes many ways; with many ways, there is a lot of bustle; and where there is a lot of bustle, there is trouble-trouble that has no remedy!" This line creates a circular, repetitive effect. Zhuangzi also paid particular attention to matching sound and meaning in his writing. For example, "Great understanding is broad and unhurried; little understanding is cramped and busy. Great words are clear and limpid; little words are shrill and quarrelsome." In Chinese, these words flow easily when read, and the repeated words add to its power. Zhuangzi also used parallel constructs in his writing. For instance, "You will find your eyes growing dazed, your color becoming composed, your mouth working to invent excuses, your attitude becoming more and more humble, until in your mind you end by supporting him. This is to pile fire on fire, to add water to water, and is called 'increasing the excessive.'" The use of parallel constructs adds to the power and persuasiveness of Zhuangzi's writing.

的人，世间里巷、家室之常，工技屠宰之末，离合背欢之态，笔笔写出，心细如许。"

以上这些都统一构成了庄子复杂，甚至有些矛盾的内心世界。

这就是庄子。他取物之大者、远者、奇怪者，以使人得以自我超拔于卑、近、凡、俗的自然物与一般器物之外。

庄子也擅长各种修辞。他擅长用表示形态、状态的修辞语，再加上"然"字，以达到鲜明、形象的修辞效果。如庄周梦蝶故事中，用"栩栩然"展现蝴蝶翩翩起舞时的轻盈与灵动；用"蘧蘧然"刻画庄周刚从梦中恍惚醒来，身体僵直的样子。轻盈与僵直形成了鲜明的对比。在《逍遥游》讲宋荣子和列子的故事中，则用"犹然"表现宋荣子嬉笑、欢喜的神态；用"未数数然"表现他为人处世方面的从容和不急促；用"泠然"展现列子神态飘然、轻妙的样子。庄子也善于运用顶真，如"夫道不欲杂，杂则多，多则扰，扰则忧，忧而不救"，达到了环环相扣的效果。庄子也讲究对仗工整，如"大知闲闲，小知间间，大言炎炎，小言詹詹。"读起来明快上口，其中的叠字又加强了气势。庄文中也有排比，如"而目将荧之，而色将平之，口将营之，容将形之，心且成之。是以火救火，以水救水，名之曰益多。"排比句的使用增加了文章的气势和雄辩力。

Zhuangzi's use of language was unique; he employed goblet-words, or natural, free-flowing words, in expounding principles, the speech of the late sages or wise men to prove veracity, and parables to expand his philosophy.

In the chapter "Metaphorical Language," Zhuangzi detailed his reasons for using these three rhetorical devices: "Of my sentences nine in ten are metaphorical; of my illustrations seven in ten are from the speech of the late sages or today's wise men. The rest of my words are like the water that daily fills the cup, tempered and harmonised by the Heavenly element in our nature. The nine sentences in ten which are metaphorical are borrowed from extraneous things to assist the comprehension of my argument. When it is said, for instance, 'A father does not act the part of matchmaker for his own son,' the meaning is that 'it is better for another man to praise the son than for his father to do so.' The use of such metaphorical language is not my fault, but the fault of men who would not otherwise readily understand me. ...The seven out of ten illustrations taken from the speech of the late sages or wise men are designed to put an end to disputations. They can do this because they are the words of my predecessors. If, however, one is ahead of others in age but does not have a grasp of the warp and woof, the root and branch of things that is commensurate with his years, then he is not really ahead of others...." These goblet words are like the water that daily issues from the cup, and are harmonised by the Heavenly Element (of our nature), may be carried on into the region of the unlimited, and employed to the end of our years.

In comparison to the parables of other pre-Qin scholars, Zhuangzi's parables are more imaginative and fictitious. Though Mencius, Han Fei, and other pre-Qin scholars employed parables and other folk stories in their writings, the majority of their parables and folk stories were already in existence, passed down by word-of-mouth, and were more connected to real life. Zhuangzi, on the other hand, consciously created fictitious parables, such as the conversation between the river god and Ruo, god of the northern sea, and Zhuangzi's dream of a skeleton.

The story of the river god and Ruo, the god of the northern sea goes like this: in autumn, a lot of rain fell. The water from the mountains ran into small streams, the streams ran into rivers, and this made the river god very pleased, because he felt that all that was good under heaven had come to him. However, as the rivers all ran into the great sea, the river god discovered that the sea did not change at all, exclaiming, "I gaze to the east and I see no end to water." His pleased expression quickly turned into a pensive one as he sighed at the immensity of the northern sea, lamenting his own base, limited vision. Ruo, the

庄子的言说方式也别出心裁，以卮言任意引申，以重言来证明可信，以寓言来推广想法。

《寓言》篇详细解释了使用这三种言说方式的缘由："寓言十九，重言十七，卮言日出，和以天倪。寓言十九，藉外论之。亲父不为其子媒；亲父誉之，不若非其父者也。非吾罪也，人之罪也。……重言十七，所以已言也，是为耆艾。年先矣，而无经纬本末，以期来者，是非先也。……卮言日出，和以天倪，因以曼衍，所以穷年。"意思是说，寓言占了全书的十分之九，其中借重先贤的话又占了全书的十分之七，自然、随意之言即卮言，合于自然的分际。寓言占了全书的十分之九，之所以要假托外人来论说，是因为亲生父亲不给自己儿子做媒，与其父亲称赞儿子，不如别人称赞可靠，这不是我的弱点，而是人性共有的弱点。……重言占了全书的十分之七，是为了中止争论，因为这些话出于前辈的见解会更可靠些。年龄虽长，但若没有什么见解的只是徒称年长。……自然随意之言，即卮言，合于自然的分际，顺应无穷的变化，悠游直至永远。

庄子的寓言和先秦其他诸子的寓言相比，多一些想象虚构。先秦其他诸子如孟子、韩非子虽在言谈中也引用寓言或民间传说等来说理，但这些寓言与民间传说大多是现成的，口耳相传的，与现实生活有一定的相关性。庄子则有意识地编造寓言，如河伯与北海若的对话、庄子梦见骷髅之事都是凭空杜撰的。

河伯与北海若的故事是这样的：秋天下了很多的雨，山上的水流汇入小溪，小溪又汇入到河里，河伯就很得意，自以为天下所有的美好全在自己身上了。可是随着河流汇入大海，河伯发现大海居然没有边，"东面而视，不见水端"，他得意的脸色马上换了一副表情，望洋兴叹，感叹北海的无穷无大，感慨自己见识鄙陋。北海之神若告诉河伯，对井底之蛙不可以同

god of the northern sea, told the river god that one cannot talk about the great ocean to a frog in a well, because it is limited by the walls of the well. One cannot talk about ice to a summer insect, because it is limited by the time of its life. One cannot talk about the greatness of the *Dao* to a prejudiced and narrow-minded man, because he is limited by man's prejudices and cannot perceive the *Dao*. After considering the river god's grasp of his own shallowness and baseness, the god of the northern sea felt that he could talk of the deep mysteries of the universe with him. Ruo told the river god that he was not the greatest in the universe. Rather, he was as insignificant as a small pebble or a small shrub on a great mountain; there was really nothing special about him. In the grand scheme of things, the four oceans compared with the heavens count as no more than an anthill in a marsh, and China's existence within the four oceans counts as no more than a small grain of rice in a great barn.

The story of Zhuangzi's conversation with a skeleton is as follows. While traveling to the State of Chu, Zhuangzi saw an empty skeleton by the side of the road. Zhuangzi struck it with his whip, asking, "How did you die? Were you executed for violating the natural order of things by trying to stay alive? Were you slaughtered when your country and family were destroyed? Did you commit suicide because of the shame of evil deeds? Did you die of sickness brought on by cold and hunger? Or did you live to the natural end of your days and perish of natural causes?" After asking these questions, Zhuangzi lay down on the skeleton like it was a pillow and soon fell asleep. In the middle of the night, he dreamt that the skull was talking to him, saying, "You speak like a debater. Your questions are the burdens of a living man. Once one dies, it is the end of all things, there is nothing more to worry about. Would you like to hear about what life is like after death?" Zhuangzi responded that he would. The skull then said, "In death, there are neither rulers commanding from above, nor worries about being court officials from below. There are no four seasons, no bitter cold or scathing heat, everything is free and natural. One lives with the heavens and the earth, and not even the happiness of the King in his court can be greater than death!" Zhuangzi was a little dubious, asking, "If I call for the ruler of our destiny to revive your physical form, return you your organs, muscles, and skin, and allow you to live with those dearest to you, would you be willing to do it?" The skull frowned, then answered sadly, "How could I forsake the happiness of a king and return to the misery of human life?"

Zhuangzi's parables had two characteristics: first, the parables hid deep

它谈论大海，因为它受到空间的约束；对夏天的虫不可以同它谈冰，因为它受到时间的限制；对褊狭之士不可以同他谈论大道，因为他被个人成见束缚，看不见大道。考虑到河泊有自知之明，认识到自身的浅薄和鄙陋，北海若觉得可以与他谈谈生生不息的宇宙。北海若说他自己在宇宙中也不是最大的，就好像大山之中的小石头、小树木这么的渺小，自己没有多么了不起。推算起来，四海存在天地之间就不过如蚁穴存在于大泽里一样，中国存在四海之内也不过如小米粒存在于大仓里一样。

庄子来到楚国，看见路边有一副空的骷髅头，就用马鞭敲打它，说："你是怎么死的呢？是因贪图生存违背了常理而被处死的？是因国破家亡而惨遭杀戮的？是作恶多端内心有愧自杀的？是挨饿受冻而病死的？还是寿限已到，自然死亡的？"庄子说完了这些话，就以骷髅当枕头很快就睡着了。到了半夜，他梦见骷髅头对他说："你说话的方式像个辩士，你所说的那些都是活人的累患，死了，一了百了，就没这些忧虑了。你想听听人死后生活的情形吗？"庄子说："好。"骷髅头说："人死了，上没有国君管辖，下没有做臣子的烦与忧，也没有四季的冷冻热晒，自由自在，与天地并生共存，就算是南面称王的快乐，也不能超过它啊！"庄子不相信，说："我叫司命官恢复你的形体，还给你骨肉肌肤，并让你与你的至亲和乡亲生活在一起，你愿意吗？"骷髅头皱起眉，忧愁地说："我怎能抛弃国王般的快乐而再次回到人间劳苦呢？"

庄子的寓言有两个特色，一是寓真于诞，二是寓实于玄。

庄子寓言显得怪诞，在于庄子寓言以神话传说作为自己的

meaning within fantastic stories, and second, they hid truth within mystical things.

If Zhuangzi's parables seem bizarre, this is because they are based in myths and legends, full of imaginative, fanciful thinking, and, "their essence bubbles like a stream, their meaning floats with the wind." They are as large as the *kun*, the roc, the great gourd, or the bullocks, as small as the leopard cat, cicadas, sparrows, and morning mushrooms. This is what makes Zhuangzi the representative of creative thinking.

Many of the parables in *Zhuangzi* were modified from ancient mythical stories. For example, the *kun* and the roc in "Free and Easy Wandering" were actually embodiments of the god of the northern sea and wind, Yu Jiang. The story in "Fit for Emperors and Kings" of Shu(Sudden) and Hu(Swift), who made seven orifices into Huntun (Chaos), was repeated from a story found in *Classics of the Mountains and Rivers: Classic of the Mountain: North*, which tells of Hundun being, "without face but skilled in singing and dancing." These lines actually describe Dijiang, the heavenly bird from Tianshan mountain. The holy man of Miaogushe Mountain in *Zhuangzi* was based on the story about Huangdi (the Yellow Emperor) who lost a string of pearls in Kunlun Mountains. In addition, Queen Mother of the West, Peng Zu, and others, were all characters from earlier myths.

Zhuangzi used a unique writing style to hide truth within mystical things; he did this because of the subject of his writing. For the most part, Zhuangzi's subject was the *Dao*. The *Dao* cannot be spoken of directly, so it must be approached from the side and from behind, using comparisons, contrasts, and other rhetorical devices to explain it. The *Dao* is not constrained by what is real, does not hold an extreme opinion, and changes depending on the situation. As such, the words used to describe it should not be restricted to real words, and Zhuangzi therefore employed "strange and mystical expressions" and "wild and extravagant words and phrases" to describe the mysteriousness of the *Dao*. Because this style of writing did not conform to what worldly people were accustomed to, it was not surprising that average people found it esoteric.

Zhuangzi employed the speech of past sages and wise men and modified existing story models, tweaking them to his own uses. Zhuangzi's writing is full of historical figures, such as Laozi, Confucius, Confucius' disciples Yan Hui and Zi Gong, and various noblemen and rulers. It contains truth as well as fiction; based on Zhuangzi's deep understanding of these historical characters, his portrayal of them is in line with their personalities as well as the logic

题材，以虚构想象为能事，"心如泉涌，意如飘风"，大至鲲鹏、大瓠、牦牛，小到狸、蜩、学鸠、朝菌等都能成为庄子思想的代言人。

《庄子》中的很多寓言，是以古代神话故事做蓝本而改写的：《逍遥游》篇的鲲鹏之变，鲲和鹏实际上都是北海海神兼风神禺彊的化身；《应帝王》篇的倏、忽为浑沌凿七窍，浑沌即《山海经·北次三经》所记的"浑敦无面目，是识歌舞"的天山神鸟帝江；藐姑射之山的神人，是在昆仑丢失玄珠的黄帝，还有西王母、彭祖等都是神话中的人物。

庄子采用"寓实于玄"的言说方式也是由其言说对象决定的。庄子言说的对象主要是"道"。道不可明说，所以只能从侧面说、反面说，用对比、映衬等修辞技巧来达到言说的目的。道不拘泥于实，不持一端之见，"随物宛转"，表达道的言辞也不得拘泥于实，因此庄子用"无端崖之辞"、"恣纵而不傥"之语表达道之玄。由于这种言说方式不合俗世陈规，在常人看来，自然感到"玄"。

庄子也借着重言对以前的故事原型加以改造，使之适合于说理的需要。庄子书中有许多历史人物，如老聃、孔子及其弟子颜回、子贡，各诸侯国君等，他们的故事中有真实，也有虚构，庄子在对他们充分认识的基础上，对这些历史人物作了合

behind their philosophies.

Zhuangzi's writing style is also shown in the form of "goblet words." A *zhi*, or goblet, was an ancient vessel used to hold wine at banquets. When it was full of wine, it would gradually tip; without wine, it would stand empty and straight. In terms of expression, goblet words refer to not deviating to any extreme and not being constricted by any particular standard or rule of expression. It means communicating without prejudice or preconceptions, just like the liquid in the vessel would form itself to the shape of the container. These words conveyed a sense of not being bound by conservative writing, but rather maintaining openness. In order to prevent his language from becoming rigid and superficial and to keep his words from meaning only one thing, Zhuangzi used negative, similar or dissimilar words to establish openness. His reason for doing this was that indescribable things, such as the *Dao*, cannot be objectified, because as soon as they are objectified they become material things; indescribable things are not material things, they surpass them.

Actually, there is no way to describe indescribable things without using the *Dao* to define them. That is not to say that all indescribable things are the *Dao*. Indescribable things can be called by other names, but *Dao* is a way to organize them. This is because in defining indescribable things, it is easy to fall into the trap of reifying them and misleading people into believing that those definitions represent the indescribable things. Thus it is necessary to negate and destroy those definitions, in order to prevent people from being misled. This is why Laozi, when speaking of indescribable things, often used negative speech structures or similar words. For example, "The Way which can be followed is not the constant way," "...Great and distant, distant and departing, departing and returning... ," "Mysterious and even more mysterious," etc. This is also the reason behind Zhuangzi's use of goblet words.

Over the past 2,000 years, Zhuangzi's literary style has influenced generations of writers. Zhuangzi employed mysterious meaning, bizarre conceptions, apt metaphors, stirring emotion, and free-flowing writing in his descriptions of starry nights and vast oceans, of flying birds and creeping beasts, of holy people and supernatural events. His writing has led generations of future scholars "to be blown away by it, caught up in it, and to go crazy because of it." Many of his stories have become idioms or set phrases. Examples of these include: "Zhuangzi Dreams of the Butterfly," "Dong Shi, the Sorry Imitator," "Treating Each Other with Equal Respect," "The Monkey Who Wanted Three Chestnuts in Morning and Four in the Afternoon," "Pao Ding Cuts the Ox," "Learns to Walk in Handan," "Spit out the Stale and Take

乎他们各自性格和思想逻辑的编造。

庄子的言说方式也体现在"卮言"上。"卮"是一种古代盛酒的器皿，倒满酒就会倾斜，不倒酒就空仰着。引申到表达上，卮言，指的是不偏向于某极又不陷于某种标准和规定的言说方式，即说话时没有成见或定见，如杯里的水，随杯之形状而给自己赋形。它传达出来的核心精神是，不执着于守故之言，它的言说永远保持着无限的开放。而为了让言说保持开放，不让其走向僵化和片面，即意义不终止在一个语词或落在一个实处上，庄子往往采用否定的方式进行言说，或引用相近或排斥性的话语让语词保持开放性。之所以这样，是因为不可说的东西不能对象化，一旦对象化就变成了物，而不可说的东西不是物，它超越于物。

甚至，不可说的东西用"道"来称谓也是不得已而为之。并不是不可说的东西就是"道"，也可以用其他的词称呼不可说的东西，"道"只不过是一个索引词。由于称谓不可说的那些词，易落到实处，导致人的错觉，以为那些词就代表不可说的东西，因而，有必要对那些称谓的词再来一次否定和破坏，给人以"警醒"。这就是为什么老子在说不可说的时，常采用否定表达式或引用相近的词语的原因，如"道可道，非常道"、"大而远，远而逝，逝而返"、"玄而又玄"，等等。庄子采用卮言的言说方式用意也在于此。

两千多年过去了，庄子的言词及言说方式影响着一代代文人。他所描绘的星空与大海、飞禽与走兽、神人与奇事，其意境之玄，构思之奇，设喻之妥，抒情之浓，文意之飘，均臻于美妙的境界，令后世文人墨客"倾倒，醉心，发狂"。尤其他寓言中所讲的故事变为了成语，如："庄生梦蝶"、"东施效颦"、"分庭抗礼"、"朝三暮四"、"庖丁解牛"、"邯郸学步"、"吐故

in the Fresh," "Lament one's littleness before the vast ocean," "The *Dao* Master Finds it Amusing," "The Roc Flies Ten Thousand *Li*," "A Self-Satisfied Expression," "The Sleek Knife Blade," "Without the Lips, the Teeth get Cold," "Courteously but without sincerity," "The Fish who Spit Bubbles to his Friend," "Walking at the Same Pace," "Stopping a Wagon with a Mantis' Arm," "A White Pony's Shadow Flashing Past a Crevice," "Capturing a Fish but Forgetting the Fish Gear," "Turn the Foul and Rotten into the Rare and Ethereal ," "The Association of Noble Men is Like Water," etc. These proverbs have become bright pearls in the treasure trove of the Chinese language and an integral part of Chinese culture.

In short, Zhuangzi was the synthesis of writing and life. Because of this, his personality and talent are evident in his writing. His pain and joy, his sincerity and freedom are displayed before us. Reading between the lines of the theories he developed, we are able to taste the richness of his life and discover his glowing personality. Mr. Wen Yiduo wrote, "In Zhuangzi's hands, words transformed into literature. His words were not only tools to express his thoughts, but they also seemed to have a purpose in and of themselves."

纳新"、"望洋兴叹"、"贻笑大方"、"鹏程万里"、"踌躇满志"、"游刃有余"、"唇亡齿寒"、"虚与委蛇"、"相濡以沫"、"亦步亦趋"、"螳臂挡车"、"白驹过隙"、"得鱼忘筌"、"化腐朽为神奇"、"君子之交淡若水",等等,已成为汉语言文学宝库中的明珠,成为代代相传的中国文化传统的一部分。

总之,写作和生命在庄子那里已融为一体。因而,他的才情和个性在他的文章中一览无余;他的痛苦和欢乐,真诚和放达一样真实地呈现在我们面前。即使在他陈述的理论中,我们也能从他理论的背后体味到他的生命情怀和掩藏不住的个性。闻一多先生说:"到他手里,辞令正式蜕化成文学了。他的文字不仅是表现思想的工具,似乎也是一种目的。"

崇尚自然是中国文人的传统
Glorifying Nature is the Tradition of Chinese Literati

八　　自然庄子

Chapter Ⅷ　　Zhuangzi and Nature

Among the various pre-Qin schools of thought, none were able to describe the process of observing and listening to nature quite like Zhuangzi's. Furthermore, none of them are able to more fully inspire human life through natural description. Zhuangzi did not hide his respect for nature, nor did he mince words in his praise for it: "The mountains and rivers, meadows and soil, how they bring joy to my soul!" He also wrote, "If the mind does not have its heavenly wanderings, then the six orifices of sensation will defeat each other... the great forests, the hills and mountains excel man in the fact that their growth is irrepressible." By this he meant that if one's spirit did not have the chance to stay in nature, then the desires of the six sensory organs-the desire of eyes to see, ears to hear, nose to smell, tongue to taste, mouth to speak, and mind to think-will become entangled and prevent people from obtaining peace. The tall trees and rolling hills are good for people because they are the place where man's spirit can become free.

Zhuangzi had good reason for placing the emotions of his heart in the great outdoors. As a hermit, he did not enjoy the complex, noisy, superficial world, but rather loved, "Walking through swamps, relaxing in nature, and fishing. (taken from the chapter "With Studious Intent"). Nature puts man's heart at ease because it brings emptiness and peace, causing the heart to distance itself from the cares of the world. On this wise, Zhuangzi had a profound influence on the poet Tao Yuanming. In "Returning to Nature, Number One," Tao Yuanming wrote, "While young, I was not used to worldly cares / And hills became my natural compeers / But by mistakes I fell in mundane snares / And thus entangled was for thirty years." Tao Yuanming was never interested in a worldly life. Rather, it was his personality to love nature, though after a mistake, he fell into the trap of worldly things where he was stuck for thirty years. After a drawn out mental debate between choosing an official career or hermitage, between choosing a royal court or mountains, Tao Yuanming finally chose the latter. After thirty years, he returned to nature, taking up residence on Zhongnan Mountain where he lived for almost ten years in a grass hut. There he listened to the cries of the birds, spent time under the elm, peach, and pear trees, and lived like a chrysanthemum flower. Ma Zhiyuan also wrote several lyrics during the Yuan Dynasty praising Zhuangzi's abandonment of worldly cares and living in nature. He wrote:

"Clear River Prelude: Nature's Joy"
Living in seclusion among the forests and streams, the wind is my constant guest.

在先秦诸多思想流派中，没有一家像庄子那样能详细描述聆听和观察大自然的过程，以及在这一过程当中所获得的人生启迪的。庄子既不隐藏自己对自然的尊重，也不吝啬对自然的赞美："山林与，皋壤与，使我欣欣然而乐与！"意思是说，山林啊，原野啊，都能使我欢欣快乐啊！又说："心无天游，则六凿相攘。大林丘山之善于人也，亦神者不胜。"意思是说，心灵若不与大自然相处，则人的六种感官所激起的欲望——眼睛欲看，耳朵欲听，鼻子欲闻，舌头欲尝，嘴巴欲说，心灵欲想，会相互缠绕，让人不能安宁和摆脱，而高大的树林，峦峦山丘之所以宜人，乃是因为在那里，人可以变得心神舒畅。

庄子把山川作为自己心灵寄予的对象，不是无缘无故的。作为隐居者，他不喜欢世俗的喧嚣与浮杂，喜爱"就薮泽，处闲旷，钓鱼闲处"（《刻意》）。山川让人心旷神怡，是因为它使人心灵虚静，从而得以使心灵远离世俗的纷扰。庄子这一点，影响了陶渊明。陶渊明在一首诗（《归园田居》其一）中写道："少无适俗韵，性本爱丘山。误落尘网中，一去三十年。"原来，陶渊明从小就对适应世俗生活没多少兴趣，生性就喜爱山林田园，一时的迷误，坠入世俗名利网中，过了三十年。在入仕与归隐，庙堂与山林之间，经过一番挣扎和深思熟虑，他最终选择了后者。于是三十年后，他返回自然，在终南山下隐居，住草屋八九间，听鸟声啾啾，与榆柳、桃李相伴，淡定如菊花般生活。元代马致远也写了几首曲，追慕庄子弃绝尘俗、浪迹山林的情趣：

林泉隐居谁到此，有客清风至。

会作山中相，不管人间事。

争甚么半张名利纸！

I am the minister of the mountains; I care not for the affairs of men. Why fight over half a piece of fame?

In the western village, the days are long and man's concerns are few; I hear the chirp of a young cicada.

I wait with joy for the blooming of the sunflower blossoms; I listen to the drone of the bees.

Carefree and untroubled, I follow the butterfly in my dreams.

The author embraced nature by melding himself into nature. The clear wind became his guest, and he himself became the master of nature. He did not fight over that "half-piece of fame" and, "cared not for the affairs of men." He loved nature. It was full of the buzz of cicadas, blooming sunflower blossoms, and humming bees. There, he was carefree, and like Zhuangzi, he followed the butterfly in his dreams, becoming one with the universe.

Zhuangzi treasured the mountains, rivers, grass, trees, birds, and animals. He became a veritable naturalist, appreciator of nature, and writer. Liu Chengji wrote, "In *Zhuangzi*, mention is made of 22 species of birds, 15 species of water animals, 32 species of land animals, 18 species of insects, 37 species of plants, 32 non-living animals, and 34 kinds of fictitious animal. These statistics show that *Zhuangzi* described almost every natural phenomenon and scene common to the warm temperate zone. As for the mythical creatures it contains, they surpass the limits of our natural understanding. The variety of life it describes also shows that Zhuangzi was a naturalist-philosopher. Natural phenomena provided a vibrant emotional form to his philosophy and aesthetics." ❶   Indeed, the gourds, butterflies, rivers, orange trees, teak trees, etc. which Zhuangzi mentioned are all plants and animals found in the warm temperate zone.

As a representative figure of Daoism, Zhuangzi, lived primarily in the marshy areas between the Heluo, Jianghuai, and Sishui rivers. There he was able to enjoy the beauty of rivers and seas, becoming familiar with all kinds of bodies of water.

In the chapter "External Things," it is recorded that Zhuangzi fished in the Pu River. In *Huainanzi: Placing Customs on a Par*, it is written that Zhuangzi fished in the Mengzhu Marsh northeast of his hometown. Furthermore, in the chapter "Autumn Floods," Zhuangzi wrote wistfully of his envy for the carefree fish swimming in the Hao River below the bridge. Also, in "Autumn Floods" is the story of the river god who sighed regretfully as he

西村日长人事少，一个新蝉噪。

恰待葵花开，又早蜂儿闹，

高枕上梦随蝶去了。

〔清江引·野兴〕

作者拥抱自然，进一步将自己融入大自然之中，清风成了他的常客，他也成了大自然的主人。他不争那"半张名利纸"，更"不管人间事"。他喜欢自然，那里有蝉鸣、葵开、蜂闹，晚则高枕无忧、梦随蝶去，就如庄子梦蝶，物我混一。

庄子欣赏山川草木、飞鸟动物。他成了名副其实的博物学家，大自然的欣赏者和书写者，"从《庄子》一书看，它涉及飞鸟计有22种，水中生物15种，陆上动物32种，虫类18种，植物37种，无生命物象32种，虚拟的神性物象34种。这些统计数字表明，《庄子》一书描述的自然物象及物候变化，几乎囊括了暖温带可能出现的大部分自然风物。至于一些虚拟的神性物象，更超出了人的感官所能把握的限度。这林林总总的物象也表明，庄子是一个博物学家型的哲学家，自然物象为他的哲学、美学提供了生动的感性形式。"[1]确实，《庄子》中所提到的葫芦、蝴蝶、水、橘树、柚树等，在地理分布上基本属于暖温带的动植物。

从地理环境来看，庄子这位道家代表人物，生长和主要活动的地方为河洛、江淮、泗水之间的水泽地带，有机会欣赏和观察河与海，所以庄子对江河湖海很熟悉。

《外物》篇记载他垂钓于濮水之上；《淮南·齐俗训》提到庄子在其故乡东北孟诸泽钓鱼；《秋水》篇中，庄子在濠水的桥上，对悠游在水中的鱼儿充满了艳羡，在该篇中还有精心

---

[1] 刘成纪：《物象美学》，郑州：郑州大学出版社，2002年版，第381页。

[1] Liu Chengji. *Phenological Aesthetics*. Zhengzhou: Zhengzhou University Press, 2002, page 381.

gazed upon in the sea. Lastly, in the chapter "Mastering Life," Zhuangzi discussed his admiration for the ferryman who guided his boat like a god, further expounding the principle, "the master swimmer need not fear water."

Through this connection with water, Zhuangzi accumulated experience and understanding. He was able to combine these experiences and understanding, finally bringing them to a higher level of understanding of the *Dao*. In other words, Zhuangzi's understanding of the Dao came in part from his daily observations of, and meditations over water. This was a deeper level of comprehension than people who lived in other areas could attain.

Zhuangzi also observed the wind rushing through the mountain forests:

> Zi You said, "May I venture to ask what this means?" Ziqi said, "The earth belches out breath and its name is wind. So long as it doesn't come forth, nothing happens. But when it does, then ten thousand hollows begin crying wildly. Can't you hear them, long and drawn out? In the mountain forests that lash and sway, there are huge trees a hundred spans around with hollows and openings like noses, like mouths, like ears, like crossbars, like railings, like mortars, like rifts, like ruts. They roar like waves, whistle like arrows, screech, gasp, cry, wail, moan, and howl. Those in the lead call out yeee! Those behind call out, yuuu! In a gentle breeze they answer faintly, but in a full gale the chorus is gigantic. And when the fierce wind has passed on, then all the hollows are empty again. Have you never seen the tossing and trembling that goes on?" (From the chapter "Discussion on Making All Things Equal").

This passage describes in vivid detail the noise of wind blowing through the cracks in the trees, the shape of the tree hollows, and the slanted form of the trees as they bend with the wind. Zhuangzi describes the cracks in the wood as being like noses, mouths, ears, wine bottles, teacups, and teeth. They are as deep as pools and as shallow as puddles. The sound of the wind blowing through the cracks is like a turbulent river, an arrow flying through the air, wind blowing through a deep crevasse, a baleful cry, and like the sound of breathing. There are great winds, little winds, and winds that shake the branches and rock the trunks of the trees. Lin Xiyi of the Song Dynasty wrote that this description of wind-a thing with neither shape nor shadow, something that can be heard but not seen-was vivid and lifelike, and conjured up a clear mental image, just as though the scene appeared before the reader. He believed that this displayed the creative artistry of the author, as well as the careful daily observation and attention that Zhuangzi paid to the environment in which he

编制的"河伯望洋兴叹"的寓言故事;《达生》篇中,他沉浸于对游者和"津人操舟若神"的观赏之中,并从中体会到了"善游者忘水"的自由境界。

因与"水"打交道,庄子积累了一些经验,悟到了一些道理,终而把这些经验、道理经过抽象、升华,上升到"道"的认识高度。换言之,庄子对"道"的认识和理解,部分来自他日常生活中与水朝夕相处过程中对水的体会、观察和思考。这是在其他地方生活的人所不具备的。

庄子也观察山林中的风:

子游曰:"敢问其方。"子綦曰:"夫大块噫气,其名为风。是唯无作,作则万窍怒号。而独不闻之翏翏乎?山林之畏佳,大木百围之窍穴,似鼻,似口,似耳,似枅,似圈,似臼,似洼者,似污者。激者,謞者,叱者,吸者,叫者,譹者,宎者,咬者,前者唱于而随者唱喁,泠风则小和,飘风则大和,厉风济则众窍为虚。而独不见之调调之刁刁乎?"(《齐物论》)

这段文字对山林中的风吹过树窍所发出的响声,树窍的形状,风吹过树林时树干倾斜的姿势都描写得非常精彩。大木之窍穴,似鼻、似口、似耳、似酒瓶、似茶杯、似石臼、似深池、似浅洼。风吹过窍穴的声音如湍急的水声,若箭飞之声,似风吹到深谷的声音,像哀切感叹的声音,仿佛呼吸的声音……有大风,有小风,风吹树木,树枝摆摆,树干摇摇。宋代林希逸认为这段描写,把无形无影之风,可闻而不可见之声,写得栩栩如生,历历在目,如身临其境,显示了作者高超的写作技巧,

lived. Finally, Lin Xiyi wrote that Zhuangzi's description showed his understanding of the true nature of things, because he was able to make manifest the sounds of heaven using the sounds of earth.

Zhuangzi was also attentive to trees. In the chapter "In the World of Men," there is a story of a carpenter named Shi who traveled to Qi. On the way there, he passed a place called Quyuan and saw a great tree. The tree was so big that it could provide shade for several thousand oxen. The circumference of its trunk was a hundred spans, and it towered far above the hills. The carpenter told his disciples that the tree was useless. If one used it to make a ship, the ship would sink in no time. If one used it to make a coffin, the coffin would soon rot. If one used it to make furniture, the furniture would soon be ruined. If one used it to make windows, the glue would soon come apart. If one used it to make beams for a roof, the beams would soon be eaten away by worms. Later on, the tree appeared in a dream to the carpenter and explained to him the value of uselessness. The carpenter sighed with regret, telling the tree that as worldly people, he and his disciples liked to use worldly logic to judge it; it was difficult for him to appreciate the tree's secret and true value. In the story just following this one, we read of a great tree near Shangqiu in Henan that was so large a thousand teams of horses could have rested under its shade. However, looking up at its branches, Nanbo Ziqi saw that they were gnarled and twisted, and thus unfit for making beams; looking down at its trunk, he saw that the trunk was pitted and rotten, thus unfit for making coffins. He licked one of its leaves, but found that it blistered his mouth; he sniffed its odor and fell into a drunken stupor for three days. Ziqi, who was already a master of *Dao*, understood the mystery and worth of the useless tree, believing that it was special because it was seen by worldly things as useless. It was not controlled or twisted by worldly things, thus able to grow without outside influences. On the other hand, pear trees, orange trees, and pomelo trees were not able to grow very large because as soon as they produced something useful, they displayed it in the form of ripe fruit. Because they had fruit, their branches were broken and grafted and their fruit was stolen from them. The useless tree was able to grow so large because it was not bound down or controlled by worldly things.

There are two main characteristics of Zhuangzi's descriptions of nature.

First, he respected the existence of all things. In the story about the sounds of earth, Zhuangzi described in stirring detail the places through which the wind blew as well as the marks and sounds of its passing. As for the bending and twisting of the tree trunks under the force of the wind, his descriptions considered every possible aspect. In comparison to Zhuangzi's description of

同时也表明了庄子对日常场景中的大自然观察之细腻和专注，并在对大自然的观察中领悟到物的某种本真存在，地籁之音中显示着天籁之音。

庄子也把目光投向自然界的树木。在《人间世》篇中，一位姓石的木匠往齐国去，路过曲辕这个地方，看见一棵很大的树木，这棵树大到可以供几千头牛遮荫，粗到"絜之百围"，高到"临山十仞而后有枝"。木匠告诉他的徒弟，这树是无用之木，用它做船，船很快就会沉没；用它做棺椁，棺椁很快就会腐烂；用它做家具，家具很快就会坏；用它做门的窗户，门的窗户很快就会流出污浆；用它做屋柱，屋柱很快就会被虫蛀。后来，这棵栎树托梦给木匠，并对他作了解释何谓无用之大用。木匠最后感叹说，像他和徒弟这样的常人喜欢用常理来衡量它，自然很难领会它存在的秘密和价值。在紧挨着的一则故事中，记载了河南商丘之大木，其枝叶可供千乘车马休息，仰看其枝条是拳曲的，无法做栋梁，俯视其大根则满是疤结不能做棺椁，尝其叶则口舌溃烂，闻其味则大醉，三天不醒。已得道的南伯子綦从中领悟到了不材之木存在的奥秘和价值，认为此木奇异的地方就是，它不被世俗看作有用处而被占领和扭折，从而成长不受影响。而梨树、橘树、柚树之所以永远不能长得更大，是因为一旦这些树以有用的方式，即以果实成熟的方式现身，这些树的树枝就遭折断、果实遭剥落。不材之木能够长得这么大，是因为免于被世俗的用处所占据和捆绑。

庄子对大自然的观察和描写有两个特点。

一是他尊重万物自身的存在。在地籁之音的故事中，庄子对山林之风所过之处、所留之迹、声音的捕捉，如神来之笔；对风吹过树林时树干倾斜的姿势的描写，体贴入微。相比对风

the wind, the afore-mentioned stories about the river god and the sea and the useless tree were not able to fully manifest his descriptive power, turning into a philosophical discussion before completing the descriptions.

Though Zhuangzi had a tendency to use nature to express his philosophical ideas, he did not typically take it beyond its limitations. He listened with great respect and admiration to all things. In this respect, he differed from many later writers who also described the forms, personalities, and habits of plants and animals. These authors, however, did not focus on the creatures themselves, but rather made them into metaphors, or vehicles for expressing the author's own intentions. The plants and animals described by these authors thus became "objective correlatives" of the authors' subjective nature. For example, Mi Heng's "Ode to the Parrot" in and Zhao Yi's "Ode to the Desperate Bird" used birds to describe the author's own situation. Du Fu's "Ode to the Eagle," Han Yu's "On Horses," Liu Zongyuan's "Three Lessons," Dai Mingshi's of Qing Dynasty "On Birds," Gong Zizhen's "Story of Sick Plum Trees," etc., all use objects or animals to express melancholy or to satirize worldly things.

In Zhuangzi's eyes, nature was more than what we think of today as "scenery." That is to say, Zhuangzi had not yet developed an understanding of nature as scenery to be appreciated in and of itself. Zhuangzi did not pay sufficient attention to the form, color, and appearance of things. It was not until the Six Dynasties Period that scenery began to be regarded as an independent source of beauty. Therefore, in Zhuangzi we do not find the kinds of diverse, many-layered beauty coupled with personal emotion that we do in the poems of post-Wei/Jin Dynasty poets. In these later poems, we read of peace and tranquility in lines such as, "The afterglow split into fine Damask / The clear river is as silent as white silk." We read of wide open spaces in verses such as, "The bright moon peeks over the mountains / Between the vast ocean of formless clouds." We read of gracefulness and smoothness in lines such as, "Under a light drizzling rain the minnows come out / Under a slight breeze the swallows dive and play." Finally, we read of vigor, force, and power in verses such as, "Broken boulders fly through the air / Billowing waves strike the shore / Throwing up a thousand piles of snow."

Second, Zhuangzi's writing is characterized by the way he connected his observation of material things and natural phenomena into a holistic view of existence and the *Dao*. In his comparisons of the portrayal of nature by Chinese and Western poets, Mr. Zhu Guangqian pointed out that poets usually have three kinds of love towards nature: "The most broad and superficial is

的描写，庄子在上述"望洋兴叹"和"无用之树"的故事中，对自然的描写还没有来得及充分展示，就被某种带有结论性的哲理所结束。

虽然，庄子存在借自然之物表达某种哲理的倾向，但总体比较节制。他对万物还保持着聆听和尊重，而不像一些后世作家也写动植物的形态、习性，但落脚点不在动植物身上，而是将动植物作为作者某种寓意、思想的载体，即作者借所托之物言自我之志，动植物成了作者主观意向的"客观对应物"。如咏物赋中，祢衡的《鹦鹉赋》、赵壹的《穷鸟赋》等借鸟自况，杜甫的《雕赋》、韩愈的《马说》、柳宗元的《三戒》、清戴名世的《鸟说》、龚自珍的《病梅馆记》等，都是借物抒发郁愤，或讥刺世俗。

大自然在庄子那里还不是今天意义上的"风景"，也就是说，作为独立的自然风景的意识在庄子那里还没有形成。庄子对物的形、色、貌也没有给予足够的关注，只有到了六朝，自然风景才作为独立的审美对象。所以，在《庄子》笔下很少有魏晋以后大自然在中国古代诗人笔下所具有的多种多样、多层次的美，并且维系着个人的情感和生命。自然界中既有"余霞散成绮，澄江静如练"的宁静与安详，也有"明月出天山，苍茫云海间"的辽阔与苍凉；既有"细雨鱼儿出，微风燕子斜"的优雅与细腻，也有"乱石穿空，惊涛拍岸，卷起千堆雪"的雄浑与大气。

二是庄子对天地、万物的观看，对日常场景中自然物象的观察，最终都与自然界的整体存在并与道联系在一起。朱光潜先生在比较中西诗人的自然观时明确地指出，诗人对自然的爱好可分三种："最粗浅的是'感官主义'，爱微风以其凉爽，爱

called 'sensualism.' This means loving wind for the coolness of its breeze, flowers for their colors and fragrance, chirpings birds and babbling springs for their pleasant sounds, as well as blue skies and clear water for their pleasant appearance. This is the natural tendency of all sane people, and poets cannot help but have a certain element of sensualism.... The second kind of love arises from the pleasant combination of interest with personality. This attitude is expressed by lines such as, 'The two gazed at each other tirelessly / Just only the Jingting Mountain remains', 'From across the wide plains one senses the wind / The young shoots carry a feeling of freshness,' and 'In stillness all things watch and are in harmony / At all times happy to be with humans.' This is the primary attitude of Chinese poets towards nature. The third category is 'pantheism', the view that all of nature is a manifestation of the gods. In observing nature we see unimaginable wonders, and we recognize a force that both surpasses man and controls him. The worship of nature thus becomes a kind of religion, encapsulating the philosophy of primitive superstitions and mysticism. This is the attitude of most western poets towards nature, and very few Chinese poets have attained this level." ❶ Among Chinese poets, Zhuangzi was the nearest to attaining the level of western poets in terms of his attitude towards nature. Zhuangzi's love of nature pushed him to search for the meaning behind its mystery. Perhaps his desire was not as strong as that of western poets, but at least he explored "the beauty of the heavens and earth, and the logic behind the existence of all things."

Zhuangzi's love and respect for the environment did not come from a desire for ecological conservation, even though by Zhuangzi's time, the Chinese people had already developed the custom and mindset of protecting nature. Furthermore, Zhuangzi's interest in nature was not limited to a leisurely pursuit of a peaceful place to live out his life. Rather, Zhuangzi's care for the environment stemmed from his realization that nature contains profound philosophical truths. Zhuangzi also acknowledged that mankind's dreams of freedom could be realized in nature as well. Through nature, man can better appreciate his own existence and rediscover himself. Zhuangzi used parables to transmit the lessons of nature to his readers. What can we learn from the pheasants in the marsh that inhabit marshy areas? Zhuangzi observed that pheasants were willing to walk ten paces for a mouthful of food and walk a hundred paces to for a sip of water; they did not desire to be kept in a cage, because they needed freedom and dignity above all else. They preferred to abandon carnal desires in favor of spiritual freedom and satisfaction. How can our perception of the world be enhanced through watching fish? In the chapter

花以其气香色美，爱鸟声泉水声以其对于听官愉快，爱青天碧水以其对于视官愉快。这是健全人所本有的倾向，凡是诗人都不免带有几分'感官主义'……诗人对于自然爱好的第二种起于情趣的默契欣合。'相看两不厌，惟有敬亭山'，'平畴交远风，良苗亦怀新'，'万物静观皆自得，四时佳兴与人同'诸诗所表现的态度都属于这一类。这是多数中国诗人对于自然的态度。第三种是泛神主义，把大自然全体看作神灵的表现，在其中看出不可思议的妙谛，觉到超于人而时时在支配人的力量。自然的崇拜于是成为一种宗教，它含有极原始的迷信和极神秘的哲学。这是多数西方诗人对于自然的态度，中国诗人很少有达到这种境界的。"❶若要在中国诗人中寻找类似于西方多数诗人对于自然的态度，庄子大概是比较接近的一个。庄子对自然的爱好有探求自然背后神秘的一面，虽没有西方诗人之强烈，但至少他有"原天地之美而达万物之理"的探询。

庄子这么喜欢和尊重大自然，不是出于生态保护的目的，虽然在庄子时代，中国人已经有了保护山林和渔猎资源的思想和惯例。自然万物之所以引起庄子的高度重视，也不仅仅是为了休闲，寻得一个人生静谧处，庄子对大自然的重视是因为庄子体悟到大自然中蕴藏着哲理，以及人类寻求自由的梦想。人类通过自然可以领悟存在，寻回自身。水泽中的野鸡能给人类什么启示呢？庄子观察到，水泽中的野鸡愿意走十步啄到一口食，走百步饮到一口水，并不祈求被养在笼子里，乃是因为它需要自由和生命的尊严，它宁愿放弃肉体上的欲望，而过一种精神上自得其乐、自由自在的生活。而鱼的生存境况又给我们

---

❶ 朱光潜：《诗论》，北京出版社，2005年版，第90页。

❶ Zhu Guangqian. *On Poetry*. Beijing Publishing Company, 2005, page 90.

"Great and Venerable Teacher," Zhuangzi observed, "When the springs dry up and the fish are left stranded on the ground, they spew each other with moisture and wet each other down with spit - but it would be much better if they could forget each other in the rivers and lakes." These lines mean that when the spring runs dry, the fish are trapped on dry land. They breathe moist water on each other and blow bubbles on each other to stay wet. However, instead of doing this, it would be better for them to forget each other in water-forget the existence of water, and forget having spent time together. This is because "to forget" symbolizes a certain degree of mental and behavioral freedom, that actions and feelings have not been bound down or limited, and represents a high level of harmony between oneself and the entirety of nature. To better understand this principle, imagine that you have a comfortable pair of shoes that fit your feet just right. When you put them on, it will be easy to forget that you even have shoes on at all. If you have a pair of shoes that do not fit your feet, then the shoes and your feet are not in harmony and you will begin to notice the shoe because it feels wrong. Fish are just like this; they swim in the water, and water becomes a part of them. When this happens, it is as if they can no longer feel the existence of the water because they have forgotten it.

Zhuangzi considered human life from the perspective of the natural universe. The power and magic of nature, the orderly succession of spring, summer, fall, and winter, the beauty and order found in the apparent chaos of life, and the natural law of birth, aging, and death were all principles that Zhuangzi incorporated into his philosophy.

In summary, the single greatest lesson that Zhuangzi gained from his observations of nature was this: the *Dao* flows through all things, all things exist in their own style, and man must respect the way of life of all things as well as the natural laws that govern the universe. This principle is exemplified in the chapter "Perfect Happiness," where we read the following story: there once was a sea bird that alighted in the suburbs of the capital of Lu. A powerful nobleman of Lu welcomed the bird into the ancestral temple, played ancient music for it, gave it fine wine, and butchered oxen and lambs to make a feast for it. But on seeing these things, the bird was sad and forlorn in its heart. It refused to eat even one piece of meat or drink even one sip of wine, and after three days it died. In Zhuangzi's opinion, this happened because the nobleman tried to raise the bird as he would a human and not after the manner of birds. Zhuangzi felt that to raise it after the manner of birds would have meant letting it return to nest in the forest, to fly above the shoals, to swoop and dive above the rivers and lakes, to catch small fish with its beak, to migrate with other

人类展现怎样的视野呢？庄子观察到，"泉涸，鱼相与处于陆，相呴（xǔ）以湿，相濡（rú）以沫，不如相忘于江湖。"（《大宗师》）意思是说，泉水干涸了，鱼被困在陆地上，它们就用湿气互相呼吸，用口沫互相湿润，它们倒不如在水里互相忘记——忘记水的存在，忘记与同伴在一起。因为"忘"表明了一种行为和心里意念的自由度，行动和感受上没有受到束缚和限制，表明了自己与整体环境所达到的深度和谐。就如你的鞋子很合你的脚，你就会遗忘鞋子正穿在脚上，一旦鞋子不合脚，即意味着鞋子与脚没有处在和谐状态，你就会注意鞋子，因为脚让你感觉不适。鱼也是这样，它在水中游，水已成为鱼的一个部分，此时，仿佛感觉不到水的存在，它已把水忘掉了。

大自然有其力量和魔力，春夏秋冬有序地更替，万物在纷杂中有秩序和大美，自然中有生老病死法则……这一切都促使庄子从自然宇宙的高度来思考人生。

总体来说，庄子从生生不息的自然界中获得的启示是：道在万物中运作，万物以自己的方式存在，人要尊重物的存在方式，尊重自然界的规律。《庄子·至乐》篇讲述了这样一个故事：从前有一只海鸟飞落在鲁国的郊外，鲁国的权贵就把它迎进了宗庙，还给它奏古乐，送美酒，宰牛羊，但海鸟看着这些东西，心生悲戚，不吃一块肉，不饮一杯酒，三天后就死了。庄子认为，这是用养人的方法来养鸟，不是用养鸟的方式来养鸟。所谓用养鸟的方式就是应该让鸟回到树林中栖息，在沙洲上飞翔，在江湖上飘游，啄着泥鳅小鱼，随鸟群迁徙，过自由

flocks of birds, and to live a free life. "Raising a bird like oneself" means to control and conquer nature, while "raising a bird like a bird" means going along with natural laws. Because of Zhuangzi's profound respect for all living things, he adopted a friendly and respectful attitude towards all creatures, living in harmony with nature.

自在的生活。"以己养鸟"是控制自然和征服自然，"以鸟养鸟"则是遵循自然的习性和规律。庄子因着对万物各自存在方式的尊重，在与一切存在物打交道的过程中采取了友好与尊重的态度，与万物和谐相处。

战国时期乐器——编钟

Musical Instrument of the Warring States Period—Chime

九　生活庄子

Chapter IX　Zhuangzi and Life

Some people live and yet never enter life; rather than truly experiencing it, they merely go through life mechanically. Some people live and yet do not ponder about life. Some people have a high standard of living and yet do not know how to experience or enjoy life. They are unable to capture the meaning and value of human life. Zhuangzi not only entered life, but he also sank his roots deep into the essence of it; he pondered on life and appreciated fully all that life had to offer him.

I. Entering Lower-class life

Throughout his life, Zhuangzi inhabited the lowest level of society. Because of this, most of his interaction was with poor laborers, and he became familiar with their skill and methods of work. In *Zhuangzi*, we read of the daily labor of many professions in the following stories: "Pao Ding Cuts the Ox," "Lun Bian Fashions the Wheel," "The Hunchback Catches Cicadas," "The Stonecutter Creates a Gust of Wind with his Axe," "The Bocheng Zigao Planting his Fields," "The Old Man who Watered his Fields with a Pitcher under his Arm," and "The Man of Song who Bleached Silk." We can also read of the customs of daily life in the following stories: "The Ferryman Navigates the Boat," "The Boy of Lü liang who Stepped in the Water," "The Soothsayers Read Palms," "Dog and Cockfights," "Fishing and Watching Fish," etc.

Zhuangzi paid careful attention to the plants and animals that he observed on a daily basis. His nearness to nature made his observations precise and his records detailed; among the pre-Qin scholars, this was very rare. In *Zhuangzi*, the following animals are mentioned: cicadas, sparrows, mantes, mosquitoes, fish, oxen, loaches, stags, wild chickens, monkeys, butterflies, moles, etc. The following plants are mentioned: pine trees, cypress trees, gourd plants, tree cracks, etc. The following natural phenomena are mentioned: wind, water, rivers, lakes, etc. Zhuangzi was also familiar with how these living creatures and natural phenomena lived and interacted with each other. In the chapter "External Things," we read of humans eating meat, stags eating grass, centipedes eating small snakes, owls and crows eating mice, macaques associating with female apes, stags associating with deer, loaches swimming with other fish, and of "fish who do not fear nets but fear pelicans."

From his observations of daily life, Zhuangzi was able to develop many of his teachings on life. In parables such as "The Monkey that Wanted Three Chestnuts in the Morning and Four at Night," "The Mantis Blocks the Wagon with His Arm," and, "The Mantis Hunts the Cicada with an Oriole Hunting

有些人有生活，却没有进入生活，他或她仅仅是经历，而不是体验生活；有些人有生活，却没有生活的思考；有些人拥有很好的生活条件，但却不会感受生活和享受生活，捕捉不到生活中溢出来的人生意义和价值感。庄子，他进入了生活，并扎根下去；他在生活中思考，也充分享受了生活所赠予他的一切。

（一） 进入底层生活

庄子一生，始终生活在社会最下层，所以他对下层劳动人民接触最多，对他们的日常生活和他们的技艺、劳作过程非常了解。《庄子》中写到各行各业从事日常生产劳动的有：庖丁解牛、轮扁斫轮、痀偻承蜩、匠石运斤成风、伯成子高耕在野、菜园老翁抱瓮灌圃、宋人漂洗丝絮为业；写到日常生活场景和生活习性的有：津人操舟、吕梁男子蹈水、神巫看相、相狗斗鸡、钓鱼观鱼等。

庄子对日常生活中所常见的各类动植物、自然景象也有近距离的观察和描摹，其观察之细，记载之详，在先秦诸子中是少有的。以《庄子》中内七篇论，提到的动物有蜩、学鸠、螳螂、蚊虫、鱼、牛、泥鳅、麋鹿、野鸡、猴子、蝴蝶、鼹鼠等；植物有松柏、大瓠（葫芦）、树窍等；自然景象有风、水、江、湖等。庄子对生物的习性很了解，提到人吃肉类，麋鹿吃青草，蜈蚣喜欢吃小蛇，猫头鹰与乌鸦喜欢吃老鼠，也提到狙与雌猿交配，麇与鹿作伴，泥鳅与鱼共游，还观察到"鱼不畏纲而畏鹈鹕"（《庄子·外物》）。

庄子也通过观察生物的规律和习性引申出人生的一些经验和教训，"朝三暮四"、"螳臂当车"和"螳螂捕蝉，黄雀在后"等成语故事讲述的都是人生的某些哲理。《庄子·齐物论》记

him," we learn truths about the nature of the human condition. In the chapter "Discussion on Making All Things Equal," we find the story of a man who raised a monkey. He gave the monkey a chestnut, saying, "You can have three in the morning, and four at night." When the monkey heard it, he was very angry, thinking that his master was giving him less food. When confronted with the displeased monkey, the master said, "Alright, you can have four in the morning and three at night." The monkey heard this and was immediately appeased. Though the amount the monkey would receive did not change, by changing the way in which it was offered, the monkey's mood changed from angry to happy. In the chapter "In the World of Men," we read the following story: "Don't you know about the mantis that waved its arms angrily in front of an approaching wagon, unaware that they were incapable of stopping it? Such was the high opinion it had of its talents." This story tells of a praying mantis that raised its arms in an effort to stop the wheels of a carriage. The mantis did not know that its own strength was not up to the task, the whole time judging itself to be very powerful. The proverb "The Mantis Blocks the Wagon with His Arm" has its origin in this story; it is used to poke fun at those people who don't know the limits to their power. "The Mantis hunts the Cicada with an Oriole Hunting him" tells of a cicada which had just found a bit of shade to relax in, when he let down his guard, not knowing that a few paces away lurked a mantis ready to attack it. At the same time, there was an oriole eyeing the mantis and preparing to pounce. Zhuangzi hid behind the oriole, sling at the ready, while behind Zhuangzi there stood the keeper of the garden, poised to arrest him for acting like a thief. This story reminds readers to not only pay attention to the prize in front, but also to be wary of the hidden dangers lurking behind.

Ⅱ. Meditating on Life

Unlike the other philosophers of the Spring Autumn and Warring States Periods-Confucius and Mencius of Confucianism, Mozi of Mohism, and Han Fei of Legalism-Zhuangzi did not devote himself to grand policies that would establish the government and bring peace. He neither attempted to prescribe a cure for securing societal order or saving the common people, nor traveled far and wide promoting his philosophy. In contrast, Zhuangzi's contemporary, Mencius, kept regular contact with such rulers as King Hui of Liang, King Xuan of Qi, and the ruler of Zhuangzi's own country, Lord Yan of Song, in order to promote his philosophy of benevolent government. Mencius even traveled to Song to push for political reform. In addition to not actively

载：有一个养猴的人拿栗子喂猴子，说："早上三升，晚上四升。"猴子听了很生气，认为主人给食少了。主人改口说："早上四升，晚上三升"，猴子听了马上就很高兴。内容实质没有改变，但语言表达的改变却可以左右猴子的喜怒。《庄子·人间世》云："汝不知夫螳螂乎？怒其臂以当车辙，不知其不胜任也，是其才之美者也。"意思是说，螳螂奋力举起手臂来抵挡车轮，不知道自己的力气是无法胜任的，还以为自己本领高强呢。"螳臂当车"的成语便由此而生，用于嘲笑那些不自量力的人。一只蝉刚刚找到可以安息的树荫，放松了警惕，忘记了自身的安全，不知道几步之外有只螳螂躲在隐秘的树林中，随时准备捕捉它，而此时怪鹊也盯着螳螂准备下手。怪鹊的背后则偷偷站着手拿弹弓的庄子，而在庄子的不远处则有守园人怀疑这一园中的可疑人物，随时准备把他当小偷盘问。"螳螂捕蝉，黄雀在后"的故事提醒人们不要只顾眼前利益而不考虑后患。

（二） 在生活中思考

在春秋战国时期，庄子不像儒家的孔子和孟子，墨家的墨子，法家的韩非子那样热衷于提出安邦定国的政治策略，开出安定社会秩序、拯救天下苍生的社会药方，也没有像他们那样到处游说，推广自己的政治理想。比如与他同时期的孟子，为了推广其"仁政"，与梁惠王、齐宣王，以及庄子国家的元首宋君偃，都有直接的交往，曾到宋国搞过政治改革；庄子也不关注历史的宏大叙事，甚至在书中也很少正面记载发生在战国

promoting his philosophy, Zhuangzi also did not care for great historical narratives; in his own writing, he rarely mentioned the earth-shattering events of the Warring States Period, such as palace coups, great battles, and political maneuverings. Rather, he turned his attention to how the wars, turbulence, and slaughters affected the safety, freedom, and happiness of individuals. Zhuangzi's answer to the ills of human life was "free and easy wandering."

Zhuangzi focused on the birth, aging, sickness, debilitation, and death of man. Zhuangzi realized that governments and the various schools of thought were unable to support the individual destinies of the people, so he paid particular attention to their lives and suffering. In *Zhuangzi*, there are many examples of the helplessness and pain that face people who deal with inexplicable sickness and disease. The following quotations relate a few of these stories:

> "All at once Zi Yu fell ill. Zi Si went to ask how he was. "Amazing" said Zi Yu. "The Creator is making me all crooked like this! My back sticks up like a hunchback and my vital organs are on top of me. My chin is hidden in my navel, my shoulders are up above my head, and my pigtail points at the sky. "
>
> Suddenly Master Lai grew ill. Gasping and wheezing, he lay at the point of death. His wife and children gathered round in a circle and began to cry.
>
> After some time had passed without event, Master Sang-hu died but had not yet been buried.
>
> Suddenly a tumour sprouted out of Uncle Lame-Gait's left elbow. He looked very startled and seemed to be annoyed.

Zhuangzi also cared for disabled people. Many of the characters in Zhuangzi's parables were people who had been handicapped as punishment for breaking the law or offending government officials. For example, he often discusses *wu*, or punishment by cutting off the feet. The Daoist monk Cheng Xuanying of the Tang Dynasty commented *wu* thus: "Cutting off one foot is called *wu*." Characters such as Wang Tai, Shentu Jia, and toeless Shu Shan are examples of characters who suffered this punishment.

Zhuangzi often pondered the meaning and value of life, believing that life had a deeper purpose than the one defined by society. In the chapter "The Sign of Virtue Complete," Zhuangzi wrote of the outstanding moral character of many disabled people. Even though these people were physically disabled, their lives were full of vigor and power, and they were thus able to inspire others. By describing the moral strength of these "incomplete" people,

时期那些惊天动地、改天换地的大事件，比如宫廷政变、征战杀伐、政治外交，而是关注在这个荒谬、动荡，到处战争杀戮，充满人生无常和苦难的世上，个人如何安身立命，个人如何在有限的生存空间中活得快乐和自由。庄子的回答是"逍遥游"。

庄子关注、思考人的生、老、病、残、死。他意识到，家与国不能承担个体自身的命运，比如人的生、老、病、残、死，所以他特别关注个体的生死爱欲与痛感。《庄子》中多次描述了无来由的疾病以及身患疾病的不幸、无奈：

> 俄而子舆有病，子祀往问之。曰："伟哉！夫造物者将以予为此拘拘也。"曲偻发背，上有五管，颐隐于齐，肩高于颈，句赘指天。❶

> 俄而子来有病，喘喘然将死。其妻子环而泣之。❷

> 莫然有间，而子桑户死，未葬。❸

> （滑介叔）俄而柳❹生其左肘，其意蹶蹶然恶之。❺

庄子也关心残疾人。庄子笔下很多寓言人物是刑残之人，如兀"兀"为断足之刑，唐代道士成玄英疏："刖一足曰兀。"者王骀、申徒嘉、叔山无趾等。

庄子思考生命的意义和价值，认为生命的意义和价值大于社会所设定的目标和功能。《德充符》篇记载了许多残畸之人的德行，他们虽身体残疾，但他们生命中所流露出的精神力量，能吸引他人。庄子通过对一大批形体残疾者的形象的塑造，来

---

❶ 不久，子舆生病了，子祀前去探望。子舆说："伟大啊！造物主竟然把我弄成这副蜷曲的样子。"子舆病得弯腰驼背，五脏挤在背部，脸颊藏在肚脐下，双肩高过头顶，发髻朝向天空。
❷ 不久，子来又病了，呼吸急促，将要死的样子，他的妻子儿女坐在床边哭泣。
❸ 过了一段日子，子桑户突然死了，还未下葬。
❹ "柳"借为"瘤"。
❺ 滑介叔左臂上生了个瘤，他本能地露出厌恶的表情。

Zhuangzi was able to bring out the significance and completeness of true morality.

In considering the complexity of society and the capriciousness of human relations, Zhuangzi's goal was to find a way to preserve the completeness of his heart, and avoid being tempted by worldly trends, bound down by mainstream culture, or hurt by the cruelty of the world.

Because of this, Zhuangzi unabashedly and untiringly criticized the Confucian concepts of benevolence, morality, and emphasis on fame. He felt that by focusing single-mindedly on these things, they had damaged and restricted the natural growth of life. This notion can be seen in the story of a high official of the state of Zheng, Zi Chan, who learned of the *Dao* from the authentic man, Bohun Wuren with his condiciple, Shentu Jia, a man who had lost one foot. Because Zi Chan enjoyed a whole and healthy body, and because of his pride in being a great man of politics, he had nothing but disdain for the cripple Shentu Jia. When walking past Jia, Zi Chan would put on airs, asking him to dodge. Shentu Jia felt that Zi Chan's actions were inappropriate. Zi Chan desired to learn of the *Dao*, but did not understand that one communicates with the *Dao* in the spiritual world within one's physical form. As long as Zi Chan evaluated the worth of others based on outward appearances and worldly position, he would be unable to truly learn the *Dao*. When Shentu Jia told this to Zi Chan, Zi Chan was deeply ashamed.

Money was another evil in life that Zhuangzi criticized. During the Warring States Period, there were many scholars who only obeyed their employers, worshipped money, and in the end, became slaves to money. Zhuangzi chose to satirize Cao Shang, a scholar who was controlled by money. Cao Shang of Song was to represent the State of Song and travel to Qin on a diplomatic mission. Before he left, the king of Song gave him several carriages. While in Qin, Cao Shang won the appreciation of the king of Qin, receiving one hundred carriages from him. On the way back to Song, Cao Shang stopped by Zhuangzi to boast of his wealth, commenting sarcastically to Zhuangzi, "You live in a shabby back alley, you weave straw sandals for a living, you are so hungry your face turns yellow and your body is wasted away; you are nowhere as good as I am. When I left from meeting with the emperor, a hundred carriages followed me. This is because of my extraordinary abilities." Zhuangzi replied, "When the king of Qin gets a hemorrhoid, he calls for a doctor. To the one who claims to be able to cure hemorrhoids by squeezing out the pus, he gives one carriage as a gift. To the doctor who licks the hemorrhoid to cure it, he gives five carriages. The more disgusting the

突显出德性的完全及意义。

在错综复杂的社会中，在险恶的人世间，如何最大限度地保全身与心的完整，而不被各种世俗流行所诱惑，不被主流文化所捆绑，不被残酷的世界所伤害，这是庄子所要思考的。

也正因为这样，庄子才不遗余力地抨击儒家的仁义道德和功名利禄，认为他们过分追求的这些东西捆绑和损害了生命内在的成长，就如郑国大夫子产与断了一只脚的申徒嘉同在真人伯昏无人门下学道，子产因着自身形体健康，又是执政大人而自傲，看不起形残位卑的同门师兄弟，在申徒嘉面前摆架子，要他回避自己。申徒嘉认为子产这样的言行有些过分，因为来这里是求学修德，是在形骸之内（精神世界中）以德相交，而子产却在形骸之外用外貌和地位来衡量人，根本不是来学道的。子产听了很惭愧。

对生命的戕害还有金钱。战国时代无数士人只认"有奶便是娘"，对金钱膜拜，结果自身成了金钱的奴隶。曹商就是一个典型的例子，庄子对此作了讽刺。宋人曹商，代表宋王出使秦国。他出发时，从宋王那里获得了几辆马车。到了秦国后曹商博得秦王欢心，秦王又赐他一百辆马车。返回宋国后，他在庄子面前炫耀自己的富贵，并讽刺庄子说："住在穷街陋巷，窘困地织草鞋为生，饿得面黄肌瘦，这是我不及的。一旦见到万乘之君，就有百辆马车跟在我后面，那是我的过人之处。"庄子说："秦王得了痔疮请医生，说能挤破痔疮消除脓肿的，

cure, the more carriages he gives. I suppose you must have licked the hemorrhoid of the king of Qin? Why else would he have given you so many carriages? Get out of my presence!"

Zhuangzi clearly understood the corrupting influence that power could have on human nature. In the chapters "Autumn Floods" and "Lie Yukou" of *Zhuangzi* as well as *Record of the Grand Historian: Biography of Laozi and Han Fei*, we find the story of the time Zhuangzi refused to be hired as prime minister of Chu. The story tells of King Wei of Chu, who, hearing of Zhuangzi's fame, sent two officials to offer him the position of prime minister. Zhuangzi was not home, but was fishing along the Pu River. When they approached Zhuangzi and recounted to him why they were there, Zhuangzi said, "Have you ever seen the sacrificial oxen before they are slaughtered? They are dressed in multicolored cloaks, they eat the finest grass and beans, and after a few years of good treatment, they are led to the ancestral temple of emperors where they are butchered and sacrificed. By that time, it is already too late for them to be simple, lonely oxen. You might as well leave; I would rather be a living turtle, dragging my tail and playing in the mud, than a dead holy turtle, put on display in the ancestral temple. I refuse to be bound down by any ruler. I am determined to live out my days outside of the court, with happiness as my life's endeavor."

Zhuangzi once passed through the State of Wei, arousing the suspicions of his friend Hui Shi, who was the prime minister of Wei at the time. Hui Shi feared that Zhuangzi would supplant him, and so for three days and three nights, he ordered men to search for Zhuangzi all throughout Wei. Zhuangzi, however, was not interested in being any kind of minister. In Zhuangzi's words, only owls are interested in rotten mice (representing the post of prime minister); Zhuangzi considered himself a *yuan* (like a phoenix) who was, "Only willing to perch in Chinese parasol trees, eat bamboo fruit, and drink sweet spring water." Not far to the west of Zhuangzi's hometown, the Jixia Academy also opened its doors to Zhuangzi. If he had wanted to, he could have easily used his talents to enter the academy and provide "consulting services" to various rulers; he never did, however, attend the academy.

Ⅲ. Appreciating Life

Of all the pre-Qin scholars, Zhuangzi was the most successful at appreciating life and living according to the dictates of his inborn nature. Confucius emphasized, "travel in art, succeed in music," holding "yearning for nature and passing one's life in quiet tranquility" as the standard for

赏车一辆；舔好痔疮的，赏车五辆；所治疗的方式越卑贱，赏赐的马车越多。你大概为秦王舔了痔疮吧？为何赏的车子竟有这么多？你快走开吧！"

庄子也清醒地意识到权力对人性的腐蚀。《庄子·秋水》、《庄子·列御寇》、《史记·老子韩非列传》都记载了庄子辞楚王聘相的史实。楚威王听说了庄子的大名，派两位大夫去聘他为相。庄子不在家，正在濮水岸边钓鱼。当听明他们来意后，庄子说："你们有没有看见祭祀用的活牛？披的是五彩绣衣，吃的是青草大豆，养了几年后被牵到太庙宰杀献祭，到那时再想做一头孤单的小牛就来不及了。你们走吧，我宁愿做活着的乌龟，拖着尾巴在污泥中快活游戏，而不愿做已死的神龟被供奉在庙堂之上。我不想被君主约束，我决意终身不仕，以快吾志。"

庄子曾路过魏国，引起当时魏国的宰相，也是他的朋友惠施对他的心存戒惧，担心庄子抢夺他的饭碗，专门派人在国内三天三夜搜捕他，但庄子对魏国的相位不感兴趣，用他自己的话说，只有猫头鹰对腐鼠（相位）感兴趣，他是鹓（凤凰），"非梧桐不止，非练实不食，非醴泉不饮"。在离庄子家乡不远的西边，当时齐国的稷下学宫的大门也向他敞开着，只要他愿意，凭他的才华，可以轻而易举加入到"为君主提供咨询服务"的行列，但他也没有去。

（三） 享受生活

在先秦诸子中懂得享受生活，率性而为的要数庄子。孔子强调"游于艺，成于乐"，有"向往自然、恬静生活"的审美情怀。但孔子一生主要成就的是道德的境界。他对后人教导和影响的是如何成为圣人，尤其是仁义道德方面的圣人。他给中国文化影响最大的是提供人伦关系和安置社会秩序。孟子则过

emotional fulfillment. However, Confucius' life was limited to the level of morality. He taught future generations how to become sages, putting special emphasis on benevolence and morality. His greatest influence on Chinese culture was his development of concepts of proper human relationships and his establishment of societal order. Mencius' opinion of his own aspirations and those ideas with which he agreed was too high, which resulted in his caustic criticism of those philosophers that did not suit him, such as Yang Zhu or Mozi. Because Yang Zhu taught to act in one's own profit, Mencius said Yang Zhu was too self-centered, that he did not put enough emphasis on the role of the ruler; because Mozi's teachings promoted unconditional love (universal love) and did not place enough emphasis on fathers, Mencius said his philosophy was "fatherless." Of these philosophers, Mencius wrote, "Rulerless and fatherless, they are just like beasts and birds." However, Mencius himself was too serious in life; he probably would not have even known how to joke around. Laozi, on the other hand, was too drawn into himself; when discussing the great events taking place in the world, he would always talk as if they had no effect on him at all, displaying an air of indifference to the changes in the world. Laozi wrote, "There is no benevolence in heaven or earth and all creatures are treated like dogs; sages are cruel, they treat commoners like dogs" (From *The Wisdom of Daoism*, chapter five). This means that heaven and earth do not play favorites, but rather allow all things to run their natural course, living or dying as they will; in the same way, the sage does not play favorites, but rather allows all people to be the masters of their own destinies instead of interfering with them. Mozi was overly focused on asceticism. Mencius wrote that Mozi was always trying to serve the people. Even if his whole body was ground to pieces, he would continue to disregard his own discomfort and work for the benefit of the people of the world. This is the principal of living without rest and struggling without cease. People like this are not able to live according to the dictates of their natures or truly appreciate life. In contrast to all these philosophers, Zhuangzi spent his life teaching, debating, traveling, transmitting knowledge of the *Dao*, fishing, receiving disciples, living in shabby alleys, weaving straw sandals, making appearances in court, mingling with the lowly people in society, and in general, living a life of freedom.

One of Zhuangzi's greatest accomplishments in life was bringing art into life. This can be seen in the following ways:

Traveling in His Mind. French author Victor Hugo once said, "The sky is broadest, the ocean is broader than the sky, and the spirit is broader than the ocean." What Zhuangzi pursued was a mental state of "heaven and earth

于看重自己的抱负和所认定的东西，对不合自己口味的如杨朱、墨家就骂。因前者提倡为我，后者提倡无等差的爱（"兼爱"），孟子就骂前者太自我中心，眼中没有皇帝，是无君也；后者不把父亲放在眼里，是无父也，"无君无父，是禽兽也"。孟子这样的人活得太正经，估计连玩笑也开不得。而老子又太内敛，在讲述天下大事时，好像与己无关，一副沧海桑田后的冷漠，所谓"天地不仁，以万物为刍狗；圣人不仁，以百姓为刍狗。"（《道德经·第五章》）意思是说，天地不会因仁慈而有所偏爱，任由万物自然运作，自生自灭；圣人不会因仁慈而有所偏爱，任由百姓自己主宰自己的命运而不加干预。墨子则太追求苦行，"墨子兼爱，摩顶放踵利天下，为之。"（《孟子·尽心上》）意思是说，墨子要永远为天下人民服务，哪怕从头顶到脚跟都磨伤了，还是不辞劳苦，不顾身体疲劳，为天下人工作。所谓生命不息，奋斗不止。这样的人也不太会率性而为，享受生活。而庄子一生讲学、论辩、游历、传道、钓鱼、授徒，居陋巷，编草鞋，出入庙堂之上，混迹于贩夫走卒之间，过着自由自在的生活。

庄子一生所成就的是人生的艺术化。庄子艺术化的人生主要体现在：

游心。法国作家雨果说过，最广阔的是天空，比天空还广阔的是海洋，比海洋更广阔的是心灵。庄子所追求的正是"天

existing with me and unity with all things." Zhuangzi desired to be at one with the Creator and at the same time make friends with people who had surpassed ordinary life and were able to "forget" all things. He wrote, "I desire only to correspond with the essence of heaven and earth." Zhuangzi looked down on all living things from the perspective of one who gazed on the universe, not from the perspective of one who crawled about on the surface of the earth. Because of the vastness of Zhuangzi's spiritual world, he had enough space for mental journeying.

Traveling for Pleasure. After resigning as manager of the lacquer tree orchard, we read in the chapters "Mountain Tree," "Perfect Happiness," and "Tian Zifang" that Zhuangzi traveled west to Wei, east to Lu, and south to Chu ❶. Zhuangzi's many travels and experiences gave him a clear view and profound understanding of the reality of society.

Zhuangzi often traveled around near his home. Examples of this include:

> The story of Zhuangzi and Hui Shi walking along the bridge on the Hao River, mentioned in the chapter "Autumn Floods." The story of Zhuangzi walking in the mountains... and stopping at the house of an old friend, mentioned in the chapter "The Mountain Tree," and the story of Zhuangzi wandering through the garden plot at Diaoling.

The complete story of Zhuangzi's walk on the bridge on the Hao River is as follows: Zhuangzi and Hui Shi were leisurely strolling along the river. Zhuangzi said, "Look at the white fish in the water. How carefree they are as they swim back and forth! This is the happiness of fish." Hui Shi said, "You are not a fish, how do you know if the fish are happy?" Zhuangzi replied, "You are not me, how do you know that I don't know if fish are happy?" Hui Shi retorted, "I am not you, of course I do not know your situation; likewise, you are not a fish, so you do not know if the fish are happy. This should be obvious." Zhuangzi countered, "Let us return to what we said in the beginning. When you asked how I know if the fish are happy, you already knew that I knew the fish were happy, that is why you asked me. You let me tell you how I know-I know it by standing on the bridge on the Hao River!"

The attitudes adopted by Zhuangzi and Hui Shi towards the same fish in the same Hao River were very different. Zhuangzi's attitude was one of

地与我并生，而万物与我为一"的境界。他在上要与造物者同游，在下与超脱生死、忘怀始终的人做朋友。"独与天地精神往来"。庄子是用宇宙人的高度来俯视芸芸众生，而不是以爬行的方式匍匐在地上生活。庄子也因着心灵世界的开阔，所以能游于心，因为游，需要足够的空间。

游历。庄子辞掉漆园吏之职后，曾经西游魏，东游鲁，南游楚❶。广泛的游历、见闻，使他对社会现实有了清醒和深刻的认识。

庄子也常在住的附近游玩：

庄子与惠子游于濠梁之上。(《庄子·秋水》)

庄子行于山中，……舍于故人之家。(《庄子·山木》)

庄周游乎雕陵之樊。(《山木》)

濠梁之游的完整故事版本是这样的：庄子与惠子在濠水的桥上游览。庄子曰："白鱼在水中，从容地游来游去，这是鱼的快乐。"惠子（即惠施）说："你不是鱼，怎么知道鱼的快乐？"庄子说："你不是我，怎么知道我不知道鱼的快乐？"惠子说："我不是你，当然不知道你的情况；而你不是鱼，所以你不知道鱼的快乐，这是很明显的。"庄子说："还是回到我们开头所谈的。你说'你怎么知道鱼快乐'这句话时，你已经知道我知道鱼快乐才来问我。现在我来告诉你，我是在濠水的桥上知道的啊！"

对于同一濠水之鱼，庄子与惠子采取了两种不同的态度。

---

❶ 分别见《庄子》中的《山木》、《至乐》、《田子方》等篇《田子方》篇记载庄子见鲁哀公，但鲁哀公与孔子同时，跟庄子相差200余年，庄子不可能见到鲁哀公。郭沫若说，哀公有可能系景公之误，则非寓言，所以，姑且存此一说。

❶ In "Tian Zifang" is the record of Zhuangzi's meeting with Duke Ai of Lu; however, this "meeting" was a fictitious one, because Duke Ai of Lu was a contemporary of Confucius, and lived over 200 years before Zhuangzi. Consequently, it was impossible for the two to have met. Guo Moruo said that using the name Duke Ai of Lu was perhaps a mistake, and therefore not a parable. Because of this, we will leave the name unchanged for now.

appreciation for beauty that sensed the happiness of the fish using subjective aesthetic emotions; Hui Shi, on the other hand, had a cognitive, logical approach to the fish in the stream. He argued that since Zhuangzi and the fish were two different kinds of beings, it was impossible for Zhuangzi to use his own knowledge or his own perception of happiness to evaluate the knowledge or happiness of other animals or people. From a logical standpoint, Hui Shi was not wrong, and from an aesthetic standpoint, Zhuangzi was not wrong. The key is, would you rather spend leisure time with Zhuangzi or Hui Shi? Most people would probably want to be with Zhuangzi, because when walking leisurely, one must use emotions to experience life, and not logic to analyze life. If not, life becomes dull and one is unable to experience the joy that comes from moving at a more leisurely pace.

Traveling to Learn. Zhuangzi received a good education and understood the philosophies of his predecessors. In his writings, he often mentioned Confucius, Laozi, and occasionally touched on other pre-Qin schools of thought, such as Mohism, Yang Zhu's philosophy, as well as the teachings of the Jixia Academy and the Logicians. Because of the breadth of Zhuangzi's learning, Sima Qian wrote in *The Records of the Grand Historian*, "There is no field to which his learning did not extend." However, Zhuangzi was one of the ancient scholars who, "learned for themselves," so his purpose in learning was to cultivate his own learning and moral character, rather than create a stepping-stone to success or to show off to others. Because of this, Zhuangzi's education was not too tiring and not very utilitarian either.

Traveling for Art. Zhuangzi's literary excellence is well-recognized by history and historians. Guo Xiang of the Jin Dynasty wrote that his literary talent was, "the champion of all the hundred schools of thought." Gao Sisun of the Song Dynasty wrote that, "His diction was meaningful, complete, and as fresh as a spring rose; he was the greatest talent of his generation." Ma Xulun of the Republican Period wrote, "His diction was interesting and profound, deeper than any of the late Zhou Dynasty scholars." Zhuangzi's training in the arts was also excellent. In the chapter "The Turning of Heaven," there is a passage that begins with "Beimen Cheng said to the Yellow Emperor..." in which Zhuangzi wrote a detailed description of music, which could only have been written by a person who was very familiar with music. The story of Pao Ding cutting the ox in "The Secret of Caring for Life" was written with a dance-like rhythm. The story tells of a chef who was to butcher an ox for Lord Wenhui. Zhuangzi described in great detail the noise made by everything that the chef touched with his hands, leaned against with his shoulders, stepped on

庄子对鱼采取审美的观照，以主观性的审美态度感受鱼的快乐；惠子则对鱼采取逻辑和认知的态度，他认为庄子与鱼是两个不同类的事物，很难从"我"的知或"我"的乐推理出他人、他物的知和乐，以及我与他人、他物共知或共乐。从逻辑学上来说，惠子也没有错，从美学角度来说，庄子也没有错。关键是，如果你与庄子、惠子共游，你喜欢与庄子在一起，还是与惠子在一起呢？相信大多人会选择与庄子在一起，因为这是在游玩，要用感觉去感受生活，而不是用逻辑去推理生活，否则人生会变得无趣，也享受不到游玩中的乐趣。

游学。庄子有很好的学问，他了解先贤们的各种思想。他在书中常提到儒家学派孔子、道家学派老子，也广涉先秦其他学派，如墨家学派、杨朱学派、稷下黄老新道家、名家等。因此司马迁在《史记》中赞扬他"于学无所不窥"。但庄子属于"古之学者为己"行列，学习的目的在于修养自己的学问和品德，而不是以学问作为敲门砖，或装饰自己给别人看，所以庄子治学不会那么累，功利性也不会太强。

游艺。庄子的文学修养是历史公认的。晋代郭象说他文学才华为"百家之冠"；宋代高似孙说他"文辞隽健，自作瑰新，亦一代之奇才乎"；民国的马叙伦说他"辞趣华深，度越晚周诸子"。庄子的艺术修养也很好，《天运》篇中的"北门成问于黄帝曰"段有关音乐的描写，只有对音乐有很深修养的人才能描绘得出。至于《养生主》篇中的"庖丁解牛"故事更是一种踏着舞蹈和音乐节奏来描写的。有一名厨师，替文惠君杀牛。他手所接触的，肩所依靠的，脚所踩踏的，膝所抵住的，无不

with his feet, or kneeled on with his knees. The chef's knife was sheathed with a scraping noise, interrupting the rhythm of the narration. This is similar to *The Mulberry Orchard* ❶ . It is also similar to *Jing Shou* ❷ .The process by which Pao Ding cut the ox was "felt with the spirit and not seen with the eyes," "according to the principles of heaven," "according to the natural way," and "followed the natural rhythm and logic of the ox." The blade which he used "had no thickness and was inserted into tiny spaces, and there was still plenty of room... more than enough for the blade to play about it." Finally, with a great crash, the ox was cut into pieces, just like mud falling onto the ground, and without knowing quite how it happened, the entire ox was cut up. This was a description of an ox being butchered, and it was also a marvelous demonstration of literary art.

Acting According to His Nature. Zhuangzi enjoyed acting according to his nature, and kept his natural spontaneity and creativity throughout his life. In *Zhuangzi* we read of numerous instances of this "natural behavior." One of the most representative stories is that of the artist who disrobed and sat in his room (found in the chapter "Tian Zifang"). The story tells of Lord Yuan of Song who wanted some pictures painted and summoned all the artists in the land to his palace to demonstrate their skills. When the artists had all arrived, they bowed and scraped and stood respectfully to one side, mixing their inks. There were so many of them that half of the artists had to wait outside. There was one artist who arrived a little later than the rest, he sauntered into the palace, and after bowing, he walked directly to the painting room without standing respectfully to the side. Lord Yuan of Song sent a servant to see what the artist was doing, and the servant reported that the artist had taken off his tunic and was sitting without a shirt, prepared to begin painting. Lord Yuan said, "I have made my decision, this man is a truly great artist." Another story is recorded in the chapter "The Great and Venerable Teacher." Zi Sanghu, Meng Zifan, and Zi Qinzhang were all friends. They lived peacefully together for a time, until one day Zi Sanghu passed away. Before he was even buried, Confucius heard the news, and sent Zi Gong to help arrange the funeral. Upon arriving where they lived, Zi Gong found Meng Zifan and Zi Qinzhang singing and playing the zither. The lyrics of their song were, "Oh Sanghu, now you have returned to the real world and left us here as humans on earth." Zi Gong was astonished at their behavior, he walked right up to them and asked, "May I ask, is it appropriate, according to the rites, to sing to the corpse?" The two friends looked at each other and said with a laugh, "Since when did you know the true

哗哗作响；刀插进去，则霍霍有声，无不切中音律：既合于《桑林》❶ 的舞曲，也合于《经首》❷ 的乐章。庖丁解牛的过程"以神遇而不以目视"，"依乎天理"，"因其固然"，顺着事物的肌理和节奏，"以无厚入有间"，"游刃有余"，最终牛哗啦解体，如同泥土散落在地上，在不知不觉中一头牛解剖完毕。这是宰割牛的过程，也是艺术展现的过程。

　　率性而动。庄子喜欢率性而动，因为它保留了生命原初的自发、自然和创造性行为。《庄子》中也提到了一些率性而动的行为，其中典型的例子是《田子方》篇中"解衣盘礴"的故事。故事叙述的是宋元君打算画一些画，请所有的画师过来一试画技。画师们来了后，都行礼作揖，毕恭毕敬地站在一旁，调理笔墨，半数的人站到门外去了。有一位画师稍晚才到，悠闲地进来，行过礼后没有毕恭毕敬地站在一旁恭候吩咐，就直接到画室去了。宋元君派人去察看，回来禀报说，他已经解开衣襟，袒露上身，盘腿端坐着了。宋元君说："行了，这才是真正的画师。"另一例子记载在《大宗师》篇中。子桑户、孟子反、子琴张三人结交为友。他们一起平静地过了一段时日。有一天子桑户死了，还未下葬。孔子听说后派子贡去帮忙料理丧事。子贡去后发现孟子反与子琴张两人，一个编曲，一个弹琴，相和唱着："桑户啊，你已回归到真实的世界中去了，而我们还要在世上为人。"子贡很纳闷，上前对他们说："请问对着尸体唱歌，合乎礼节吗？"这两人相视而笑，说："你哪里知道礼的真正意思？"子贡回去后把这个事情说给孔子听，并请教孔子他们是什么人，竟然对着尸体唱歌。孔子回答说：

---

❶ 《桑林》，因汤祈祷于桑林而有《桑林》之舞乐。
❷ 《经首》，尧时作《咸池》乐章，《经首》为其名。

❶ Tang prayed in a mulberry orchard and created the "Dance of the Mulberry Orchard."
❷ The name of musical composition of XianChi in Yao's time.

meaning of the rites?" Zi Gong returned and recounted what had happened to Confucius, asking Confucius what kind of people they were who would sing songs to corpses. Confucius replied, "They are people who wander beyond the realm of worldly things, while I am confined to this world. Being among worldly things and beyond worldly things are two different states of being, it was a mistake for me to have sent you to mourn with them! Truly they are the companions of the Creator, wandering between heaven and earth. They see life as a tumor-like growth and death as the draining of a sore or bursting of a boil. How can people such as these care for life or death? They allow life to change according to natural cycles, idly wandering beyond the dust of this world. They despise performing rites to please worldly people."

The philosophy of acting according to one's nature, which Zhuangzi promoted, became popular during the Wei and Jin Dynasties. In *New Tales, Retold and the Book of Jin*, there are many stories of renowned scholars who allowed themselves to act according to their natures. One representative story, found in *New Tales, Retold*, is of Wang Ziyou, who went to visit Dai Kui on a snowy night. In the story, Wang Ziyou returned before arriving at Dai Kui's house. People asked why he did this, and he answered, "I left for his house on a whim, but then my desire to see him diminished; why then should I continue to journey to his house?" With this one sentence he revealed the carefree nature of many famous scholars. Another story, called "The Seven Sages of the Bamboo Grove," is found in the *Book of Jin*. It tells of Ruan Ji's tears when encountering the dead end. It also tells of Ji Kang's firm honesty and hatred of evil, his chivalrous acts for the poor, his travels through the wilderness, and his natural, easy-going manner, as well as Liu Ling's addiction to alcohol.

"他们是遨游于世俗之外的人，而我是拘泥于世俗之内的人。世俗之内与世俗之外是不同的，而我却派你去吊唁，这是我的浅陋啊！他们正要和造物者为伴，遨游于天地之间。他们把生看成多余的赘瘤，把死看成脓疮溃破一般。像这样的人，又怎么在意生死呢？……让生命随着自然循环变化，安闲无牵挂地神游于尘世之外。他们厌烦将世俗的礼节，表演给众人来观看。"

由庄子所倡导的率性而动，在魏晋成了一种风气。《世说新语》和《晋书》记载了诸多名士任情恣性的逸事。典型的如《世说新语》所载王子猷雪夜访戴安道,未至而返,人们问之,他答道："吾本乘兴而来,兴尽何必见戴?"一语道出了名士潇洒自适的真性情。《晋书》记载"竹林七贤"中阮籍的穷途之哭、善使青白眼；嵇康的刚肠嫉恶、任侠尚奇以及游弋山水、恬淡自得；刘伶的嗜酒如命；等等。

《逍遥游》画意（徐君陶　作）
Painting According to "Free and Easy Wandering"
(Painter: Xu Juntao)

余论
Further Discussion

Zhuangzi was a philosopher, a thinker, and a writer; he was also a man who knew how to appreciate life. From his high vantage point in the universe, he looked down upon human life, using his "carnal heart" to understand life, pursuing spiritual freedom, expanding his understanding of life, avoiding worldly cares, and exerting great influence on future generations.

Zhuangzi was not against fulfilling the basic needs of human life. What he opposed was the emotional or physical harm that could befall someone who desired too much from the outside world. He taught that empowerment came from peace and tranquility. If a person's heart became entangled or bound down by outside things, it would be difficult for him to obtain peace and power. Only those who succumbed naturally to the changes in the outside world and who placed little importance on winning and losing, glory and shame, or life and death, were the ones who could live easily and happily. Zhuangzi taught the worldly man to walk out of darkness and confusion, to face reality with an open mind, to handle fame and fortune with a disinterested heart, and to embrace life with calm tenacity. Once a person is able to release himself from the bonds of his cares, what he gains in return are respite and satisfaction.

To pursue spiritual freedom and avoid being weighed down by wordly cares, one must learn how to "refuse" and "let go." One cannot single-mindedly pursue the accolades of society by currying favor with others, but rather must live according to the dictates of one's nature. One must learn to reject such things as posturing to save face, doing favors simply to get something in return, eating foods one does not like, making friends one does not want to have, going to banquets one does not want to attend, and doing things that one does not want to do. It is okay to say no to the obsessive pursuit of wealth, to excessive competition, and to social intercourse beyond one's ability.

When we give in to worldly opinions and popular ways of thinking, when we wear ourselves out in pursuit of standards and values set forth by the world, when we do not allow our hearts and minds to rest, then we are unable to enjoy a carefree life, unable to give our spirit the room it needs, and unable to allow our true selves to grow into who we really want to be. In the midst of our frenetic bustle, we often forget to listen to the voice which speaks to us from deep in our hearts. We run along the road of life at top speed, but along the way, we forget who we are, why we are alive, and what we really need from life.

Tao Yuanming, Ji Kang, Bai Juyi, Su Dongpo, Lin Yutang are just some of

　　庄子是哲学家、思想家和文学家，也是一个会享受生活的人。他从宇宙的高度俯视人生，以"肉心"体悟生活，追求精神的自由，旷达的人生，不被物累，对后世影响甚大。

　　庄子不反对人的基本需要，他反对的是因对外部世界过度需求而导致对身、心的损害。得力在于平静安稳，如果人的心灵被外物纠缠、束缚，就难以使身心获得安宁和力量。只有那些顺应外界变化，看轻人生得失，看淡生活的荣与辱，看破生与死界限的人，才有可能从容地活着。庄子让世俗之人从迷茫中走出来，以旷达的态度去面对现实，以淡漠之心去对待名利，以沉着坚韧的情感去拥抱生活。当人解除了个体心灵的缠累和束缚，换来的将是轻松与自得。

　　追求精神自由，不被物累，意味着在生活中要学会拒绝和放手，不再一味地寻求社会的喝彩，讨他人欢喜，而是依自己的本性而活。对一文不值的面子，对讨厌的人情世故、不想吃的食品、不想交往的朋友、不想去的宴会、不喜欢做的事情，学会拒绝；对世人趋之若鹜的生财之道，对超过自己能力范围的竞争，对自己力不从心的应酬，可以说不。

　　当我们常常屈从于世俗的意见和流行的想法，在世界给定的标准、是非中疲于奔命，不愿意让自己内心安静下来时，我们就没法让自己享受悠闲的生活，没法给心灵多留一些空间，让内心真正的我长成自己想要长成的那个样子；我们也会在忙碌中忽略了去聆听内心深处的声音；我们在成长道路上一路厮杀和奔跑，但忘记了我是谁，我究竟为何活着，我生命中真正需要的是什么？

　　陶渊明、嵇康、白居易、苏东坡、林语堂……历史上很多

the famous scholars and poets who were able to find themselves through the teachings of Zhuangzi. Tao Yuanming was not willing to bow and scrape to get five dou❶ of rice, but rather chose to live in fields apart from society. In his poem "In the Ancient Manner: Number Eight," he wrote, "I see no one I recognize, only ancient hills / Along the sides of the road are tall gravestones, those of Bo Ya and Zhuangzi / There will never be another scholar like them, When I do what my heart desires, what more can I ask for?" Bai Juyi wrote, "I left my country and departed for faraway lands, I blame myself for not seeing the corruption of the court / I read *Zhuangzi* and learned how to deal with this situation, I will wander freely and easily to find freedom." When Su Shi was young, he read *Zhuangzi* and lamented, "I once saw Zhuangzi, but I was unable to speak of it; now I read his book, and it touches my heart deeply." Lin Yutang commented, "All too often, in our busy, daily pursuits, we forget our true selves, just like the bird in Zhuangzi's marvelous parable forgot the danger it was in because of its desire to eat the mantis and just like that same mantis who wanted to eat the cicada and forgot the danger lurking behind it."

Zhuangzi lived without restraint, according to his own conscience and nature. People today, however, are so obsessed with the unimportant things of life that they forget how to live. Perhaps through reading Zhuangzi, you too can find your true self again, allow yourself to find respite from the cares of the world, and protect the simplicity of your spirit in this cacophonous, ever-changing world?

人通过庄子找回了"自己"。陶渊明不为五斗❶米折腰，选择了归园田居。他在《拟故·其八》中说："不见相知人，惟见古时丘。路边两高坟，伯牙与庄周。此士难再得，吾行欲何求！"白居易云："去国辞家谪异方，中心自怪少忧伤；为寻庄子知归处，认得无何是本乡。"苏轼少时读《庄子》叹曰："吾昔有见于中，口未能言；今见是书，得吾心矣。"林语堂说："我们往往在生活的追求中忘记了真正的自我，正如庄子在一个美妙的譬喻里所讲的那只鸟一样，为了要吃一只螳螂而忘记自身的危险，而那只螳螂又为了要捕捉一只蝉也忘了自身的危险。"

庄子，自我、自然、自在地活着，而今天的人们太为生存而奔波，忽视了生活。你是否通过阅读《庄子》，找回了自我，让自己在忙碌中有闲适，在喧嚣、变幻的世上永葆精神的简朴呢?

---

❶ 译者注：斗，中国容量单位。

❶ Translator's note: "dou" is a measure for grain, equal to 7.5kg in East Jin.

Recommended Reading

1. Sun Yikai, and Zhen Changsong. *General Criticism of Zhuangzi*. Orient Publishing House, 1995.

2. Yan Shian.*Critical Biography of Zhuangzi*. Nanjing University Press, 1999.

3. Huang Zhengyu. *Natural Sound of The Flageolet*.Yunnan People's Publishing House, 1999.

4. Yang Kuan. *History of the Warring States*. Shang hai People's Publishing House, 2003.

5. Wang Bo. *Zhuangzi's Philosophy*. Beijing University Press, 2004.

6. Fu Peirong. *Fu Peirong's Experience about Zhuangzi*.International Culture Publishing Corporation, 2007.

7. Chen Guying. *The Present Annotation and Translation of Zhuangzi*. (Volume I - II), The Commercial Press, 2007.

8. Author:Bi Laide. ［Switzerland］/ Translator:Song Gang. *Four Studies about Zhuangzi*.Zhong Hua Book Company, 2009.

延伸阅读书目

一、孙以楷、甄长松《**庄子通论**》，东方出版社1995年版

二、颜世安《**庄子评传**》，南京大学出版社1999年版

三、黄正雨《**自然的箫声：〈庄子〉**》，云南人民出版社1999年版

四、杨宽《**战国史**》，上海人民出版社2003年版

五、王博《**庄子哲学**》，北京大学出版社2004年版

六、傅佩荣《**傅佩荣〈庄子〉心得**》，国际文化出版公司2007年版

七、陈鼓应《**庄子今注今译**》（上、下），商务印书馆2007年版

八、毕来德［瑞士］《**庄子四讲**》，宋刚译，中华书局2009年版

Translator's Note

Zhuangzi's imagination, wisdom, and literary skill have earned him an undisputed place among the great Chinese philosophers of the pre-Qin period. Furthermore, the interpretation of Daoism that he presents in his masterpiece *Zhuangzi* has exerted tremendous influence on Chinese culture in the centuries since his death. As such, a careful study of Zhuangzi's life and philosophy is essential for any student of China and Chinese culture. This concise edition of the original biography of Zhuangzi, from the Collection of *Critical Biographies of Chinese Thinkers*, provides students of Chinese culture with an excellent gateway into the world of Zhuangzi. It incorporates what little is known about his actual life with the stories and teachings found in his writings, drawing connections to modern philosophers and the contemporary world in a way that brings Zhuangzi to life for readers today. The author's rich prose and vivid imagery mimics Zhuangzi's expansive style of writing, adding an additional layer of depth to the work that makes it a truly enjoyable read.

However, as the English translator for this version, I came across numerous passages that I realized would seem foreign and perhaps a little silly in the eyes of those unfamiliar with Zhuangzi's unique manner of expression. In translating, I have attempted to stray as little as possible from the intent of the author, both to aid students of Chinese in their comprehension of the original text, as well as to do some measure of justice to the author's distinctive style. As a result, readers of the English text may notice occasional disjointed ideas, inapt adjectives, or other sources of confusion. To those who would scoff at the bizarre metaphors, fantastic imagery, and distinctly "Chinese" writing style, I would advise, as Zhuangzi might himself, humility and an open-minded attitude; both are qualities which will serve diligent students well as they broaden their understanding of Chinese culture.

I would like to acknowledge the authoritative translation of *Zhuangzi*, entitled *The Complete Works of Chuang-Tzu* by Burton Watson, which I used as a reference throughout the translation process and in which can be found all the direct quotes from Zhuangzi's work cited in this book. I thank my wife,

Jessica Mitchell, for her untiring patience and the invaluable editorial work that she provided throughout the translation process. I also acknowledge the helpful revisions by Professors Wang Zhengwen and Cheng Aimin of Nanjing University.

I hope that this English translation will be an adequate guide to the reader's appreciation of Zhuangzi's life and philosophy. With Zhuangzi, I sincerely pray that we all may "broaden our minds," "live without restraint," and "act according to our natures."

Thomas Wen-Yen Mitchell
March 2010

图书在版编目(CIP)数据

庄子/包兆会著；(美)米歇尔(Mitchell, T.)译
.—南京:南京大学出版社，2010.6
(中国思想家评传简明读本:中英文版)
ISBN 978-7-305-07177-5

Ⅰ.①庄… Ⅱ.①包…②米… Ⅲ.①庄周(前369～
前286)—评传—汉、英 Ⅳ.B223.55

中国版本图书馆CIP数据核字(2010)第108244号

出版发行　南京大学出版社
社　　址　南京汉口路22号　邮　编　210093
网　　址　http://www.NjupCo.com
出 版 人　左　健

丛 书 名　《中国思想家评传》简明读本(中英文版)
书　　名　庄　子
著　　者　包兆会
译　　者　Thomas Mitchell
审　　校　王正文
审　　读　石云龙
责任编辑　芮逸敏　　　　编辑热线 025-83593962

照　　排　江苏凤凰制版印务中心
印　　刷　丹阳市教育印刷厂
开　　本　787×1092　1/16　印张 14　字数 257千
版　　次　2010年6月第1版　2010年6月第1次印刷
ISBN 978-7-305-07177-5
定　　价　28.00元

发行热线　025-83594756
电子邮箱　Press@NjupCo.com
　　　　　Sales@NjupCo.com (市场部)